THE FATE OF
EARLY MEMORIES

THE FATE OF EARLY MEMORIES

Developmental Science and the Retention of Childhood Experiences

MARK L. HOWE

AMERICAN PSYCHOLOGICAL ASSOCIATION
Washington, DC

Published by
American Psychological Association
750 First Street, NE
Washington, DC 20002

Copies may be ordered from
APA Order Department
P.O. Box 92984
Washington, DC 20090-2984

In the U.K., Europe, Africa, and the Middle East, copies may be ordered from
American Psychological Association
3 Henrietta Street
Covent Garden, London
WC2E 8LU England

Typeset in Goudy by EPS Group Inc., Easton, MD

Printer: Data Reproductions, Auburn Hills, MI
Cover Designer: DRI Consulting, Chevy Chase, MD
Technical/Production Editor: Allison L. Risko

Library of Congress Cataloging-in-Publication Data
Howe, Mark L.
    The fate of early memories: developmental science and the retention of childhood experiences/Mark L. Howe
        p.   cm.
    Includes bibliographical references and indexes.
    ISBN 1-55798-628-2 (cloth: alk. paper)
    1. Early memories.   2. Memory in children.   I. Title.
BF378.E17H69   1999
153.1′2—dc21   99-43252
                                                                    CIP

British Library Cataloguing-in-Publication Data
A CIP record is available from the British Library.

Printed in the United States of America
First Edition

For Julia, Galen, and Reilly

CONTENTS

ACKNOWLEDGMENTS

There are a number of institutions and individuals who have contributed to my research over the years—research that has culminated in the publication of this book—whom I would like to thank. This book would not have been possible without the support of the Natural Sciences and Engineering Research Council of Canada. Throughout my career, their support of my research initiatives has been unwavering, and without it, many of the ideas presented in this book may not have received the empirical scrutiny that they did.

I also thank the children, their parents, and their teachers for participating in the research that is described in this book. Without their joyful cooperation in what sometimes must seem like very strange "memory games" played by adults, my colleagues and I would know much less than we do about early memory and its development. It is only through their generous participation in all of our research projects that we have learned so much, and for this I am especially grateful.

This book was written during my tenure at Memorial University in St. John's, Newfoundland. To all of the research personnel who have helped during these years, thank you. I would also like to thank my students, graduate and undergraduate, past and present, who have contributed to my thinking about early memory development. I am particularly grateful to a number of these students who, through no fault of their own, suffered through an earlier draft of this book as the text for a graduate course on early memory development. Their comments, insights, and patience have been invaluable to my own thinking.

A number of colleagues also have played an important role in the research that has led to this book. I thank F. Michael Rabinowitz, who always loves a spirited discussion and theoretical challenge, especially when it comes to issues of consciousness and implicit–explicit memory and learning. I am also deeply grateful to Charles J. Brainerd, who has been a constant source of support and encouragement. Not only is he a dear personal friend and mentor, one who has taught me much, but he is also a valued colleague and critic.

Finally, I would especially like to thank Mary L. Courage, who has been a great friend, colleague, and partner in the discovery of what early memory is and how it develops. Her tireless scrutiny of the manuscript, suggestions for improvement, and patience with me when I simply did not want to hear about any more changes will be forever appreciated. Many of the good things about this book are due to her perseverance, but all of the mistakes are mine. For all of these things, but particularly for her friendship, I am deeply indebted.

INTRODUCTION

It is a capital mistake to theorize before one has the data. Insensibly one begins to twist facts to suit theories, instead of theories to suit facts.

—Sherlock Holmes in Sir Arthur Conan Doyle's
A Scandal in Bohemia (1891)

Many people would agree with the idea that events experienced early in their lives are not only formative but also remain with them somewhere in memory, continuing to exert their influence throughout their lives. Many more would agree with this assertion if they were talking about traumatic experiences. These views are not only found in everyday folk beliefs but also are popular in theories about the effects of early experience on later behavior in adulthood. Indeed, any number of theories concerning personality development, neuroses, and other mental illnesses contain either implicit or explicit references to the important role of early experiences. Many popular books (e.g., Bass & Davis, 1988) and television shows (e.g., John Bradshaw on PBS) about the problems that afflict people in adulthood contain similar references. Although there appears to be agreement, at least in current folklore, that early experience plays an important role in later development, there is considerably less scientific evidence to substantiate such claims (see the chapters in this book; see also Bjorklund, 1997; Kagan, 1996).

There is also considerable disagreement about whether people can remember these early experiences and whether such "explicit" remembering is necessary for these experiences to exert their influence. For example, there have been many reports over the past decade or so concerning the impact of remembered traumatic events from childhood on behavior later in adulthood. The popular literature and media have also been rife with stories about individuals whose behavior was apparently adversely influenced by early childhood trauma but who failed, at least initially or without some "help," to provide an explicit recounting of the critical events. In the latter case, as goes the argument, memories must still have been in storage as they were eventually "recalled" but simply inaccessible to consciousness (e.g., see arguments by Pope & Brown, 1996). Thus, according to this synopsis, early experiences, at least traumatic ones, can exert their influence on later adult behavior and do exist in memory regardless of whether they can be recalled.

The purpose of this book is to examine this hypothesis in light of current scientific evidence. In this sense, this book is not so much about the acquisition of memories, although this, too, is essential to any interpretation of how well memories are retained. Rather, this book is about the development of the survival of memories in long-term storage and their subsequent recollection.

This is a particularly fortuitous time to write such a book because there has been a groundswell of activity in many researchers' laboratories concerning the nature of the early development of long-term retention. Although this research agenda is by no means complete, and many of the conclusions reached in this book are subject to potential revision, there is now a sufficient corpus of evidence from which several reasonably firm conclusions can be made. This is particularly critical because many important claims, both scientific and legal, have been made on the basis of folk beliefs. The reason a scientific perspective is important is because, as Sagan (1996) has pointed out, for every science there exists a "pseudoscience," one that gains considerable currency in the popular media and that constitutes many a layperson's folk beliefs about that science.

In the area of early memory, for example, there are frequent reports made by otherwise "normal" adults that unremembered experiences from early childhood suddenly were recalled in vivid detail. Such autobiographical memories are said by some to have originally taken place in the first year of life, and some have even claimed remembering experiences from the womb (e.g., see Loftus & Ketcham, 1994). Moreover, it has been claimed that these events, consciously remembered or not, are at the root of an individual's current and perhaps long-standing psychological problems. It is this belief that early experiences can exert such a powerful influence over people's lives, and that these so-called formative events can be remembered, that served as the impetus for writing this book. As the quotation at the beginning of this chapter so aptly indicates, there is a need to counteract these beliefs about early memories of experiences with the empirical facts. As I discuss throughout this book, much of what is currently known about early memory serves to dispel many of these notions that are commonly found in the pseudoscience of early memory, ones that I hope will be replaced, after reading this book, with theories built on the scientific evidence. Although science, too, has its warts, it does

> teach how something gets known, what is not known, to what extent things *are* known (for nothing is known absolutely), how to handle doubt and uncertainty, what the rules of evidence are, how to think about things so that judgements can be made, how to distinguish truth

from fraud, from show. (R. Feynman, cited in Gribbin & Gribbin, 1997, p. 145)

In this book I try to present a balanced perspective of what the data indicate, leaving much of the theoretical speculation until the final chapter. I begin in chapter 1 by reviewing what is known about memory development from a developmental neuroscience perspective. I also summarize some of the changes in sensation, perception, attention, and motor skills that either directly or indirectly affect memory. Much of the hardware necessary for the basic operation of memory (e.g., encoding, storage, retrieval) is in place early in life. This includes the neurological hardware that supports different aspects of memory, including declarative (i.e., memories that are consciously accessible on demand; also called *explicit memory*) and nondeclarative (i.e., memories that may not be consciously recalled on demand; also called *implicit memory* or *procedural memory*) components. Although additional developments in this hardware may not be purely epiphenomenal to subsequent improvements in memory, they have not been demonstrated to have causal links to these memory improvements, at least those that typify the development of long-term retention.

In chapter 2, I provide an overview of the development of long-term retention between birth and 2 years of age. What is shown in this chapter is that early memory is considerably more robust than what has been historically thought. For example, there is evidence for long-term retention of prosodic information (e.g., characteristics of the cat in *The Cat in the Hat* as read by one's mother) in newborns even though such information had been presented to them only in utero. Similarly, even 6-month-olds can recognize stimuli (e.g., dynamic visual patterns) that had been presented to them 3 months earlier, when they were 3-month-olds. As remarkable as these findings are, such recollections are not the same as what people usually mean when they talk about recalling events that have happed to them in their lives. That is, although these studies do show that memory is operative early in life, what is remembered is not the event per se but some of the sensory–perceptual characteristics of those events.

This chapter also establishes the existence of an extraordinary continuity in memory from early infancy to later childhood. Indeed, although there are changes in how well children maintain information in memory storage with age, many of the variables that affect older children's and adults' long-term retention performance also affect infant's memory. For example, infants, children, and adults are subject to the effects of retroactive interference, a phenomenon in which information already in memory can be disrupted by subsequent events. Such effects lie at the heart of the well-known misinformation effect in eyewitness memory. Here, incorrect or misleading suggestions can interfere with a witness's recall of what actually happened, a phenomenon that has exasperated many of those involved in the legal system.

Chapter 3 is an overview of preschool children's long-term retention, and this chapter illustrates some of the important achievements in early memory development that contribute to the stability of memories over time. For example, it is during the early preschool years that memories for events in one's life become memorable as more than simple sensory–perceptual configurations or amalgams of conditioned or imitative responses and become events that are meaningful and important to a "self." It is this extraction of meaning, especially one that is relevant to a relatively enduring structure such as the self, that imbues these memories with greater longevity. Although 18-month-olds can reenact from memory events that have occurred earlier in their lives, the nature and durability of those memories are qualitatively different from those memories constructed during the preschool years. Indeed, as shown in chapter 3, one of the fundamental developments in memory during this age range concerns changes in what children know and how they use this knowledge. As children learn more about how the world operates, they can reorganize and better integrate information in memory, a phenomenon that also leads to greater durability of those memories over time.

Coincidentally, these gains in knowledge are also associated with inaccuracies in children's (and adults') memories. That is, because memory is reconstructive (i.e., people use what they know to "fill in the gaps" in their memories for events), gains in knowledge may lead to new kinds of false memories, ones that, although consistent with what usually happens, are inconsistent with what actually happened. Of course, individual episodes can remain memorable and not become confused with other like events when they are different in important ways from what usually happens. Indeed, what people often remember best are those events that are unique and distinct, especially when those events are also personally consequential. These two themes—knowledge and distinctiveness—are critical to understanding memory and its development and are discussed in detail in this chapter and in chapters 4 and 5.

In chapter 4, I examine early memory for experiences that are stressful or traumatic and show how reactions to stress can modulate memories for these experiences. I also demonstrate how other factors (e.g., knowledge, attachment) can mediate the stress reaction to some experiences, which in turn can affect memory for a particular event. In this context I review the neuroscience of stress as it relates to memory and show how stress reactivity is linked to both improvements and declines in memory. That is, although moderate levels of stress can enhance memory for the stressful event, extremely high levels of stress can actually hurt memory for that event. In fact, what this review shows is that highly traumatic experiences may not remain in memory at all; questions concerning later recovery of such memories may be moot because such memories may never have been adequately stored. However, for those experiences that are stored, it appears that the moderate increase in stress may lead to corresponding increases in memory accessibility and durability. This increased longevity is like that afforded by gains in knowledge, and in the latter part of this chapter, I link long-term retention for traumatic experiences to that for other distinctive or personally consequential events, integrating this memory phenomenon with more general models of long-term retention functioning.

In chapter 5, I detail how autobiographical memory emerges from ongoing, basic-level processes that have been operating since birth. That is, although the onset of autobiographical memory heralds the offset of infantile amnesia, an apparent discontinuity in memory development, the argument put forward in chapter 5 is that memory and other underlying processes that have been active since early in life, ones that lead to the emergence of the cognitive self at 18–24 months of age, conspire to alter what was simply memories for events to personalized memories for events. It is this personalization of event memory that, like other organizational mnemonic devices, leads to the greater longevity of memories for experiences. That is, like other memory phenomena, events become more durable in memory (i.e., are better maintained in storage) because they can be organized. Indeed, like other memories, the gist of experiences that are repeated can become represented generically with respect to the self, and even one-time experiences that are unique or particularly important to this self may be well remembered.

In chapter 6, I present an overview of the role of consciousness in memory and long-term retention and, like in other areas of this book, contend again that there is little compelling evidence that researchers need to propose models that have more than a single memory system. Indeed, throughout this book I argue that the weight of the evidence rests on the side of a single memory system, one that appears to develop, at least in basic-process terms, in a continuous fashion. Whether one is talking about declarative or nondeclarative aspects of memory, there are few developmental data to show that these represent anything more than differences in memory tasks. Even if additional evidence comes to light showing that they are different memory systems, the current evidence indicates that they probably emerge contiguously in development and follow parallel developmental trajectories.

In chapter 7, I deal with several methodological and statistical problems that have plagued some of the research on early memory development, particularly the development of long-term retention. For example, in all of the research on long-term retention, whether it is about remembering word lists from a laboratory experiment or recalling experiences from one's days in a concentration camp, conclusions about what was forgotten, falsely remembered, and correctly remembered are contingent on knowing what was in memory to begin with. Although comparing the current memory report with some objective record of the events (e.g., the word list itself, records written at the time of the events) is useful at a pragmatic and forensic level, it does not indicate how memory for the words or events changed with time and experience. What is needed is a *memory record* taken at the time the information was initially acquired (e.g., a record of words recalled initially in the experiment, a written diary). Thus, although the objective record may show with a certain degree of accuracy what was supposed to have been in memory initially, it does not indicate what actually got into memory. This is because, as discussed throughout this book, memory is constructive and reconstructive, with events being interpreted as they enter storage and reinterpreted as they are being retrieved. Thus, what gets into memory differs from the objective record in many ways, depending on how people interpret the event. Indeed, it is because memory is not like an objective record that this issue is so important, and it is only by obtaining an initial memory record that people are able to evaluate what was forgotten. Throughout this chapter, similar problems are examined, solutions are suggested, and studies in which those solutions have been implemented are reviewed.

Finally, in chapter 8, I present a synthesis and an integrative perspective on the early development of long-term retention. I argue that memory is operative from even the earliest of days and that what can be remembered in these early months is remarkable. Despite this, these early memories are not the sort of recollections researchers refer to in people's everyday discourse about memory for their life experiences. Nor is it similar to the types of recollections needed in forensic settings. Indeed, there is little doubt that such recollections are not available until the early preschool years (i.e., around 2 years of age). It is only around this time, after the emergence of a more structured cognitive sense of self, that memories can be organized autobiographically. Given this achievement, children can begin to recount events they have experienced in a manner more typical of what is meant by the term *autobiographical recall*.

These facts about memory and its development are then organized into an integrative perspective. In this perspective, I develop the idea that memory is best suited to retain the gist of people's experiences and impose some organizational structure on these meanings so that people may better understand, predict, and interpret the world they live in. In this perspective there is no need for more than a single memory system, nor is there a need to establish separate rules governing what happens to memories that are currently (or potentially) conscious from those that are not. What does remain to be better understood is the process by which the dynamic storage medium researchers call *memory* changes and reorganizes itself as a function of extracting new knowledge. As new domains of knowledge are acquired, recent and extant memories can be organized as cohesive and dynamic structures, ones that not only gain in longevity but also serve to beget new memories from subsequent experiences. It is this self-organizing principle of memory that researchers need to understand better, a principle that serves memory from its very inception.

Of course, before I discuss this integrative perspective, I must begin at the beginning. The beginning, as in a good Sherlock Holmes book, starts with a puzzle—in the present case, the nature, onset, and development of early memory. This is followed by an examination of the evidence that, when wholly unearthed, leads ineluctably to the puzzle's resolution. In this case, although the ultimate solution may require additional research, the chapters that follow reveal many of the clues necessary for discovering the fate of early memories.

THE FATE OF
EARLY MEMORIES

1

OVERVIEW OF DEVELOPMENTS IN SYSTEMS RELATED TO EARLY MEMORY

In this chapter I provide a synopsis of what is known about the development of sensory-perceptual, attentional, motoric, and neural mechanisms linked to the ontogeny of memory. There are at least three reasons for presenting this information at this point in the book. First, it is pointless to talk about early memory until the age at which the systems involved in the encoding, storage, and retrieval of information are mature enough to support the formation and subsequent retention of memories. Second, although I show that some memories can be formed early in life (even in utero), there are several theories in which the onset of specific, more mature memory systems (e.g., declarative or consciously accessible memory, autobiographical memory, or memory from our personal life) is linked to later (particularly neurological) developments. As I show, developments in the neurological systems that subserve memory are advanced enough within the first postnatal year of life that they are probably not limiting factors in memory development after this time (for a review, see Howe & Courage, 1993, 1997b; C. A. Nelson, 1995). Furthermore, the empirical evidence needed to support claims that different memory systems (e.g., implicit vs. explicit, procedural vs. declarative) have fundamentally distinct developmental trajectories within this first year (or later) is weak at best (also see

3

reviews by Howe & Courage, 1993, 1997b; Rovee-Collier, 1997). Thus, if developmental changes in neurophysiological functioning are associated with changes in memory then such changes should affect memory uniformly rather than turning on or off select systems. Finally, it is important to have at least a working knowledge of the development of the neural substrates of memory because these systems, in interaction with neurohormonal systems, can modulate the storage of memories. This is particularly important in later chapters, when the discussion turns to issues relevant to remembering traumatic experiences, and the role of cortisol and norepinephrine is considered in the establishment and retention of these memories. I begin with a brief overview of the early capacities and development of sensory-perceptual and attentional systems and then discuss neurological mechanisms.

EARLY SENSORY-PERCEPTUAL DEVELOPMENTS

The status of sensory and perceptual systems is key because information must travel through the human senses before being converted into memories. Similarly, attention to different aspects of the environment (e.g., scanning) is often crucial to establishing some memories. If these systems lack the maturity to support encoding, storage, and retrieval of information from the environment, then surely memories for early experiences would be absent, or at best, extremely impoverished.

I first consider the evidence that early sensory or perceptual limitations may restrict memory. Most of the research has focused on visual development, perhaps because it is one of humans' most important but least well-developed systems at birth. This is fortunate because most researchers of memory development have used visually encoded materials. Of course, it is important to summarize what is known about the development of the other senses because one purpose of this book is to consider memories for experiences that may involve numerous senses (e.g., as in real-life traumatic events). Unlike vision, people's other senses are reasonably well developed at birth or shortly thereafter in normally developing fetuses. For example, the structural mechanisms critical to auditory discrimination, detection, and localization are well developed within the last trimester of gestation (e.g., Aslin, 1987). In fact, at 25 weeks' gestation the fetal brain will respond to sound, and by 28 weeks reflexive movements and heart rate changes can be elicited (Parmelee & Sigman, 1983). Within a few days after birth (after fluid has drained from the ears), the infant's auditory threshold is only about 10–20 dB higher than that of the adult, although sensitivity varies as a function of sound frequency. For example, longitudinal research has shown that at 6 months of age, infants' thresholds are somewhat higher than those of adults at low (200 Hz) and high (10000

Hz) frequencies and approach adult levels at midrange (1000 Hz) and very high (19000 Hz) frequencies, with fine-tuning in sensitivity continuing for several years (see Aslin, 1987; Trehub & Schneider, 1983). Consistent with their proficient sound detection, very young infants also are able to discriminate among sounds along the dimensions of intensity, frequency, duration, and timing (see Fernald, 1992). For example, by 5 months of age infants can discriminate among pairs of tones in the mid-frequency and high-frequency ranges almost as precisely as adults can, but thresholds for low-frequency discriminations are still twice that of adults (Olsho, 1984).

Infants' ability to localize the source of sound also has been investigated. An early case study by Wertheimer (1961) showed that his newborn infant reliably oriented toward the source of a clicking sound in the delivery room. However, subsequent research has shown that the ability to localize sound follows a U-shaped function, with performance declining toward 2 months of age and reemerging after about 4 months. This pattern has been attributed to a shift from subcortical to cortical controlling mechanisms over this time period (Muir & Clifton, 1985), with precision in localizing the source of a sound continuing to improve over the first postnatal year (Morrongiello, 1988).

Infants are particularly sensitive to the sounds of human speech and show a remarkable ability to discriminate a wide range of phonemic contrasts in the neonatal period (Eimas, Siqueland, Jusczyk, & Vigorito, 1971). Interestingly, infants are even better than English-speaking adults at discriminating certain phonemes not found in the English language, an advantage they lose during the second half of the first postnatal year (Werker & Tees, 1984). Furthermore, by 4 months of age they can discriminate and show a preference for "motherese" over adult-directed speech with its high pitch and exaggerated intonations (Fernald, 1985). Subsequent work by DeCasper and his colleagues has shown that the infants' early facility with speech discrimination is evident even during the prenatal period. They found that 3-day-old neonates can not only discriminate their mother's voice from that of a female stranger but that they can also recognize the prosodic characteristics of a story read to them during the last trimester of gestation (DeCasper & Fifer, 1980; DeCasper, Lecanuet, Busnel, Granier-Deferre, & Maugeais, 1994; DeCasper & Prescott, 1984). Newborns also can remember a familiarized word for 24 hr (Swain, Zelazo, & Clifton, 1993), and by 6 weeks of age they can recognize a familiar nursery rhyme after 3 days (M. J. Spence, 1996).

I next consider information processing through the chemical senses (taste and olfaction). Specifically, the taste buds are structurally mature long before birth (Bradley, 1972), enabling neonates not only to discriminate among sweet, sour, salty, and bitter substances when placed on their tongues but also to discriminate within these taste categories (e.g., Crook, 1987; Rosenstein & Oster, 1988). Olfactory receptors are also well developed at birth (Sarnat, 1978), and consequently olfaction, which has been linked by several investigators to emotional distinctiveness in memory (e.g., Herz, 1997; Herz & Cupchik, 1995), is also well developed early in life. For example, neonates can discriminate a variety of food odors (e.g., bananas, vanilla, fish, rotten eggs) as well as discriminate their own mother's odor from that of another female (e.g., Cernoch & Porter, 1985; MacFarlane, 1975). Finally, concerning tactile sensitivity, fetuses react to a foot touch with a limb movement in the second trimester (e.g., Windle, 1971), neonates can discriminate shapes on the basis of oral exploration (Meltzoff & Borton, 1979), and touch fosters soothing and facilitates growth in preterm infants (e.g., Scafidi et al., 1990).

In contrast to the maturity of the auditory, chemical, and tactile senses, the visual system of the human neonate is immature both structurally and functionally at birth. Although the major optical and anatomical components of the eye are in place, there are considerable neurological immaturities in the structures of the retino–geniculo–cortical system (i.e., the constellation of neural structures, pathways, and their interconnections that lie between the retina and the cortex; for reviews, see Aslin, 1987; Banks & Salapatek, 1983; Hickey & Peduzzi, 1987). In particular, the foveal region (i.e., an indentation at the back of the retina where the greatest concentration of photoreceptors is found) of the retina is poorly articulated; cone cells are sparsely distributed; and cell bodies in the lateral geniculate nucleus (i.e., a thalamic relay station along the retino–geniculo–cortical system) are small, sluggish, and fatigue easily. Despite the completion of neurogenesis of cells in the primary visual (striate) cortex and the visibility of the laminar structure, there is only a skeletal organization of mature cortical receptive fields (e.g., retinotopicity, direction and orientation selectivity, binocularity), and ocular dominance columns are unformed. Myelenation is incomplete and, although axons and dendrites are recognizable in the cortex, the latter are short and poorly arborized. These early immaturities do not last long, with the first 3 postnatal months constituting a period of rapid development. Although the end of this time marks the point at which much of the basic neural hardware is in place, at least in rudimentary form, considerable fine-tuning occurs throughout the first postnatal year.

These early limitations constrain visual function and perception in the early months of life. For example, newborn infants have poor visual acuity, contrast sensitivity, and color vision. Despite the presence of visual reflexes (e.g., saccadic and pursuit movements), general visuomotor immaturities limit neonates' scanning and their abilities to detect stimuli beyond approximately 30° in the peripheral visual field. Fortunately, rapid neurological developments coincide with substantial improvements in all of these visual functions, so that beginning around 3 months of age, infants begin to (a) recognize objects and determine their spatial layout, (b) use binocular and monocular cues to determine the location of objects, (c) perceive objects as constant in their size and shape despite variable information projected to the eye, (d) perceive forms as such rather than as component parts, and (e) recognize faces (Aslin, 1987; Banks & Salapatek, 1983).

In summary, although there are early immaturities that constrain young infants' visual perceptual abilities, and visual development continues over the first year with perception becoming more and more adult-like, it is clear that like the other senses, babies are fully capable of extracting visual information. It would therefore appear that, although sensory-perceptual systems may undergo considerable and rapid development, such systems are often intact early in life and, although they may limit what may be encoded, they do not preclude the formation of long-term memories.

EARLY ATTENTIONAL AND MOTOR CHANGES

In what way do early shifts in attentional and motor mechanisms constrain memory in the early months of life? Like the question concerning memory limitations imposed by early developments in sensory-perceptual mechanisms, this question encompasses a vast literature—one that cannot possibly be covered here. Moreover, it should be evident that growth in neurological and sensory-perceptual systems is related to changes in attentional and motor mechanisms early in infancy. That is, all of these systems are highly interconnected, with developments in one often being dynamically related to changes in another. Again, my intent here is simply to highlight some of the basic findings and show that these factors do not preclude the establishment of traces in long-term memory but may serve to constrain the types of features that can be incorporated into memory traces. For a more in-depth review of this area, readers should consult Adolph (1997); Bertenthal, Campos, and Barrett (1984); Ruff and Rothbart (1996); Thelen et al. (1993); and Thelen and Ulrich (1991).

Even newborns orient to sounds and sights and will remove their attention (e.g., close their eyes) when the stimuli are too intense or abrupt (e.g., Finlay & Ivinskis, 1987). More important, the expansive literature on infant perception and recognition memory attests to their early selectivity (for reviews, see Cohen & Salapatek, 1987; Howe & Courage, 1997b), although the extent to which this selectivity is voluntary or driven by involuntary neurological mechanisms (at least in the neonatal period) is unclear (see Banks & Ginsberg, 1985). Although young infants actively direct their attention to certain classes of visual stimuli (e.g., patterned over unpatterned, novel over familiarized), their attention is constrained in the early months by limitations in oculomotor control and scanning (for reviews, see Aslin, 1987; Haith, 1980). For example, before 2 months of age, infants direct their fixations (and presumably their attention) to the external boundaries of objects and patterns (e.g., toward faces) that are rich in contour information and generally ignore internal details (however, see Maurer, 1983). This "externality effect" diminishes after 2 months of age and fixations become distributed more broadly (Bronson, 1991; Salapatek, 1975), after which time infants can begin putting things together to perceive forms as such rather than as separate component parts (Bertenthal, Campos, & Haith, 1980; Van Giffen & Haith, 1984). At this time, too, infants begin to deploy (i.e., engage and disengage) their attention more flexibly, are influenced by experience, and develop expectations not only about what to anticipate but also where stimulus events might occur (Haith, Hazan, & Goodman, 1988; M. H. Johnson, Posner, & Rothbart, 1991). These behavioral changes in attention reflect rapid and extensive development in the underlying neurological structures (for a review, see Ruff & Rothbart, 1996).

Attentional developments in the duration, distribution, and efficiency of looking are enhanced by the subsequent emergence of motor skills such as manual exploration and locomotion, abilities that serve to expand the infant's vista and provide a new arena for information processing. With newly acquired proficiencies in visually directed reaching, eye–hand coordination, and fine finger control, infants from about 5 or 6 months of age are increasingly drawn by the graspability and manipulability of objects. This, in tandem with visual inspection, allows them to actively take in information and focus their attention while simultaneously developing the capacity for resisting distraction (Oakes & Tellinghuisen, 1994; Ruff, 1986). This latter ability may signal the presence of inhibitory mechanisms essential to directed attention, something that has been thought to play an important role in the control of memory processing (e.g., Dempster & Brainerd, 1995).

The emergence of crawling and other modes of self-produced locomotion is related to further developments in selective attention, as the new perspective provided by these achievements reveals different aspects of the physical and social environment. For example, the onset of crawling in the second half of the first year leads to changes in attention to the now-critical spatial relationships of objects in the environment. Not surprisingly, crawlers are better able to discriminate changes in spatial layout than are noncrawlers (Bertenthal et al., 1984). Developments in independent locomotion also are related to the onset of attentiveness to and wariness of drop-offs (Campos, Bertenthal, & Kermoian, 1992) and to increased use of social referencing as a source of information (Walden & Ogan, 1988). Subsequent developments in attention primarily concern advances in control, including better deployment, the ability to resist distraction, and the use of more systematic scanning strategies. Although early developments are more of the "hardware" variety (e.g., neurologically based advances in attentional and motoric mechanisms), many of these later developments are based more on "software" changes brought about primarily by advances in knowledge that direct attentional strategies.

In summary, changes in attention and motor performance provide the infant with a greater breadth of experience and access to new and increasing numbers of features of objects, people, and the physical environment. Although such breadth should surely influence the quality and quantity of features available for encoding into memory, early attentional and motoric limitations do not prevent the encoding and storage of information in long-term memory. Thus, like changes in sensory-perceptual systems, attentional and motoric developments may lead to richer encodings and therefore more durable traces for retention, but their immaturities do not preclude the establishment of long-term memories.

DEVELOPMENTAL NEUROSCIENCE

Although the encoding limitations imposed on early memory by the factors mentioned earlier are typically short-lived, it has been suggested that neurophysiological immaturity may be at the heart of any early memory inadequacies, particularly infantile amnesia. Although I simply want to provide a synopsis of what is known about early neurological development as it relates to memory, a more complete and highly readable exegesis of this area can be found in Elman et al. (1996, particularly chap. 5) or the more technical series of chapters, in Dawson and Fischer (1994).

Historically, the idea that neurological immaturities underlie limitations associated with early memory development can be traced to clinical observations of patients with amnesia. Indeed, much of the data for this comes from studies of human memory pathology, particularly patients with bilateral damage to the medial aspect of the temporal lobe (especially the hippocampus and amygdala) or other subcortical structures related to memory (e.g., the diencephalic structures, especially the mammillary bodies and the dorsomedial nucleus of the thalamus). Despite intact immediate and remote memories, as well as an ability to retain perceptual, motor, and some cognitive skills, these patients experience marked anterograde amnesia wherein they are unable to consciously access (or perhaps store, as originally proposed) recently experienced events (for reviews, see Squire, 1986; Squire & Cohen, 1984; Squire & Frambach, 1990; Squire & Zola-Morgan, 1988). Such dissociation of memory suggested that memory was not a unified phenomenon and that there may be at least two different types of memory: *procedural* (spared in amnesia) and *declarative* (lost in amnesia; e.g., Cohen & Squire, 1980). Thus, to the extent that the structures damaged in amnesic syndromes are immature in infancy, neonates should have difficulty establishing declarative, but not procedural, memories. Subsequently, investigators sought evidence for the immaturity of this hippocampal complex that appeared to be integrally important in learning and memory early in life and one that may be responsible for memory deficiencies in infancy, including later infantile amnesia (e.g., Mishkin, Malamut, & Bachevalier, 1984; Nadel & Zola-Morgan, 1984; Schacter & Moscovitch, 1984; Squire, 1987).

To provide experimental confirmation of this hypothesis, researchers posited animal models of early memory function. For example, researchers have used rhesus monkeys with medial temporal or diencephalic lesions, or both, in tasks thought to be sensitive to those elements of memory that have been spared or lost in human amnesias (for reviews, see Mishkin et al., 1984; Squire & Cohen, 1984; Squire & Zola-Morgan, 1983; Zola-Morgan & Squire, 1985). Using these animal models, Mishkin and his associates (Aggleton & Mishkin, 1983; Malamut, Saunders, & Mishkin, 1984; Mishkin et al., 1984; Mishkin, Spiegler, Saunders, & Malamut, 1982; Zola-Morgan, Squire, & Mishkin, 1982) proposed two retention systems that store experiences in fundamentally different ways: a cortico–limbic "memory" system (analogous to declarative memory) and a cortico–striatal "habit" system (analogous to procedural memory). It is the former system that is contingent on the integrity of the medial temporal and diencephalic regions and is lost in amnesia and the latter system that is independent of these regions (perhaps being served by the striatum or basal ganglia) and is spared in amnesia. For example, studies on the development of these memory and habit systems (e.g., Bachevalier & Mishkin, 1984) in 3-, 6-, and 12-month-old monkeys showed that the monkeys had equal proficiency in tasks involving the habit system, with older groups being better only in tasks involving the memory system (e.g., delayed nonmatching to sample). (For a more in-depth review of this diverse and extensive literature on experimental work with animal models, see Squire, 1987.)

As attractive as these ideas are, there are several shortcomings associated with them. There is a fundamental problem with comparing the performance of an adult (particularly one with a brain injury) with same-species developing organisms who are neurologically intact. Interestingly, there is even recent evidence that current models of adult memory abilities that are lost (i.e., declarative, explicit) or spared (i.e., procedural, implicit) in amnesia may be inadequate. For example, Hamann and Squire (1995) reported that under specific acquisition conditions (the study-only as opposed to the more usual study–test method), patients with amnesia acquired new word knowledge (albeit more slowly than is usual for this declarative memory task), that this knowledge generalized, and that it persisted over a 1-month delay period. That patients with amnesia (which included individuals who had damage to the medial temporal lobe and the midline diencephalic structures) can acquire new declarative memories implies that despite their brain pathologies, a simple change in the conditions of learning altered the deficits to declarative memory often observed in patients with amnesia. Clearly, then, conclusions concerning the different-aged onsets of memory abilities based on data from adults with amnesia is extremely limited given the current uncertainty about which models of memory and amnesia are appropriate as well as the available evidence.

There are also problems associated with evidence from the animal model research. For example, the database rests on a diverse array of tasks that are said to provide independent measures of memory (declarative) and habit (procedural) processes (for descriptions of these tasks, see Squire & Shimamura, 1986; Squire & Zola-Morgan, 1983). Although a medley of tasks is not necessarily a negative thing, the absence of comprehensive task analyses makes their utility questionable (also see chap. 7 in this book). That is, the critical difference between the different tasks is supposed to be that those tapping habit (procedural) processes are based on simple skill learning that involves conditioning and strengthening of stimulus–response bonds. Alternatively, those tapping memory (declarative) processes are thought to depend on the earlier storage of knowledge and the absence of external cues to guide performance. The missing link here is that there is no independent confirmation that such a distinction is appropriate. Moreover, there are several inconsistencies (a) in performance on tasks said to measure the same process, (b) between studies using the same tasks, and (c) in determining what process a specific task is said to measure (Malamut et al., 1984; Squire & Zola-Morgan, 1983). These problems are further exacerbated by the fact that most tasks probably reflect a mixture of both procedural and declarative memory, varying perhaps only in the degree to which one or the other system is engaged (Squire, 1987). Although some recent progress has been made in these areas, clarity will not be achieved until task standardization has been resolved (also see Howe & Courage, 1993). Until this happens, legitimate cross-species and cross-age generalizations about the role that developing neural structures play in performance on tasks meant to measure different memory and habit processes will remain limited.

These problems notwithstanding, Schacter and Moscovitch (1984) were among the first to attempt to apply these findings to memory development in infants. Here, early retention was based on a habit or procedural system that emerges first, perhaps at birth, and accounts for performance on conditioning, novelty preference, and habituation tasks. A late-developing retention system (memory or declarative) emerges gradually around 8 months of age and accounts for older infants' performance on more complex conditioning, novelty preference, and habituation paradigms involving spatiotemporal contexts (Millar & Schaffer, 1972), longer intervals or delays (Millar, 1972; Ramey & Ourth, 1971), or cross-modal memory (Rose, Gottfried, & Bridger, 1979). Although Schacter and Moscovitch admitted that this simple dichotomy underestimates the complexity of development (both neural and cognitive), there are several noteworthy limitations. For example, Schacter and Moscovitch's model seriously overestimates the age (8 months) at which spatiotemporal skills appear. Indeed, as seen in the next chapter, even 3-month-olds encode and retain contextual information (e.g., Rovee-Collier & Shyi, 1992) and 4- to 6-month-olds can retain spatiotemporal information for at least a week (Smith, Arehart, Haaf, & deSaintVictor, 1989). There is also an extensive literature on event memory during the first 2 years of life that shows that performance is more sophisticated than prescribed in this model (e.g., Bauer, 1995; also see chap. 2 in this book). Thus, whatever neurological structures are needed to mediate a variety of nonprocedural memories, they must be intact earlier than Schacter and Moscovitch's model would suggest.

Although this more recent evidence may serve to infirm older depictions of the neurological underpinnings of early memory development, C. A. Nelson (1995) has provided an up-to-date neuroscience accounting of these changes, one that retains the notion of multiple memory systems that come on stream at different times. For example, like the multiple memory proposals just discussed, C. A. Nelson argued that neurological structures that develop early in postnatal life (e.g., the hippocampus, striatum, cerebellum, olivary–cerebellar complex) are sufficient to sustain what he called a "preexplicit" (or procedural) memory system. Here, different types of recognition memory performance are available and can be observed in certain early novelty preferences, habituation, instrumental and classical conditioning, and visual expectancy tasks. Performance on certain other "explicit" memory tasks (e.g., delayed nonmatching to sample, cross-modal recognition, deferred and elicited imitation) and working memory tasks (e.g., A not B delayed response) is said to also require the later developing structures of the medial temporal lobe (e.g., the amygdala), inferior temporal cortical regions, and regions of the prefrontal cortex, which do not begin to come on stream until the latter half of the first postnatal year. These structures continue to mature across infancy and childhood and, in conjunction with related achievements in the cognitive and linguistic domains, form the foundation for improvements in memory performance observed in the early years.

In effect, then, C. A. Nelson (1995) also suggested that there is a qualitative shift in the development of early memory that occurs during the last half of the first postnatal year, one that is coincident with (or perhaps enabled by) qualitative changes in neurological maturation. This shift from preexplicit to explicit memory, which occurs between 6- and 12-months of age, heralds a shift from recognition to recall in infancy. It is not clear, however, how such a qualitative shift squares with Meltzoff and Moore's (1994) finding that 6-week-old infants showed deferred imitation of facial expressions after a 24-hr delay. Given that these findings demonstrate that infants can recall motor actions on the basis of stored (but not overtly practiced) representations (however, see Anisfeld, 1996), it would seem that recall is possible much earlier than anticipated in this developmental neuroscience model.

If C. A. Nelson's (1995) argument is that different kinds of memory performance are supported by different neural substrates that have parallel developmental histories, many would agree. However, if the stronger assertion is made that these memory systems are independent and have different developmental trajectories, then many would disagree that the evidence marshaled to date justifies this stronger claim (e.g., Roediger, Rajaram, & Srinvas, 1990; Rovee-Collier, 1990). As C. A. Nelson acknowledged, the connection between brain structure and memory function is not isomorphic and, regardless of age, memory behavior, or species, the brain works as an integrated system receiving inputs from and sending outputs to both local and distal structures (also see Elman et al., 1996).

The fact that memory performance may be an emergent property of numerous, distant, and distinct but dynamic neural interconnections is crucial when trying to decipher the link between neurological events and memory behavior. Indeed, the nature of this integrated neurocognitive system is currently the subject of considerable active research. For example, as already discussed, the hippocampus (and its related structures in the medial temporal region) historically has been considered a late-developing structure whose maturation was viewed as the likely source of the delayed onset of an explicit or declarative memory system (Nadel & Zola-Morgan, 1984; Schacter & Moscovitch, 1984). More recent evidence has shown that the hippocampus and its surrounding structures (except for the dentate area, where development is protracted over the first 3 or 4 postnatal years) in human and nonhuman primates mature relatively early in postnatal life (Berger & Alvarez, 1994; Chugani, 1994; Chugani & Phelps, 1986; Kretschmann, Kammradt, Krauthausen, Sauer, & Wingert, 1986; O'Neil, Friedman, Bachevalier, & Ungerleider, 1986). Although components of the hippocampal formation become functional in early infancy, it is also clear that some neocortical (e.g., inferotemporal) components, as well as their reciprocal connections with the hippocampus, develop more slowly (Bachevalier, Brickson, & Hagger, 1993; Bachevalier & Mishkin, 1984). These latter structures, along with the hippocampus, mediate performance on more complex memory tasks that emerge over the period of infancy (e.g., cross-modal recognition, deferred imitation, and delayed nonmatching to sample). Thus, although the hippocampus plays a changing role in mediating memory performance, it may contribute to the apparent underlying continuity of memory processes across infancy and childhood (see Bauer, 1995; Howe & Courage, 1997b). Aspects of this continuity are discussed more fully in the other chapters in this book.

New findings have become possible in recent years given rapid technological advances, particularly in the area of neuroimaging. In a recent review of this area, C. A. Nelson and Bloom (1997) suggested that it may be through this new technology of functional neuroimaging (e.g., positron emission technology and functional magnetic resonance imaging) that the neurobiological mechanisms related to memory (and cognitive) development may be more precisely identified (also see Wheeler, Stuss, & Tulving, 1997). Interestingly, one of the important outcomes of this approach has been the recognition that many areas of the brain are often involved in mediating even the simplest of memory functions. For example, in a recent review of findings using positron emission tomography imaging, Nyberg, Cabeza, and Tulving (1996) showed that the entire right prefrontal cortex was preferentially involved in a number of different episodic retrieval tasks (e.g., cued recall using word stems, word recognition, face recognition). Using similar techniques, Kapur et al. (1994; also see Tulving et al., 1994) concluded that memory processes, rather than being localized in specific structures, tend to involve large neural regions. This position is consistent with one recently articulated by R. A. Swain et al. (1995), who extended it even further to include other components of brain tissue. That is, they suggested that the term *brain adaptation* be used when discussing memory to better reflect the myriad simultaneous brain changes that occur in response to experience including glia, blood vessels, neurons, and their synapses.

One potential outcome of this new research is the possibility of illuminating the dynamic interplay between maturation and experience in the developing brain (also see Elman et al., 1996). In particular, many aspects of brain development are contingent on experience, including the creation of neural connections. For example, Greenough and his associates (Greenough, 1990; Greenough & Bailey, 1988; Greenough & Black, 1992; Greenough, Black, & Wallace, 1987) have identified two mechanisms by which new synaptic connections are established through experience: experience-expectant synaptogenesis and experience-dependent synaptogenesis. In the *experience-expectant synaptogenesis*, synapses form given a required but limited exposure to some environmental conditions. Here, there may be an initial overproduction of synapses followed by a pruning back to only those connections that are adaptive. In *experience-dependent synaptogenesis*, synaptic formation optimizes adaptation to specific (and perhaps unique) aspects of the environment. This latter form of synaptogenesis is perhaps most relevant here because it concerns learning and memory. That is, depending on experience, different neural connections will be established in memory, giving rise to individual differences in learning and knowledge. Indeed, early positive and negative experiences can influence not only what is stored but also alter brain structure and function (this is discussed in greater depth in chap. 5, when I consider the effects of stress and trauma on memory). The important point is that maturation does not determine developmental outcomes in brain development but instead conjoins with experience to alter both structure and function (also see Howe & Courage, 1997b).

To summarize, knowledge of the dynamics of structure–function relationships in the early development of human memory is itself in a state of development. Indeed, as C. A. Nelson and Bloom (1997; also see Wheeler et al., 1997) pointed out, there are several serious methodological and analytical problems that need to be worked out before the various neuroimaging techniques will produce data that unambiguously specify the role neurobiological factors play in early memory development. Until then, the question of whether there are multiple memory systems with differential ontogenetic time courses remains unresolved. Perhaps, as I have argued previously (Howe & Courage, 1993, 1997b), it is more parsimonious to consider the development of memory in infancy in terms of a unitary memory system in the absence of incontrovertible evidence to the contrary. This is certainly consistent with the evidence that is presented in subsequent chapters that shows considerable continuity in memory functioning across infancy and childhood. In any event, even if there is a qualitative shift in early memory from preexplicit to explicit memory in the last half of the first postnatal year, this does not preclude the idea that such a behavioral-level discontinuity cannot be driven by an underlying continuous process (e.g., see Bates & Carnevale, 1993; Courage & Howe, 1998a; Elman et al., 1996). Neither would such a shift provide evidence that preexplicit and explicit systems are independent after the onset of explicit memory. Indeed, there may be no reason to think that previously preexplicit memories cannot be converted to explicit ones late in the first year of life. Regardless of the outcome of subsequent research in the area of developmental neuroscience, it is clear from this review that encoding, storage, and retrieval are functioning early in life. Thus, memories can be and are formed early in life. Whether this early memory remains strictly preexplicit and inaccessible to conscious recollection later in life is a matter for future research, some of which will occur in the arena of developmental neuroscience. Behavioral evidence of what can be exhumed from people's early life experiences is discussed in depth in other chapters of this book.

CONCLUSION

In this chapter I have shown that much of the human information-processing system relevant to memory is intact and functional early in life. I have traced a number of changes in sensory-perceptual, attentional, motoric, and neural systems that permit greater flexibility and range in the types of events and features that are available for potential encoding in memory. Although more events and greater numbers of features become available for encoding as development unfolds, particularly during the first year of life as attentional and motoric advances occur, the fundamental systems involved in encoding, storing, and retrieving memories are apparent early in life.

There are two important elements of the preceding conclusion that require clarification. First, if memory traces consist of aggregations of features encoded from experiences, a claim common to most current models of memory (for recent reviews, see Estes, 1997; Howe & Courage, 1997b; Howe & O'Sullivan, 1997), then the fact that neonates are capable of encoding and retaining information over protracted retention intervals (e.g., see DeCasper & Prescott, 1984) suggests that the basic feature-extraction mechanisms involved in the establishment and retention of long-term memory traces are operative early. Subsequent developments in the systems outlined in this chapter simply allow greater augmentation of traces with more features. Similar growth occurs as children develop more extensive knowledge bases, which in turn allows them to direct attention to critical features of an event for retention (e.g., the color of a robber's eyes and hair). Although such developments permit a more exhaustive survey of the features of an event, the same basic feature-encoding mechanisms are being used to encode and retain the event. Indeed, these developments in feature extraction and encoding may lead to more durable traces in memory storage, the main development that occurs in children's long-term retention (see Howe & Courage, 1997b; Howe & O'Sullivan, 1997). I discuss this further in later chapters.

Second, much has been made of the question, What constitutes memory? This question is critical here because some claim that memory requires detailed verbal recall of an entire event, including perhaps the time of that event (particularly if it is to be called "autobiographical memory"). Clearly, if this definition were adopted, memory would not exist until at least the time when language is acquired. A less conservative view might hold that simple behavioral responses (e.g., avoiding a person who has been unkind) should suffice. The problem with behavioral evidence such as this is that the "memory" that is causing the behavior must be inferred indirectly and in a circular manner. In better controlled circumstances, some of which are considered in subsequent chapters, the link is noncircular and direct. Even here, though, there is debate about whether purely behavioral reenactments constitute evidence for memory.

Throughout much of the remainder of this book, I elucidate this debate in the context of behavioral evidence for very long-term retention of early events. I argue that there is a fundamental continuity in basic memory processes (encoding, storage, retrieval) across development (also see Howe & Courage, 1993, 1997b). By this, I do not mean to imply that the many diverse aspects of mnemonic competence (assessed through recognition, recall, or savings measures) that are used to evaluate the status of information in memory are "created equal" in their cognitive prerequisites, neurological underpinnings, or developmental trajectory. Rather, I simply mean that the evidence marshaled to date, in terms of both the neurological underpinnings of early memory development and the memory performance data, can easily be accommodated by a model in which there is a single memory system that develops continuously.

2

MEMORY DEVELOPMENT FROM BIRTH TO 2 YEARS OF AGE

To address questions concerning the fate of early memories, particularly the notion that infants' encoding, storage, and retrieval are somehow too immature to lay down sustainable memory traces of events for later recall, I review the early development of retention skills. In this chapter, I examine the literature on memory up to the age of 2 years, beginning with an overview of the different procedures that are used to assess infant memory. The results from these various paradigms are presented along with a discussion of what type of memory is being measured and the implications of these findings for long-term retention of events from this age. As I show, although considerable work needs to be done to adequately answer the questions posed earlier, one can come to some tentative conclusions that have implications for more general theories of the development of memory.

The growing consensus from the literature on very early memory development is that from the earliest days of life infants can encode, store, and retrieve a great deal of information about events in the world that they experience and that they retain this information over considerable time periods (for recent reviews, see, e.g., Bauer, 1996; Howe & Courage, 1993, 1997b; Rovee-Collier, 1997). Although there are clear developments in long-term retention skills (to be discussed shortly), infants are capable of storing and later retrieving information about events that occur in their lives. In fact, there is some evidence that information encoded prenatally can be retrieved in the first few postnatal hours. For example, DeCasper, Spence, and their colleagues (DeCasper & Prescott, 1984; DeCasper & Spence, 1986, 1991; Spence & Freeman, 1996) showed that long-term memory and retention were functional before birth by having mothers-to-be read passages (e.g., *The Cat in the Hat, The Gingerbread Man*) out loud at regular intervals to their fetuses during the last trimester of pregnancy. Within 33 hr of being born, these newborns showed a preference for the prenatally exposed auditory stimuli. Because considerable research has gone into eliminating other possible explanations for such preferences and because postnatal auditory experience could not be used to explain such preferences, it seems reasonable to conclude that long-term memory is operational before birth.

Although exhibiting recognition for fairly specific prosodic patterns is impressive, it is a far cry from remembering one's life events while in utero. However, it does mark what may be the beginning of early memory. Unfortunately, researchers do not know how long such memories last because it is not obvious how the relevant follow-up experiments can be conducted without the influence of continued exposure to the maternal voice nor is it apparent whether such auditory recognition memory is similar to the type of memory researchers mean when they refer to recollection of events. That is, such memories may be more like conditioned responses or fragmentary associations than memories of events in one's life. Although I defer discussion of this issue until later in this chapter, it is clear that for learning to occur memory must be present (also see recent discussions by, e.g., Mandler & McDonough, 1997). However, the question remains, although people may perform a learned response (e.g., riding a bicycle) or exhibit an acquired preference (e.g., preferring the maternal voice reading *The Cat in the Hat*), do they remember the events that produced that learning (e.g., hearing *The Cat in the Hat* being read in utero) and, if not, does this constitute evidence that these are two distinct aspects of memory? Whether researchers consider what was learned (e.g., procedural memory) to be a different form of memory from recollection of the learning experience itself (e.g., declarative memory) or simply refer to them as different aspects of a single stored memory, is fundamentally irrelevant to whether such aspects of memories are dissociable. That is, researchers can apparently recall one without recalling the other, and one type or component of memory (e.g., procedural) may be preserved even in cases of amnesia, whereas the other (e.g., declarative) may not be (also see McDonough, Mandler, McKee, & Squire, 1995). Regardless, although it would seem prudent to conjecture that retaining prenatal auditory preferences into the first few hours of postnatal life is not akin to recalling in utero experiences as part of one's autobiography, these results do suggest that the potential for some form of long-term memory is operational before birth.

This same issue is of concern whenever memory is assessed nonverbally, which means it is normally a problem in the age range being discussed in this chapter. Indeed, this issue is more broadly related to the general concern of whether memory development consists of the continuous development of a single memory system or the discontinuous development of numerous memory systems and is a problem that has vexed this field for some time (e.g., for recent overviews see Bauer, 1995; Howe & Courage, 1993, 1997b; C. A. Nelson, 1995; Rovee-Collier, 1997). Information pertinent to behavioral aspects of this debate unfolds across the different sections in this chapter. I begin with an exegesis of what is known about early memory development, starting with an overview of findings from the mobile conjugate reinforcement paradigm. This is followed by a discussion of other research on early memory including deferred imitation, elicited imitation, and novelty preference. Finally, I conclude that there is little evidence, neurophysiological or behavioral, that supports the idea that separate memory systems exist with different developmental trajectories.

EARLY MEMORY DEVELOPMENT PARADIGMS

Mobile Conjugate Reinforcement

Nowhere have the issues introduced in the preceding paragraphs been more hotly debated than with regard to the work of Rovee-Collier and her colleagues (for recent overviews, see Rovee-Collier, 1997; Rovee-Collier & Boller, 1995; Rovee-Collier & Shyi, 1992). In her mobile conjugate reinforcement paradigm, infants learn a contingency between their own foot-kick response and the movement of an overhead mobile (the reinforcing event). Following acquisition of this contingency, there is a retention interval followed, in experimental conditions, by a reactivation treatment 24 hr before a test of retention. Reactivation simply involves the re-presentation of an aspect of the original event (e.g., the motion of the mobile, the bumper pad used in the crib during acquisition), not the entire conditioning event (as one might see in a savings paradigm, e.g., where the difference between the original time to learn and relearning is used as an index of retention). If the reminder used at reactivation is a component of the stored trace, it can presumably be used to flesh out the trace again, making it active in memory and hence retrievable. In general, because infants who receive the reactivation treatment remember the contingency better than control infants who do not receive reactivation, one can use this procedure not only to evaluate what features were encoded in the original memory trace but also, by varying the length of the pre-reactivation interval, evaluate the "decay" function for the various features. Presumably faster decaying features (e.g., peripheral information) will not be very stable reactivators over time, a finding that should tell researchers what elements of an event are important and preserved in memory with time.

With this procedure, Rovee-Collier and her colleagues have established the course of very early memory development from 2 to 6 months of age and isolated a number of factors that are critical in the maturation of early long-term memory and retention. Prominent among these findings is that infant age and length of the retention interval are positively correlated, and differences in retention are larger in earlier months than in later months (e.g., see Rovee-Collier & Shyi, 1992). Indeed, 2-month-olds exhibit considerable forgetting after a single day and little or no retention after 3 days (Greco, Rovee-Collier, Hayne, Griesler, & Early, 1986); 3-month-olds show minimal forgetting after 4 days and little or no retention after about 13 days (Sullivan, Rovee-Collier, & Tynes, 1979); and 6-month-olds have a relatively shallow forgetting slope with an asymptote near 21 days (W. L. Hill, Borovsky, & Rovee-Collier, 1988). Of course, the poor retention of even 2-month-olds can be alleviated with additional training (Hayne, Greco, Early, Griesler, & Rovee-Collier, 1986), particularly if that training is distributed across time rather than all at once (Ohr, Fagen, Rovee-Collier, Hayne, & Vander Linde, 1989; Vander Linde, Morrongiello, & Rovee-Collier, 1985), a ubiquitous finding with infants of other species (e.g., R. Richardson, Riccio, & McKenney, 1988; Solheim, Hensler, & Spear, 1980), children (e.g., Dempster, 1988), and adults (e.g., Postman & Knecht, 1983). These effects are usually attributed to greater variation in feature sampling over time, leading to a greater variety of features being encoded into memory traces with more distributed study opportunities, something that should lead to less labile traces, which should in turn lead to a higher probability of retrieval as the additional features increase the number of potential cues that could lead to trace recovery (e.g., Rovee-Collier, Early, & Stafford, 1989). Unfortunately, there is little unambiguous evidence to indicate that younger infants benefit more from distributed practice than older infants (contrast Enright, Rovee-Collier, Fagen, & Caniglia, 1983, with Ohr et al., 1989).

Of course, work with older infants using this paradigm shows that retention continues to improve with age. Furthermore, like older children and adults, infants' retention is affected by variables such as the extent to which proximal (mobile) and distal (context) cues match at training and tests of retention and are subject to both reinstating and interfering effects of information presented during the retention interval (for reviews, see Rovee-Collier & Bhatt, 1993; Rovee-Collier & Boller, 1995). These latter findings are particularly important. Consider reactivation first. Here, simply providing partial information about the original training and context can facilitate retention in infancy. What this means is that considerable information remains in memory even after forgetting sets in, including information about the display itself (e.g., the properties of the mobile) as well as the surrounding context (e.g., the crib bumper pad; Rovee-Collier & Shyi, 1992). Interestingly, older infants (e.g., 6-month-olds) require more specific information than younger infants (e.g., 3-month-olds). Regardless of age, however, the effectiveness of reactivation is determined by how closely the reactivating stimulus matches the current contents of the memory trace, which is in turn correlated with the nature of the events (interfering or reinstating) that have intervened during the retention interval as well as the length of the retention interval itself. However, once a trace is reactivated, it can be retained for at least as long as it could after training. All other things being equal, it is theoretically possible that given continued reactivation of an event such an experience might be remembered over a lifetime (see Rovee-Collier & Hayne, 1987).

However, all things are rarely, if ever, equal. For example, analogous to older children's and adults' source misattribution errors (for a review, see M. K. Johnson, Hashtroudi, & Lindsay, 1993), 6-month-old infants' memory for the context of an earlier learned event may not be accurate even though the event itself can be remembered. That is, when aspects of a previous event are encountered in a new context, that context may be falsely remembered as the event location, with the original context being forgotten altogether (e.g., Boller, Rovee-Collier, Gulya, & Prete, 1996). Similarly, there is now considerable evidence that even 3-month-olds are highly susceptible to retroactive interference even after a brief exposure to new information during the retention interval (Rovee-Collier & Boller, 1995). This finding is similar to that in older children (Howe, 1995), adults (Postman & Knecht, 1983), and the eyewitness memory literature (e.g., Loftus, 1993). As Rovee-Collier and Boller (1995) pointed out, however, memory updating of the sort that occurs with interference, regardless of one's preferred mechanism (e.g., whether it involves the blending of new and old information in the same trace, the erasure of old by new information, or the construction of a newer trace that is appended to and may supplant the old one), may be particularly adaptive early in development, when much of the information encountered is novel.

The research that has emerged from Rovee-Collier's laboratory shows that the mechanisms (neural and otherwise) that are essential for the establishment (encoding and storage) and subsequent retention and behavioral display (retrieval) of early conditioning experiences are functional early in life (e.g., see Rovee-Collier & Shyi, 1992). Hartshorn and Rovee-Collier (1997) have recently shown that these findings are not confined to the use of the mobile conjugate reinforcement paradigm, at least for 6-month-olds. Using an alternative operant lever-pulling task involving the movement of a toy train, comparable patterns of long-term retention, memory reactivation, and cue specificity at retention were obtained. Similarly, using an analog of the traditional paired-associates task in which arm or leg movements were associated with the activation of a mobile or a music box, Timmons (1994) found that 6-month-olds required reactivation for 3-week, but not 3-day, retention intervals. Importantly, then, the findings from Rovee-Collier's laboratory may be task independent.

Moreover, the data generated from this research group define memory continuity by many of the variables that affect infant memory performance having similar effects in childhood and adulthood (also see reviews in Howe & Courage, 1993, 1997b). Although I return to the issue of continuity and discontinuity in memory development later, it is important to note its presence in this context, because there is some question about whether Rovee-Collier's procedure provides a measure of declarative memory, the type of memory functioning usually associated with event recall. As already noted, this issue is particularly bothersome when nonverbal or behavioral measures of recollection are used which, by definition, they must be in this age range. Thus, despite the similarity in the effects of variables across ages, as well as the similarity in their effects in the conjugate reinforcement paradigm and in more traditional declarative memory tasks, the question remains, Is there a way in which the conjugate reinforcement paradigm can be integrated into the declarative memory literature?

First, although it would be nice to argue that because the effects of memory variables in this conditioning procedure and more traditional procedures that assess declarative memory are similar that both tasks are therefore tapping the same type of memory, such an argument is overly simplistic. In fact, such similarities do not constitute evidence that both tasks are tapping the same type of memory at all. This is because it could simply be that regardless of how memory is measured, these variables have a uniform effect. Second, because conditioning procedures have been more often associated with procedural, not declarative, memory, it may be prudent to view the conjugate reinforcement paradigm as tapping procedural memory and view the similar effects as evidence for overlap or cross-talk between different measures of memory. Again, however, this dichotomy is not as clear-cut as some might wish. As Barr, Dowden, and Hayne (1996) suggested, because even 3-month-olds can learn and retain the contingency between kicking and the movement of the mobile through simple observation in the absence of prior practice (e.g., Greco, Hayne, & Rovee-Collier, 1990; Hayne, Greco-Vigorito, & Rovee-Collier, 1993; Rovee-Collier, Greco-Vigorito, & Hayne, 1993), something that is said to occur in memory tasks that are deemed declarative (see the subsequent discussion), the mobile conjugate reinforcement paradigm may provide a measure of declarative memory. Indeed, Rovee-Collier (1997) has cogently argued that her task does tap, in young infants, declarative (explicit) memory because it satisfies the criteria normally used to distinguish procedural (implicit) and declarative (explicit) memory. Regardless of how one views the preceding argument, it does portend an important theme in memory development: Are there really distinct forms of memory—ones that come on-line at different times and have distinct developmental courses—or is there a single memory system whose development is fundamentally continuous? According to Rovee-Collier, there is no evidence to support the claim that different memory systems with dissociable developmental patterns exist. If there are different memory systems, they must surely exhibit similar developmental trajectories. Before elaborating on this theme, I turn to a consideration of results from paradigms that are, less arguably, tapping what researchers consider to be "declarative memory."

Deferred Imitation

There is almost unanimous agreement that the deferred imitation task represents a measure of declarative memory and that it is this latter type of memory that researchers are referring to when they use the term *recall*. When researchers use the term *recall*, they generally mean that perceptually absent information is brought into conscious awareness (see Mandler & McDonough, 1997). Because the information being recalled is not perceptually available, it must be represented in some manner in memory. Thus, information in declarative memory must have been interpreted and represented at some earlier point in time, a process that required that the individual conceptually represent the past experience in memory. When individuals can verbally express these memories, they convey that they have represented that experience in memory and are making explicit their conceptualization of the past event. However, when only nonverbal measures are available, infants must show their conceptualization behaviorally. More important, if researchers are to establish that the memory is not based simply on a conditioned, procedural (motoric) response, then, according to some, it must also be shown that recall is based on a cognitive representation and not on a behaviorally practiced maneuver.

Deferred imitation fulfills these requirements because a behavioral event is demonstrated to the infant who does not get the opportunity to perform the behavior immediately. Following a 24-hr or longer retention interval, the infant is given the opportunity to imitate or reenact the behavior that was witnessed earlier. For example, a 6- to 18-month-old watches an adult remove a mitten from a puppet, shake the mitten to make a hidden bell ring, and then replace the mitten. Alternatively, the adult might light up a panel by touching it with their forehead. Using procedures like these, there is now ample evidence that infants will successfully imitate novel actions witnessed, but not performed, 24 hr earlier. Deferred imitation has been demonstrated in 9-, 14-, and 24-month-old infants and toddlers with retention intervals ranging from 24 hr to 1 week (Meltzoff, 1985, 1988a, 1988b, 1990). Indeed, Meltzoff (1995) has shown that 14- and 16-month-old infants can reenact modeled events after delays of 4 months. Interestingly, deferred imitation generalizes across changes in the imitated object's size and color as well as the context in which imitation is tested (Barnat, Klein, & Meltzoff, 1996). Finally, Meltzoff and Moore (1994) showed that infants as young as 6 weeks of age exhibit deferred imitation of facial expressions following a 24-hr delay, although the nature of this imitation may not be the same as that found in older infants.

Interestingly, deferred imitation occurs not only from watching live models but also, as many parents know, from television. For example, Meltzoff (1985) has shown that 14-month-olds exhibit deferred imitation for televised actions, although Barr and Hayne (1996b) found that it was not until 18 months of age that infants showed deferred imitation of videotaped actions. The difference here may lie more in the difficulty of the actions being imitated than in the ability to imitate from videotaped rather than live displays.

Barr et al. (1996) have also shown that organization is important in deferred imitation in young infants. Here, 6- to 24-month-olds were shown three specific actions with a puppet and demonstrated excellent retention of these actions when asked to imitate them 24 hr later. Using a 1-week retention interval, Barr and Hayne (1996a) showed that 18-month-olds were sensitive to the temporal structure of events in a deferred imitation task. Here, relationships between modeled actions either followed a causal sequence (e.g., put a plank on a block, put a toy frog at one end of the plank, push the other end of the plank to make the frog "jump") or were arbitrary (e.g., put a block on the plank, put the frog on the plank, push the frog). Causally related sequences were better imitated by the 18-month-olds 1 week later than were the arbitrary sequences. Thus, despite variation in event complexity, ranging from simply removing a puppet's mitten, shaking its hand, and then replacing the mitten (e.g., with 12-month-olds in Barr et al., 1996) to making a frog jump by constructing a teeter-totter (using a small board and a wedge), placing a frog at one end, and hitting the other end of the board (e.g., with 18-month-olds in Barr & Hayne, 1996a), infants in the first 2 years of life are well able to store in and later retrieve from memory earlier witnessed events. Unfortunately, although this procedure does provide information about the infant's ability to represent and recall information, it does not indicate directly the infant's knowledge about when or where the event happened (something that becomes important later in discussing the nature of autobiographical recall).

Elicited Imitation

In a closely related paradigm, infants and toddlers are shown a modeled target action or actions that they are required to imitate immediately as well as after retention intervals of varying lengths. Here again, modeled events can consist of causally linked sequences or simply be arbitrarily associated. Like the results from deferred imitation studies, elicited imitation studies have clearly shown that recall is superior for causally rather than arbitrarily organized events and that 11- to 24-month-olds use this causal information in their recall of events involving sequences of up to five components (for reviews, see Bauer, 1995, 1996). Moreover, recall can be facilitated and extended by several hours (young infants) to several weeks (older infants) when these event components are causally structured, familiar, and verbal cues accompany the retention test (Bauer & Dow, 1994; Bauer & Hertsgaard, 1993; Bauer, Hertsgaard, & Wewerka, 1995; Bauer & Mandler, 1989, 1992; Bauer & Shore, 1987; Bauer & Thal, 1990; Bauer & Travis, 1993). Indeed, at least for 18-month-olds, causal structure seems to be more important than prior practice with the action sequence (Barr & Hayne, 1996a). Some event sequences can be remembered up to 3 months by 11-month-olds (Mandler & McDonough, 1995) and 12-month-olds (Howe & Courage, 1997a) and over an 8-month interval by 13- to 21-month-olds (Bauer, Hertsgaard, & Dow, 1994), and there is some evidence that individual object-specific actions that were acquired at 11 months of age can be remembered up to 24 months of age (McDonough & Mandler, 1994).

More recently, Mandler and McDonough (1997) reported that the relative advantage of causally organized over arbitrary sequences may be present as early as 9 months. Nine-month-olds reproduce two-action causal sequences after a 24-hr interval but have difficulty reproducing such sequences when they are arbitrary. Similar findings have been reported for deferred imitation in 6-month-olds (Barr et al., 1996). That is, 6-month-olds could imitate as well as 12-month-olds immediately after modeling and, with additional exposure to the modeled actions, could reproduce at least one of those actions following a 24-hr delay. As Mandler and McDonough (1997) pointed out, such findings are consistent with the claim that a conceptual, not simply motoric, representation is a prerequisite for deferred imitation and that both nonverbal and verbal expressions of recall are influenced by the same variables from early in life. Although children are exposed to the same number of actions and objects for the same amount of time, action–object pairings that are causally linked (e.g., one must open the box before retrieving the toy that is inside it) tap into conceptual knowledge the child already has about how the world works, whereas arbitrary orderings (e.g., placing the toy next to the box and then tapping the top of the box) do not. Such differences between meaningful events (e.g., causally sequenced) and nonmeaningful (e.g., arbitrary sequences) events are routinely observed in recall throughout the life span (e.g., Bjorklund, 1987). In fact, it is well-known that when people encode and store information in memory, they do so by interpreting, organizing, and imposing meaning on that information (e.g., Tulving, 1984). Indeed, as new knowledge structures become available, people may recode or reorganize information already in storage (e.g., Howe & Brainerd, 1989; Howe & O'Sullivan, 1997). Note that meaningfulness is important in recall by at least 9 months of age, if not at 6 months of age (Barr et al., 1996) or earlier.

These findings show that young infants can retain information about events for up to at least 8 months. Is there any evidence that events can be remembered for longer periods of time, especially when intentional learning or conditioning was apparently not involved? Interestingly, in this context, Perris, Myers, and Clifton (1990) found evidence that some aspects of an experience at 6 months of age were retained over a 1-year span. However, a longitudinal study of infants' memories of a toy-play event experienced at home at 10 and 14 months of age and in a laboratory setting at 32 and 60 months of age revealed less, not more, event recollection with time (Meyers, Perris, & Speaker, 1994). Boyer, Barron, and Farrar (1994) also failed to find evidence of memory for a nine-action event sequence learned at 20 months of age and recalled 12 and 22 months later. Although the research is somewhat sparse and is methodologically heterogeneous at this point, it would seem that very long-term retention of early experiences is more the exception than the rule. Although infants can certainly retain information over long periods of time, what is retained appears to be fragmentary, especially over protracted retention intervals (also see Howe & Courage, 1997b).

An interesting exception to this can be found in some recent work by Bauer and her colleagues (Bauer, Kroupina, Schwade, Dropik, & Wewerka, 1998). Those authors have recently provided evidence of verbal recall of events that were most likely encoded and stored before productive language. However, there is an important caveat to this finding, namely whether what was being recalled was in fact autobiographical (i.e., children were reporting on contrived events sequences they had learned 12 months earlier in a laboratory setting, events whose causal sequencing, not the experience itself, could have been derived from a generic representation). As Bauer et al. (1998) pointed out, although the memories did contain some specific episodic features, it was not clear that they could be classified as autobiographical.

Interestingly, like Rovee-Collier's (e.g., 1997) finding that reactivation extends retention in young infants, a number of researchers have established that reinstatement (partial re-presentation of the original learning event) and reenactment (complete re-presentation of the learning event) forestall forgetting in older infants and toddlers. For example, using an 8- to 10-week retention interval, Sheffield and Hudson (1994) found that events reenacted 24 hr before a retention test were better remembered than nonreenacted events by 14- and 18-month-olds. Similarly, Hudson and Sheffield found that reenactment produced near perfect retention in 18-month-olds for events learned 6 months earlier. Indeed, it has been shown that some reenacted events that were originally learned at 18 months of age are remembered 1 year later (Sheffield & Hudson, 1994). Thus, like younger infants, older infants' and toddlers' memories can be extended over considerable intervals given the opportunity to reexperience part or all of the original event. Note here that subsequent reencounters with events do not always lead to better memory for the original event. In fact, as shown in subsequent chapters, such reexperiencing can often result in recall that "blends" a number of experiences together rather than being a faithful recollection of the individual events (also see Howe, Courage, & Peterson, 1995).

Novelty Preference

Another set of procedures that has been used to examine infant memory, ones that are probably among the earliest to be used in this field, involves the examination of early recognition as exemplified in the habituation–dishabituation and paired-comparisons paradigms. Arguably, the preceding methods (i.e., mobile conjugate reinforcement, deferred imitation, and elicited imitation paradigms) involve measures of cued recall in that the presentation of the ribbon and mobile (among other cues in the mobile conjugate reinforcement paradigm), like the presentation of the objects involved in the modeled events (among other cues in the imitation procedures), serve as cues for infants to recall the associated actions. (Note in this context that Rovee-Collier preferred to think of her paradigm as a measure of delayed recognition as opposed to cued recall.) In the habituation–dishabituation and paired-comparisons methods, both of which are novelty preference paradigms, infants are presented with stimuli that they have experienced before and must recognize those stimuli through some sort of (typically visual) preference response. That is, like recognition memory tasks used with older children and adults, infants must either "recognize" a stimulus as old or new when presented singly (as in the habituation–dishabituation method) or indicate which of two stimuli is the new stimulus when pairs of old and new stimuli are presented simultaneously (as in the paired-comparisons method). For example, in the habituation–dishabituation design, infants are either continuously or repeatedly exposed to a visual stimulus (e.g., a checkerboard pattern) until their attention to that stimulus declines to some predetermined absolute or relative level that is indicative of having encoded, stored, and recognized that stimulus. After this habituation, the infant is successively presented the old habituated stimulus (the checkerboard) or a new previously unseen stimulus (e.g., concentric circles forming a bull's-eye). If attention remains low to the old stimulus and high to the new stimulus, the infant is said to have recognized the old stimulus.

In the paired-comparisons variant of this procedure, infants are exposed to an identical pair of stimuli (e.g., two checkerboards) for a fixed familiarization period. After this familiarization period, infants are presented with the old (checkerboard) and new (bull's-eye) stimuli simultaneously. Here, like before, continued inattention to the familiarized stimulus coupled with heightened attention to the new stimulus was said to be an index of the infant's recognition of the familiarized pattern as having been seen previously (for an overview of both of these procedures, see Courage & Howe, 1998b).

Using either of these paradigms, information about the early development of recognition memory can be obtained. For example, research based on these paradigms has revealed that at and even before birth (e.g., DeCasper & Spence, 1991), infants exhibit robust immediate recognition memory for visual, auditory, tactile, and olfactory stimuli (for a review, see e.g., Olson & Sherman, 1983). Interestingly, when stimulus complexity and time to encode are controlled across age, developmental differences in recognition measures are few (e.g., Hunter & Ames, 1988), and infant recognition memory appears to be resistant to interference from stimuli presented during the retention interval (e.g., Cohen, DeLoache, & Pearl, 1977). These results echo those found with older children (e.g., W. Schneider & Pressley, 1989), in which developmental advances using recognition memory measures tend to be considerably smaller than those associated with measures of recall (free or cued).

Several criticisms have been leveled at the habituation and paired-comparisons procedures, ones that may compromise the interpretation of findings from this literature. For example, to exhibit recognition memory for an item, infants must not only have the familiarized stimulus in memory but also find the alternative or new stimulus "interesting" enough to attend to (e.g., Rovee-Collier, 1987). That is, not only must there be memory for the old stimulus, but there must also be a preference for the new stimulus. If the alternative stimulus is not interesting, or at least not as interesting as the familiarized one, infants might not exhibit "memory" not because they have forgotten the original stimulus but simply because they prefer the familiarized one. Clearly, stimulus preference (among other variables) needs to be carefully controlled in studies of this sort.

Despite problems with recognition memory studies, including the ones reviewed here, the novelty preference paradigm is enjoying a recent resurgence and is being used effectively as a technique for assessing infant long-term retention. The thinking here is that if infants' preference for novel stimuli immediately after familiarization is an index of the strength of the familiarized stimulus in memory, then examining the *pattern of change* in infants' preference for novel and familiar stimuli over time might similarly track the course of long-term retention. That is, as time passes and the trace for the familiarized stimulus weakens, attention to the novel stimulus declines and a preference for the familiar stimulus reemerges. Using this logic, Bahrick and Pickens (1995) examined changes in 3-month-olds' novelty preference over a 3-month interval. Using memory for object motion (e.g., an object moving in a horizontal or circular motion), retention of a familiarized stimulus was measured using the paired-comparisons method in which separate groups of infants were tested at 1 min, 1 day, 2 weeks, 1 month, and 3 months. They found novelty preference at the 1-min delay, no preference at the 1-day and 2-week delays, and a familiarity preference at the 1- and 3-month delays. Using a similar paired-comparisons procedure and auditory stimuli (e.g., the nursery rhymes "Humpty Dumpty," "Crooked Life") with 7-week-olds, Spence (1996) found that infants showed a preference for a novel rhyme after a 1-day interval, no preference after 2 days, and a familiarity preference after 3 days.

Both of these patterns can be interpreted as indicating an initial phase characterized by novelty preference in which memory for the familiarized stimulus is robust, a second or transitory phase characterized by no preference in which memory for the familiarized stimulus is waning, and a third phase characterized by familiarity preference in which features associated with the familiarized stimulus are being refreshed or perhaps updated. Of course, there is a possible fourth stage in which responding returns to no preference, wherein the familiarized stimulus may be completely forgotten. Interestingly, this pattern seems to hold regardless of whether test intervals are manipulated between or within subjects. That is, using a paradigm much like that of Bahrick and Pickens (1995), but manipulating test intervals within as well as between infants, Courage and Howe (1998b) found a similar pattern of forgetting by 3-month-olds over a 3-month retention interval. These findings not only provide converging evidence on the ability of young infants to retain information in memory over protracted retention intervals but also extend the duration of these intervals considerably over those established using other recognition paradigms (e.g., Rovee-Collier, 1997).

Although studies of long-term infant recognition are making a resurgence only now, it is important to note that several researchers consider the novelty preference paradigm to be a measure of declarative memory (McKee & Squire, 1993). McKee and Squire's foundation for asserting that novelty preference taps declarative memory comes from the area of neuroscience research, particularly research with adults with and without amnesia. Although there is disagreement about the generalizability of research with adults to conclusions about infants and toddlers (e.g., Rovee-Collier, 1997), surely the analysis of task demands should be the same regardless of age. Thus, like other findings reviewed in this chapter, there appears to be converging evidence supporting the conclusion that declarative memory may be present by at least 3 months of age, if not before.

CONCLUSION

Research shows that infant and toddler memory is exceedingly robust. Although there certainly are key developments in the type and amount of information retained, as well as increases in the length of the retention interval over which information can be maintained, it is clear that even 3-month-olds can remember information over protracted intervals.

The studies reviewed in this chapter provide little behavioral evidence favoring the view that more than a single memory system emerges over the first 2 years of life. Regardless of how the distinction between implicit and explicit memory or between procedural and declarative memory was framed, infants as young as 3 months of age may well have both. That is, using both recognition and (cued) recall tests, infants as young as 3 months of age exhibit long-term retention of memories formed solely on witnessed, but not practiced, experiences, a phenomenon held up by many to be the sine qua non of declarative memory. Thus, although memory may often appear to be discontinuous on the surface (e.g., a change in recall from purely nonverbal to one that permits verbal recall of past events), the underlying processes and mechanisms that are memory are perhaps best conceived of, at least if one wishes to be consistent with the empirical facts, as a unified constellation, one whose growth is continuous. Consistent with this perspective, events stored during an individual's "preverbal" phase (for current purposes, before the onset of productive language) can be subsequently reported using words once the individual becomes more facile with the linguistic expression of the contents of memory (Bauer et al., 1998; West & Bauer, 1999). Although other developments (e.g., the personalization of event memory with the establishment of autobiographical recall; see chap. 5 in this book) certainly lead to changes in memory that can, for example, lead to increased capacity and longevity of memory, these changes do not represent fundamental alterations in the hardware or architecture of memory. Rather, such changes herald alterations in the cognitive software that drives memory organization, ones that augment the types of features available for extraction, storage, and retrieval within a unified memory system.

Overall, then, it is more parsimonious to conclude that there is only a single, unitary memory system from birth (or before), one that can encode, store, and retrieve information needed to perform both procedural (implicit) and declarative (explicit) memory tasks. Indeed, this system is robust enough to support recognition of visual displays in 3-month-olds over a 3-month retention interval as well as cued recall of reenacted information over a 1-year (and perhaps longer) interval by 18-month-olds. Although such accomplishments are remarkable, they are certainly not on the same order of magnitude as the recall feats of older children and adults and do not constitute the type of memory usually associated with autobiographical event recollection. Clearly, subsequent developments in memory do occur, ones that I argue are fundamentally of the cognitive software variety and that serve only to augment an already robust, unitary memory system. Indeed, these subsequent developments, rather than bringing new hardware, new processes, or new mechanisms on-line, simply serve to improve an already efficient system. It is this set of changes (e.g., in knowledge, strategies, metamemory, etc.), ones that serve to augment the implementation of an already functioning memory system and give rise to apparent discontinuities in memory development at the level of behavior (e.g., more detailed, although not necessarily more accurate, recall of an event; more efficient organization of information in storage), that is the focus of the next chapter.

3

MEMORY DEVELOPMENT DURING THE PRESCHOOL YEARS

As discussed in the preceding chapters, memory functioning is remarkable early in life, at least relative to what has been held historically. Indeed, it appears that all of the basic mechanisms necessary for encoding, storage, and retrieval are present and functioning at or even before birth. However, this does not mean that memory is complete in infancy. To the contrary, there are numerous advances that occur in memory development, ones that help children take full advantage of these basic mechanisms. In particular, changes in the cognitive "software" that engage these basic processes lead to increases in the rates of information acquisition, duration of information in storage, and reliability in accessing that information. This occurs in part because children gain access to new features that can be encoded and used for storing, recoding, and retrieving information in memory (e.g., see Howe & O'Sullivan, 1997). These advances in turn are brought about in large measure by more global gains in children's cognitive and social functioning, including changes in knowledge (e.g., acquisition of new semantic and conceptual representations), acquisition and fine-tuning of strategies (e.g., focusing and deployment of attention), and metamemory (e.g., replacing naive beliefs about memory and the mind with those that are more realistic; see O'Sullivan & Howe, 1998).

Nowhere are all of these changes better illustrated than in the advances that culminate in the emergence of the "cognitive self," an event that heralds the onset of autobiographical memory (see Howe & Courage, 1993, 1997b). It is not until features of the cognitive self are available and recognizable to toddlers that they can even begin to use these self-features in their encoding of events, organization of events in storage, and retrieval of those events in long-term memory. As discussed in chapter 2, it is not that young infants and toddlers cannot remember events over fairly extended retention intervals but that it is only when the cognitive self emerges that these memories become personalized and hence autobiographical. Note that this "onset" of autobiographical memory does not require a cataclysmic neurological development or the addition of a new and independent memory system. Rather, according to this theory, autobiographical memory arises as a simple consequence of coincident social and cognitive achievements, ones that permit toddlers to use newly discovered self-features to benefit memory.

Because autobiographical memory is central to the theme of this book, I present a much more detailed discussion of that topic in chapter 5. Here, discussion of memory development during the preschool years is centered on how changes in cognitive software, although oftentimes appearing to affect memory functioning and performance in discontinuous ways, are in fact consistent with the underlying assumption that memory development is fundamentally continuous. Because a number of such topics have already received extensive and recent coverage—children's metamemory and strategy development (e.g., W. Schneider & Pressley, 1997) and children's memory for eyewitnessed events (e.g., Ceci & Bruck, 1995) —here I focus on achievements in other, related domains. In particular, I emphasize several issues that are relevant not only to immediate concerns of understanding early memory development but also serve as an important backdrop to topics addressed in later chapters (particularly memory for traumatic experiences and autobiographical memory). I begin with a synopsis of some general changes that occur in memory performance during the preschool years, ones that illustrate the inherent continuity of memory development. I then focus on two contemporary ideas about memory development (i.e., models of cognitive inhibition and fuzzy-trace theory) and some new research generated to examine these ideas (e.g., children's directed forgetting, false memories). Finally, I provide an overview of changes in knowledge that influence which features are encrypted into memory and which features facilitate long-term retention, a basic appreciation of which is essential to understanding how changes occur in autobiographical memory. It is against this background that a discussion of the influence of distinctiveness in memory makes sense, a topic that forms the last section of this chapter.

GENERAL TRENDS IN PRESCHOOL MEMORY DEVELOPMENT

The sophistication and variety of memory behaviors increase dramatically during the preschool years in terms of both what is acquired and retained as well as how memory is organized and expressed. As already indicated, children become more strategic and acquire considerable information about how memory operates, information that becomes useful in guiding the acquisition and retention of information (W. Schneider & Pressley, 1997). Furthermore, not only can memories be organized autobiographically, but with improvements in productive language skills, most memories can be expressed verbally (a discussion of the role of language is deferred until chapter 5, where theories of autobiographical memory are discussed). In addition, although 8- and 9-month-olds can successfully search for and retrieve hidden objects (for reviews, see P. L. Harris, 1987; Willatts, 1990), studies with children over the first 5 years of life show substantial improvement in memory for location. These improvements have been found to be due to the increasing sophistication of children's search strategies rather than to an increase in memory per se (e.g., DeLoache & Brown, 1983; DeLoache & Todd, 1988). Indeed, 3- and 4-year-old children can use location information to retrieve objects (e.g., hidden toys) in large-scale environments and use spatial context to facilitate recall (e.g., Hazen & Volk-Hudson, 1984).

Children's memory for events also continues to improve including eyewitnessed incidents (Ceci & Bruck, 1995). Many of these improvements are confined to relating (peripheral) details of episodes in recall narratives rather than recalling the gist or central details of the event. For example, younger (2-year-old) children are more likely to forget (or fail to report) objects involved in an event, but not the event itself, than older children (Jones, Swift, & Johnson, 1988). Indeed, older children's reports are often richer than younger children's not because they actually recalled more of what happened but because they are better at using their general knowledge to reconstruct details of the events that occurred (e.g., see Myles-Worsley, Cromer, & Dodd, 1986). For example, even though a young girl might not explicitly remember opening a door to get from her bedroom to the hallway, when recalling such an event she may infer that she must have opened the door; otherwise, how could she have gotten from her bedroom to the hall? Often, such inferences are not separated from what was really remembered in recall narratives and may even be mistaken by the rememberer as something he or she actually remembered.

Although children's recall of events improves with additional knowledge (see later sections in this chapter), it also improves in terms of the types of cues that can be used to reinstate those memories. For example, Howe, Courage, and Bryant-Brown (1993) found that 3.5-year-olds' recall in a memory-for-location task could be improved simply by having the experimenter visit the children before the retention test. Salmon and Pipe (1997; Salmon, Bidrose, & Pipe, 1995) found that under some circumstances, even 3-year-olds can benefit from seeing toylike representations of real objects to aid recall even after a 1-year delay.

Despite clear improvements in preschool children's ability to store and retain information used in laboratory tasks (e.g., word lists, picture lists, paired associates) as well as more naturalistic events (e.g., going to the museum), like infants and toddlers, preschool children's memory performance still varies in the same predictable manner in response to changes in the amount and distribution of practice, organization, reinstatement, postevent information and retroactive interference, encoding conditions, and the effects of being tested (see the section on false memories). For example, like older children and adults, Howe (1995) found that preschoolers' performance on picture lists decreased reliably under conditions in which retroactive interference was induced. Howe (1998c) found similar interference effects when preschoolers recalled stories. These findings are akin to those obtained with infants (e.g., Rovee-Collier & Boller, 1995). Similarly, retention is improved in adults (e.g., Postman & Knecht, 1983), children (e.g., Dempster, 1988), and infants (e.g., Rovee-Collier & Bhatt, 1993) as practice on the to-be-remembered information is distributed rather than massed across time. Again, the point is simply that despite developmental advances in areas such as speed of encoding and retrieval, amount retained, and periods over which information can be held in long-term storage, most variables continue to affect basic memory processes in the same manner throughout childhood. This same pattern holds for other areas of memory development discussed in this chapter. Indeed, nowhere is this better illustrated than in research on the role changes in children's inhibitory abilities play in memory development.

CONTEMPORARY MODELS AND RESEARCH

Cognitive Inhibition and Directed Forgetting

Although the idea that inhibitory processes are important in learning (e.g., classical conditioning), memory, and cognition has been around for some time, the popularity of this explanation has gained considerably in recent years (e.g., see the book by Dempster & Brainerd, 1995). Indeed, changes in inhibition and inhibitory mechanisms have been used to account for improvements in performance during infancy (e.g., Diamond, 1988, 1990a, 1990b, 1991), toddlerhood (e.g., Luria, 1961), the preschool and early elementary school years (e.g., Harnishfeger, 1995), adolescence (e.g., Schiff & Knopf, 1985), as well as declines in performance that occur during later adulthood (e.g., Hasher, Stoltzfus, Zacks, & Rypma, 1991;

Hasher & Zacks, 1988; McDowd, Oseas-Kreger, & Filion, 1995). Essentially, the notion is that because the amount of information people can process is limited, they must have some mechanism by which they can keep out task-irrelevant information. For example, if one is trying to remember the name of a male friend, one would want to selectively search only male names of people one has met and ignore the names of women or people whom one has heard of (e.g., through the media) but not met. Similarly, when one is at a party in which there are numerous auditory and visual inputs occurring simultaneously, one must screen out many of those inputs (e.g., conversations, noise) so that one can selectively attend to the conversation one wishes to participate in.

More formally,

> cognitive inhibition [italics added] is the suppression of previously activated cognitive contents or processes, the clearing of irrelevant actions or attention from consciousness, and resistance to interference from potentially attention-capturing processes or contents. At a basic level, inhibitory processes control the contents of consciousness as well as the operation of processing activities, restricting attention to only the relevant aspects of the environment and limiting processing to only those necessary for the task at hand. (Bjorklund & Harnishfeger, 1995, p. 143)

The ability to inhibit behavior and cognition is something that develops and that, at least in terms of behavioral inhibition, may be linked to age-correlated changes in the prefrontal cortex, an area of the brain with extensive reciprocal interconnections with just about every part of the nervous system (e.g., Fuster, 1980, 1984, 1989). The prefrontal cortex is one of the last areas of the brain to reach full maturity and enjoys a period of rapid development between birth and 2 years and again between 4 and 7 years, with subsequent growth being more gradual into young adulthood (Luria, 1973). These neurological changes, which include changes in the size and complexity of individual neurons as well as mylenation, are associated with behavioral changes in inhibition. For example, Diamond (1988, 1990a, 1990b, 1991) found that over the first 2 years, infants are better able to inhibit inappropriate reaching responses en route to a goal of retrieving a toy.

Dempster (1993), Bjorklund and Harnishfeger (1995), and Harnishfeger (1995; Harnishfeger & Bjorklund, 1993) have argued that these neurological changes also underlie advances in children's ability to suppress or inhibit cognitive responses. For example, Harnishfeger and Bjorklund (1993) found that in a categorized cued-recall task, there were fewer intrusions in recall for older (i.e., grades 3 and 6) than younger (i.e., preschool and kindergarten) students, where task-inappropriate intrusions index a failure to inhibit competing material. Moreover, when these intrusions were classified as being task relevant (i.e., belonging to the same category as the cue) versus task irrelevant (i.e., not belonging to the same category as the cue), more of the younger children's responses were from the latter than the former grouping. Similar findings were obtained under free-recall conditions. Thus, younger children are less able than older children to inhibit the production, or at least the output, of inappropriate responses in free- and cued-recall settings.

There are several other findings that show that older children are better at inhibiting both behavioral as well as cognitive and memory responses than younger children. The issue is whether and in what manner these differences are related to neurobiological developments in the frontal lobes. Again, the problem is that the link between hypothesized neurobiological changes and cognitive development is constrained, at least in part, by the fact that much of the direct evidence (as noted in chap. 1 in this book) is based on data from animal models or humans who have brain pathologies. Moreover, although it is clear that neural inhibition is an important property of brain functioning, it demands a considerable leap of faith to say that changes in these properties (e.g., changes at the level of the synapse) are directly related to changes in cognitive inhibition. Finally, but perhaps most seriously, changes in frontal lobe functioning have become an explanatory panacea for a wide range of limitations and advances in cognitive functioning, making it a viable explanation of none. For example, changes in frontal lobe inhibitory mechanism functioning have been posited to underlie the development of self-control, which in turn is important to a developing sense of self (e.g., Mischel, Shoda, & Rodriguez, 1989). In a similar vein, changes in frontal lobe functioning are said to be critical to autonoetic consciousness, the capacity to represent and be aware of personal experiences in the past, present, and future (Wheeler, Stuss, & Tulving, 1997). Such changes are said to contribute to psychiatric disorders (e.g., obsessive–compulsive disorders; Malloy, 1987); individual differences in IQ measures (e.g., McCall & Carriger, 1993); individual differences in working memory tasks (e.g., Harnishfeger & Bjorklund, 1993); evolution of human intelligence (e.g., Bjorklund & Harnishfeger, 1995); and a variety of motor, perceptual, and linguistic tasks each with its own developmental course (e.g., Dempster, 1993). Although neurobiological changes might indeed have such far-reaching consequences, the evidence certainly does not support such a claim. Thus, although changes in children's ability to inhibit (or direct) cognitive activity is clearly important, its link to changes in the prefrontal cortex is somewhat precarious.

As a result of the recent interest in the role of inhibitory processes in cognitive development, there has been a resurgence of research on directed (intentional) forgetting. The ability to forget information (through conscious or unconscious means) has been an important component of theories about the fate of early memories, particularly if those memories are ones for traumatic incidents. In addition, though, directed forgetting is of interest in its own right simply because it provides a window on how well, if at all, children (as well as adults) can control their own forgetting. Forgetting of information may be important in a number of everyday circumstances, particularly if prior information interferes with learning new information (see Bjorklund, 1997). Moreover, forgetting old information may be critical when updating outdated information. For example, when moving to a new home, it is important to replace an old address with a new one and an old telephone number with a new one. Similarly, when switching from one computer operating system to another or updating to a more current version of a particular program (whether it be a graphics or word-processing package), it may be helpful to extinguish old commands before learning the new ones associated with the change or upgrade.

Although there are many theories concerning the mechanisms underlying intentional forgetting (for a review, see H. M. Johnson, 1994, as well as chapters in Golding & MacLeod, 1998), some of which suggest that differential rehearsal of information may be at the heart of selective forgetting, many other models emphasize the importance of inhibiting previously learned information. In the classic paradigm used to examine directed forgetting, participants are presented with some material that is to be studied and, after study, are told to remember some items and to forget others (e.g., Bjork, 1972). Although such information may not in fact be forgotten, the goal is to recall the to-be-remembered items with little or no intrusions from the to-be-forgotten materials. This can be achieved by selectively rehearsing the to-be-remembered items, devising a search algorithm that locates only to-be-remembered items, or inhibiting (suppressing) retrieval of the to-be-forgotten items. Given that directed forgetting involves inhibition and that younger children are less able than older children to inhibit cognitive activity, younger children should be less able to engage in directed forgetting than older children.

Most of the studies conducted to date have been with children older than preschoolers, perhaps because it has been believed that inhibition is not sufficiently well developed until well after the preschool years (e.g., Harnishfeger & Pope, 1996, pp. 297–298). In any event, these data do tend to tell a consistent story about the locus of children's directed forgetting effects, namely that like adults (e.g., Bjork, 1989), they appear to be due to retrieval inhibition (Harnishfeger & Pope, 1996; Lehman & Bovasso, 1993; Lehman, McKinley-Pace, Wilson, Slavsky, & Woodson, 1997; Lehman, Morath, Franklin, & Elbaz, 1998). However, they tell a less consistent story about developmental changes in directed forgetting. Although Harnishfeger and Pope (1996) found that directed forgetting improved gradually over the elementary school years (i.e., from grades 1–5), with retrieval inhibition still requiring further modification even after grade 5, Lehman and her associates (Lehman & Bovasso, 1993; Lehman et al., 1997, 1998) found effective retrieval inhibition in children as young as 7 years of age, although there were improvements between childhood and adulthood.

Interestingly, Lehman et al. (1998) suggested that differences between children and adults in retrieval inhibition may be due to differences in discriminating items in memory. In their research, Lehman et al. (1997, 1998) used a story about a honeybee who needed to find honey to save his hive. Children were invited to help the bee remember places where he found honey and forget places where there was no honey. Each of the locations was represented by a picture (black-and-white line drawings of objects such as a lamp, tree, etc.) and if honey was at that location it was represented by showing the child a honeypot. In general, the authors found support for the retrieval inhibition hypothesis, that is, directed forgetting occurs because children, regardless of age, actively inhibit access to information stored in memory. However, results also suggest that children may be worse at retrieval inhibition than adults not because of differences in the ability to inhibit information per se but because children may exhibit poorer encoding of items than adults, something that may contribute to their poorer item differentiation in memory (i.e., discriminating those locations to be forgotten from those to be remembered; see Lehman et al., 1998). Although poorer encoding may contribute to age differences in directed forgetting, a stronger case for this hypothesis could be made under conditions in which age and learning rates were not confounded. (This is a serious methodological problem and one that complicates much of the research on early memory development, not just directed forgetting. A more formal treatment of this problem, and its solution, is presented later in chap. 7.)

Note that in much of this research, forgetting instructions targeted specific items. Although analogous to the examples given earlier in which someone is trying to forget an old telephone number, it is not akin to trying to forget entire (traumatic) events. In a more recent series of experiments, Howe (1997b, 1998c) examined preschoolers' ability to forget entire episodes after they had been learned to a criterion of perfect recall. Here, a retroactive interference paradigm was used in which two sets of information were learned sequentially and, after a delay, recall of the first-learned information was requested. Specifically, 4-year-olds were asked to learn two stories, one at a time, with study and test trials continuing until they could recall both stories without error. Other children, those in the control group, learned only a single story. Normally, when asked to recall the first (or only, in the case of control children) story learned 24 hr later, children in the control condition do much better than children in the retroactive interference condition (also see Howe, 1995). This is because information from the second story intrudes or interferes with recall of the first story, something that happens not only in experimental circumstances such as these but also in more naturalistic settings with emotional events (see Howe et al., 1995).

The idea behind the directed forgetting manipulation was that if preschoolers could "forget" the interfering material (i.e., the second story), their performance 24 hr later should be like that of the control children. To examine this release from retroactive interference hypothesis, some of the children, after learning the second story, saw the experimenter act flustered, telling the children that she had made a mistake and that they were not supposed to have learned this second story. She then instructed the children to simply forget the second story. The next day, when the experimenter returned and asked the children to recall the first story they had learned, consistent with the hypothesis, preschoolers in the directed forgetting condition did significantly better when recalling the first story they had learned than their counterparts who had learned both stories but had not received the directed forgetting instruction. Compared with the control condition, however, directed forgetting had reduced, but not eliminated, retroactive interference. There was also evidence that the underlying source of preschoolers' failures during recall was attributable to processes operating at the level of storage. Like Lehman et al. (1998), the data from this experiment suggested that preschoolers had difficulties recoding or discriminating information already present in memory that was to be recalled from that which was not. Interestingly, when the directed forgetting manipulation was presented at the time of retention testing rather than at the end of acquisition, preschoolers showed little or no release from retroactive interference. To the extent that effective directed forgetting requires isolation of the information designated "to be remembered" from information that is "to be forgotten," such directed forgetting instructions seem more useful for preschoolers at the time the information is acquired rather than after the information has been consolidated 24 hr later. This flexibility in recoding information in memory may be one aspect of memory that develops between childhood and adulthood, as it is well-known that adults have little difficulty with such recoding operations at the time of a retention test (e.g., Bower & Mann, 1992). Indeed, in a recent series of experiments it was found that older children were better able than younger children to use category cues to reorganize interfering information in storage to reduce retroactive interference (Howe, Peddle, & Wadwahan, 1999).

What these findings indicate is that both storage and retrieval processes are important in directed forgetting regardless of whether one is referring to individual items or entire episodes. That is, retrieval inhibition is implicated as a direct source of intentional forgetting, with recoding of information in storage (i.e., discriminating or isolating information to be recalled from information not to be recalled) contributing to the effectiveness of these inhibitory processes (Howe, 1997b, 1998c; Lehman et al.,

1998). It is also clear that the term *directed forgetting* is a misnomer in that it is not forgetting at all that happens but directed remembering. That is, the to-be-forgotten material still resides in memory; it is simply a matter of attempting to direct one's retrieval attempts to other to-be-remembered items. This is a critical point because, as seen later when memory for traumatic experiences is considered (see chap. 4 in this book), there is evidence that individuals with a history of childhood abuse are better than those without such a history at directed remembering, a process that is, arguably, the one studied here. Regardless, it is clear that whatever one calls this phenomenon, even preschoolers have sufficient inhibitory abilities to engage in directed forgetting, something previously thought extremely unlikely (e.g., Harnishfeger & Pope, 1996). Furthermore, further developments in directed forgetting appear to involve memory discrimination processes rather than necessarily additional refinements in inhibitory processes. Thus, although inhibition skills may develop in several domains, it is not clear what role they have in explaining the development of early memory.

Fuzzy-Trace Theory and False Memories

Another global model of memory development, *fuzzy-trace theory*, takes advantage of the distinction between verbatim memory and memory for the gist of events (for recent reviews, see Brainerd, Howe, & Reyna, in press; Brainerd & Reyna, 1998; Reyna & Brainerd, 1995). In essence, the argument is that children store separate memory traces of the to-be-remembered target's verbatim information (its surface forms and other item-specific properties) and gist (its semantic, relational, and elaborative properties). These representations have different life spans with verbatim representations being forgotten more rapidly than gist representations. Finally, verbatim and gist memories of the same inputs develop at different rates. In terms of acquiring information, the usual assumption is that memory for the gist undergoes a more protracted developmental course, as it is to a large extent knowledge driven, than verbatim memory. There is also evidence, from recognition memory studies, that verbatim memories also undergo considerable development (for a review, see Brainerd et al., in press). Concerning long-term retention, it has been argued that developmental changes in verbatim memories are more pronounced than those in gist memories (e.g., Bjorklund, 1995). That is, because retention improves between childhood and adulthood and then declines during later adulthood and because verbatim traces are inherently more forgettable than gist traces, age fluctuations in retention are probably more a matter of changes in verbatim memories than gist memories (see Brainerd et al., in press). Empirically, the adequacy of this assumption is unknown because the data that bear on this proposal have yet to be collected.

Although this theory is intended to cover a variety of memory development phenomena (e.g., discussed in chap. 5 on autobiographical memory), it is perhaps best exemplified by its unique and comprehensive account of the ontogeny of false memories in childhood (see Brainerd & Reyna, 1998). This is an extremely important issue in memory development, one that has both theoretical and legal ramifications. Recall that the effects of misinformation are thought to decline with age, including those that are due solely to memory factors (see Ceci & Bruck, 1995). For example, older children are less likely than younger children (particularly preschoolers) to confuse something they were told happened during an event they witnessed with what it was they actually witnessed. Although such effects can arise because of source monitoring failures (e.g., forgetting that the source of one memory was something that one was told, whereas the other memory was for the event actually witnessed; for a review, see M. K. Johnson, Hashtroudi, & Lindsay, 1993), they can also arise because of differential access to verbatim and gist traces in memory. Indeed, this latter account can not only explain how suggestibility arises and how false memories occur as a result of external and internal stimuli but it can also explain developmental trends in both.

Before turning to this account, consider the nature of false memories and their developmental course. False memories arise because of the external suggestion that it is often indirect as well as internal processes that give rise to feelings that one has memories for things that have occurred when they have not (see contributions in Pezdek & Banks, 1996, and Schacter, 1995; also see Spanos, 1996). In the former case, the suggestion can be about an aspect of an event that actually occurred (as in the traditional eyewitness memory experiment) or an entire event can be suggested or implanted. For example, Ceci and his colleagues (Ceci, Huffman, Smith, & Loftus, 1994; Ceci, Loftus, Leichtman, & Bruck, 1994; Huffman, Crossman, & Ceci, 1996) had children who were 3–6 years old "think real hard" about and report whether they could remember events they had experienced in their past as well as an event (provided by the experimenters) that had not happened. Typically, 10 such sessions were held, with each separated by a 7- to 10-day period. The event that had not happened involved a child getting his finger caught in a mousetrap and subsequently having to go to the hospital. The initial results showed that the younger children made more false reports that this fictitious event had in fact really happened than did the older children, an outcome that did not change across repeated interviews. In fact, using a procedure designed to mimic the use of visualization techniques often used in psychotherapy, the number of false reports increased across interviews.

Over time in the absence of repeated interviewing, however, the number of false reports tended to decline for the older but not the younger children. Interestingly, a similar pattern was observed for true reports. For the older children, there was a substantial decline in reports of events that had actually happened, whereas for younger children, there was actually a modest increase over the 2-year interval. Not only were there different trends at long-term retention for the younger and older children, it may be that false memories are more durable than true memories, at least under some conditions (cf. Huffman et al., 1996, and Reyna & Lloyd, 1997).

Alternatively, like retroactive interference effects in which material experienced most recently interferes with recall of earlier learned information (e.g., see Howe, 1995), more recent experiences can intrude when children are trying to recall a specific event that happened sometime in the past. Although these effects are considered again in chapters 5 and 6, such interference is important here because these intrusions are not always detected by the person remembering, with the two events becoming "blended" in their recall narrative forming—for all intents and purposes —a false memory. For example, Howe et al. (1995) studied preschool children's recall of a traumatic childhood event. Children's (30-, 36-, and 48-month-olds') recall of an emergency room experience and the event that precipitated the visit was assessed initially and after a 6-month retention interval. Interestingly, although children's recall was extremely accurate at both interviews, especially for the gist of the event, there were also a number of intrusions produced at the 6-month recall interview, ones that originated from additional medical experiences that occurred during the 6-month interval. For instance, one child was relating the target event in which she had an eye injury and said that "I got a lollipop when I hurt my arm and went to the hospital (p. 131)." The problem in many circumstances in which children are being interviewed is that the interviewer would not be able to detect that this was an intrusion, especially if the child is not aware of it either. (Note that in this study, the experimenters knew a priori what the target event was, something that investigators and interviewers rarely know for certain ahead of time. As well, Howe et al. were able to confirm that the intruded event was from an additional medical experience by checking with the child's parents and medical records when appropriate.) Such memory blends amount to false memories inasmuch as the blended event never occurred. Importantly, however, although children of all ages produced intrusions, the number of intrusions declined with age. Thus, like the "mousetrap memories," memory "blends" based on intrusions of other "real-life" events behave similarly to true memories. Indeed, false memories and real memories share a number of similarities, including the fact that they are both durable over some long period of time, with persistence having been reported for up to 2 years.

How can these trends be explained? According to fuzzy-trace theory, false memories and suggestibility arise either because gist memories are retrieved when verbatim memories are called for or because the wrong verbatim memories get recalled (Brainerd & Reyna, 1998). Using experimental analogs of these real-life examples, Brainerd and Reyna (1998) have shown that children's false recognition memories can be due to the similarity between the gist representation of a target memory (what was studied) and the subsequently presented misinformation. Simply stated, if the correct verbatim memory for the original event is not present or not retrieved or the wrong verbatim memory is retrieved, then children (and adults) may rely on the gist representation of the original event to judge whether the memory probe (e.g., interviewer's question, retrieval cue, recognition item) is correct. To the extent that the probe resembles the gist representation of the original event, the more likely it is that the probe will be falsely judged as having happened in the original experience.

Interestingly, this model predicts both developmental increases and decreases in false memories depending on the context in which memories are examined. That is, to the extent that a task engages gist representations, developmental increases in false memories can occur when age increases in gist retrieval exceed age increases in verbatim retrieval. On the other hand, to the extent that a task necessitates the use of verbatim traces, developmental decreases in false memories can occur when age increases in verbatim retrieval exceed age increases in gist retrieval. For example, in studies in which extremely long retention intervals are used (e.g., 6 months to 2 years), task demands will be greater on gist representations than verbatim representations because the latter are forgotten more quickly than the former. If developments in gist retrieval exceed developments in verbatim retrieval, then one should observe the pattern of false memory decline found in Howe et al. (1995) over long (6-month) retention intervals.

What this research indicates, particularly in terms of long-term retention, is that the capacity to retain both true and false memories develops. Indeed, the durability of false memories matches that of true memories, at least over a 2-year interval. Moreover, there are reasons to expect that the development of false memories closely parallels the development of true memories. This is because both "types" of memories use the same general principles, something that also turns out to be true for autobiographical memories and memories for traumatic experiences. As already mentioned in the context of fuzzy-trace theory, some of these important principles have to do with how children process information on the basis of similarity and distinctiveness (also see Howe, 1998d).

KNOWLEDGE AND LONG-TERM MEMORY

School-Age Children

For several decades, age differences in memory (both acquisition and long-term retention) have been attributed to age-correlated growth in knowledge base (for a review, see Bjorklund, 1987; Bjorklund & Schneider, in press). What children know affects what they encode, how that information is organized in storage, and the manner in which it is retrieved. Regardless of whether the task involves simple memory span (e.g., Dempster, 1978), free or cued recall (e.g., Howe, Brainerd, & Kingma, 1985a), or memory for events (e.g., Fivush, 1993; see contributions in Fivush & Hudson, 1990), the greater the background knowledge about the to-be-encoded information the better that information is remembered. Moreover, it is because older children have more (and differently organized) knowledge than younger children, that older children outperform younger children in most memory tasks. Indeed, studies in the 1970s and 1980s seemed to show that when familiarity and meaningfulness of the material were equated across age, developmental differences in memory performance vanished (e.g., Bjorklund & Bjorklund, 1985; Chechile & Richman, 1982; Ghatala, 1984; Richman, Nida, & Pittman, 1976).

Although knowledge may have been seen as a panacea by some, it is clearly not the only factor to influence developmental changes in memory performance. Indeed, children's use of memory strategies and the development of metamemorial skills (e.g., O'Sullivan & Howe, 1998) are also instrumental in age-related changes in memory, particularly in the later childhood years. It can be argued, however, that metamemory and mnemonic strategy use are by-products of changes in knowledge. In fact, O'Sullivan and Howe argued persuasively that metamemory is simply one type of knowledge: knowledge about memory, accurate and naive. Moreover, knowledge, strategies, and metamemory are highly intercorrelated in memory research (see the review by Bjorklund & Schneider, in press). Interestingly, in studies in which all of these variables have been measured, it is the variation in levels of knowledge that routinely account for the majority of the variance in memory performance (e.g., Alexander & Schwanenflugel, 1994; Hasselhorn, 1992; W. Schneider, 1993).

Given the importance of changes in knowledge, the following question remains: How does it influence memory? According to Bjorklund's (1987) original formulation, it did so in three ways: by affecting retrieval, by facilitating spread of activation among related items in memory, and by facilitating the use of strategies. To this list I could add that knowledge also facilitates the initial encoding of information inasmuch as knowledge directs the encoder to specific features in the to-be-remembered display. Moreover, knowledge can add considerable elaborative detail to an item's encoding when it is stored with other similar items in a knowledge space. That is, not only does an item's encoding potentially set off a series of between-items elaborations (as noted by Bjorklund, 1987), but it may also set off within-items elaboration in which an item might receive considerable embellishment because of its category membership (e.g., if the encoded item were *robin*, the information stored about the item might go beyond what was encoded using one's already existing knowledge about robins to add to and thereby strengthen the information stored in memory about item). The effects of greater between- and within-items elaboration on memory performance are well-known (e.g., Ackerman, 1984).

Clearly, not only does knowledge increase encoding efficiency, but it also provides for better elaborated and therefore generally more durable traces in storage. As it appears to be maintenance of trace storage that is the hallmark of developmental improvements in long-term retention from infancy to adulthood (see Howe & O'Sullivan, 1997), knowledge most likely exerts its effect through improving trace durability. Of course, trace accessibility on demand is also important, although less so in the development of long-term retention than the initial acquisition of information. To the extent that knowledge provides a basis by which information can be retrieved, changes in knowledge must also be related to improvements in children's retrieval skills. However, it is becoming clear that maintaining information in storage is the hallmark of the development of children's long-term retention (Howe & O'Sullivan, 1997) and that the primary influence of knowledge on children's long-term retention resides in the enhancement of this storage maintenance. Although this represents a shift away from Bjorklund's (1987) emphasis on retrieval effects, it is not inconsistent with his basic position.

Although knowledge may drive the development of memory in general and long-term retention in particular, measuring knowledge is not an easy task (see Chi & Ceci, 1987). One way to evaluate knowledge or expertise is to give children a test of their knowledge in a particular domain (e.g., football, hockey) and then to assess their performance on a memory task associated with that domain (e.g., see Clark, 1993; Gaultney, Bjorklund, & Schneider, 1992). Clark and Howe (1990; also see Clark, 1993) did just that by testing 8- to 10-year-old children's knowledge in a specific domain (biology in Clark & Howe, 1990, soccer in Clark, 1993) and having children who were more and less expert in these domains learn and retain stories about their areas of expertise and about areas in which they were not experts (e.g., the solar system). As predicted, there was a Story × Expertise interaction, both at acquisition and at retention. Specifically, stories that matched the children's expertise were learned more quickly and were better retained over a 1-month interval than stories not in the child's area of expertise. Moreover, there were no differences between experts and novices in their acquisition or retention of stories unrelated to their areas of varying expertise. Thus, having more knowledge in a particular domain is related to better memory (both acquisition and long-term retention) for information related to that expertise but not to better memory in general.

In addition, though, simply having more knowledge may not suffice unless that knowledge is organized efficiently. That is, two children could have the same amount of knowledge but perform differently on the same memory task. This performance difference may be because one child had his or her knowledge structured more efficiently than the other, evincing better performance on some related cognitive or memory task (see Chi & Ceci, 1987). Although there are several techniques for extricating knowledge structure (e.g., Falmange, Claude, & Doignon, 1988), many confound descriptions of the knowledge structure with the statistical technique used to measure the structure. A number of recent advances have been made in this area, ones that have appeared in the literature on children's memory for emotional and traumatic events and are discussed further in chapter 5. Note here that knowledge can have a wide-ranging impact on memory (both acquisition and retention) at all ages.

Preschool Children

Much of what has been reviewed in this section concerns children beyond preschool age. Indeed, for some time, the role of knowledge in memory development was examined mainly with children in the primary and elementary school years. Over the past decade or so, this situation has changed, and there are now considerable data showing that knowledge acquisition during infancy and the preschool years affects memory performance similarly to how it does in later childhood. Unlike the research with older children, the work with infants, and to some extent with preschoolers, has been one of establishing whether and what type of conceptual representations exist, with less attention being paid to how this knowledge is used to facilitate (or inhibit) memory functioning more generally. For example, work with infants has shown that even 7-month-olds can conceptually differentiate between categories such as animals (e.g., birds) and vehicles (e.g., airplanes; e.g., Mandler & McDonough, 1993). Although infants' concepts may be crude by adult standards, they nevertheless allow infants to make meaningful semantic distinctions, ones that are not available through perceptual categorization skills. Indeed, infants can differentiate things belonging to a kitchen and things belonging to a bathroom (Mandler, Fivush, & Reznick, 1987). At the least, these categories serve as the basis for early knowledge development, ones that organize information in storage and influence subsequent encoding.

Although the influence of this early knowledge on subsequent acquisition and retention performance has not been examined directly in young infants, their ability to use this information in generalization and inference tasks has been established. For example, Bauer and Dow (1994) demonstrated that 16- and 20-month-olds generalize props used in an event sequence (e.g., a teddy bear put to bed in a toy crib) with props from the same class (e.g., Big Bird and a toy bed). Similarly, Mandler and McDonough (1996) showed that 14-month-olds can generalize actions performed on models of animals (e.g., a dog drinking from a cup) or vehicles (e.g., starting a car with a key) to other animals (e.g., giving a bird a drink) or vehicles (e.g., starting an airplane with a key).

There is also some evidence that this knowledge can be used, at least by older (24-month-old) toddlers, to facilitate the subsequent acquisition and retention of information. For example, Ratner and Myers (1981) have shown that 2-year-olds' knowledge of which objects belong in which rooms of a house can facilitate memory performance on a task in which objects and their rooms serve as the to-be-remembered information. In a similar vein, the work by Bauer and her colleagues (Bauer, 1995, 1996) shows that even young toddlers can use their knowledge of temporal (causal) ordering to facilitate recall of event sequences. That is, causally ordered events tend to be better remembered than arbitrarily ordered events.

It is not simply knowledge itself that can alter retention performance but also how well that knowledge is structured. Recall that with older children, Chi and Ceci (1987) argued that it may not be the amount of knowledge per se that aids acquisition and subsequent retention but how that information is structured. To evaluate this hypothesis, Chi and Koeske (1983) examined the structure of a preschool child's (a 4.5-year-old's) knowledge of 40 dinosaurs. They identified two distinct knowledge structures for this information, one that was better organized (e.g., more elaborate and greater cohesion among elements) than the other. Of importance here is that the child's recall and long-term retention of dinosaurs over a 1-year interval was better for the more integrated information than for the less structured set of dinosaurs. Thus, cohesion of knowledge is important to long-term retention, not simply the amount of information (also see Howe & Brainerd, 1989).

Familiarity with and repetition of an experience, although not affecting accuracy directly, do influence the organization and (hence) durability of that information in storage for preschoolers and older children alike (e.g., Fivush, 1984; Fivush & Mandler, 1985; Hudson, 1986, 1990). Fivush and Hamond (1989) found that children who had experienced an event twice recalled the event better 3 months later than did children who had experienced it only once. Moreover, the children's recall was as good at 3 months as it had been during a test just 2 weeks after the experiences.

There is now a considerable body of evidence concerning the growth of knowledge base in preschoolers (aged 2–5 years), including children's knowledge of motion (e.g., Gelman & Gottfried, 1996), growth cycles in plants (e.g., Hickling & Gelman, 1995), and growth of animals (e.g., Rosengren, Gelman, Kalish, & McCormick, 1991). Although this research documents the growth of knowledge in a variety of domains, there is little research that addresses questions concerning the influence of this knowledge on memory acquisition and long-term retention. Like other knowledge, perhaps growth in these areas is matched with the development of better integrated and organized structures in storage, ones that may in turn give rise to more durable memories. Indeed, in some instances, repeated experiences may result in the extraction of a generic representation of an event, one that preserves the gist of like experiences at the expense of memory for each individual episode.

Concerning the emergence of generic representations, it has been argued that schemas or scripts are learned (or extracted from experience) by children and that these representations may be among the first to characterize the manner in which the world operates (e.g., K. Nelson & Gruendel, 1981). For example, children learn sequences of actions that commonly occur when going to the grocery store, to birthday parties, or to preschool. Specifically, much like the acquisition of conceptual categories, children may extract a common representational structure for these different events based either on their first experience (plus subsequent modifications) or on some abstraction that occurs after a number of similar experiences. These representations serve to guide behavior and expectations in similar circumstances and to save the child from having to represent each individual episode in memory. Indeed, adults may store only episodic information about frequently experienced events when something unexpected or unique occurs (e.g., something that does not match one's script).

Whether children store scripts (e.g., K. Nelson & Gruendel, 1981) or simply store gistlike generic representations of events (e.g., Reyna & Brainerd, 1995), the importance of knowledge in memory and long-term retention is without dispute. Although the exact parameters controlling the connection between knowledge and retention have not been specified precisely enough to chronicle the course of developmental changes in the knowledge–memory relationship from infancy through childhood, the pioneering work that does exist not only demonstrates the utility of studying knowledge base when trying to understand early (and later) memory development, but it also suggests several fruitful avenues for future investigations. Indeed, by understanding the nature of symbolic representations in infancy as well as the generic representations of experiences in preschool, researchers should be able to determine, to a large extent, the constraints on the types of information that infants, toddlers, and preschoolers will likely be able to encode, store, and later retrieve about their early life experiences. As seen in the following section, what children know plays an important role not only as an organizer for incoming information in children's memory but also by providing the background against which information receives distinctive processing, something that makes that information more durable in memory.

THE ROLE OF DISTINCTIVENESS

Perhaps one of the keys to understanding retention is that, more often than not, what is remembered best (at least in terms of individual experiences) is that which is distinctive from what is already known. Such information stands out from the background "noise" of one's other experiences and knowledge. Distinctive experiences or aspects of an event that are distinctive are best remembered not only over the short haul (e.g., immediate recall) but also over the long term (e.g., 1 year later). Indeed, such experiences are often maintained for a lifetime, especially when they are personally consequential and distinctive (Brewer, 1988; Linton, 1979; see also chap. 5 in this book).

Distinctiveness is important to memory and its longevity, but what exactly is it? Medin, Goldstone, and Gentner (1993) defined *distinctiveness* as the processing of differences relative to some context. In traditional list learning experiments, this might mean that children, for example, would learn a list comprised mainly of concepts from a single category, say animals. One item, the isolate, on that list would belong to a different category, say furniture. Here, the list of animal concepts serves as the context, and the lone item from the furniture category would receive distinctive processing relative to the background context. Thus, distinctiveness is determined dynamically because what is distinctive is inextricably bound to a background context, one that changes in time (especially for autobiographical experiences; see chap. 5 in this book).

In a typical experiment of the sort just outlined, the outcome is often that the isolate tends to be memorized more quickly, and is retained better, than the items forming the context. Few studies of this von Restorff effect (for an overview of the original work by von Restorff, see Hunt, 1995) have been conducted with children (cf. Rabinowitz & Andrews, 1973), and I know of no published studies on the effects for children's long-term retention. The only exception I could find is the recently completed study (reported briefly in Howe, 1997a) in which 5- and 7-year-olds found a distinctive item easier to learn and retain over a 3-week interval than items belonging to the context-setting category. Interestingly, as predicted, younger children did not benefit as much as older children when the isolate came from a different semantic category (e.g., a tool rather than an animal), but both groups benefited from a perceptual change (e.g., a shift from black-and-white pictures of objects to color pictures). Such differences are well-known in the literature on children's spontaneous use of semantic categories (e.g., Bjorklund, 1987) and illustrate the point that differences in what children know will influence what types of information receive distinctive processing. Although these findings hold for children older than preschoolers, preliminary results from experiments currently under way indicate that the same sorts of effects exist with younger children.

Outside of these more traditional laboratory experiments, distinctive processing plays an equally important role. However, it is much more difficult to control and measure the background context against which distinctive processing occurs. Although these issues are considered in greater detail in chapters 4 and 5, note here that the better researchers understand what knowledge, experiences, and expectations children bring with them to an event, the better position they are in to predict (and not simply postdict) what it is that children might remember from that event. If it is people's personal history and knowledge that serve as the backdrop against which distinctive processing occurs, then it is paramount that researchers find a reliable and valid measure of that background. More important, because this background changes with development and potentially with each new experience, it is important that these measures embody the inherently dynamic properties that define distinctiveness.

One approximation might be to ask what types of knowledge younger and older children have within a specific domain (e.g., as outlined in the previous section) and then to determine what might be distinctive from that information. To do this, consider the sorts of knowledge young children have, how that knowledge develops, and what sort of information differs from it in significant ways. In other words, consider what is known about the development of generic representations.

Developmentally, it has been speculated that although generic representations may be age invariant and easy to form early in life, younger children (e.g., 2-year-olds) are more likely to encode, store, and retrieve more typical aspects of events than elements that are discrepant. This may be because they are still novices when it comes to understanding how certain events unfold. During the preschool years, the argument continues, novices turn into experts whose representations contain both the generic representation and any instances in which violations have occurred. It is this transition during the preschool years that is thought to produce a developmental shift in recall from remembering the familiar to remembering the distinctive (see Fivush & Hamond, 1990).

Does such a shift exist? It has been argued that these effects are evident in children's recall of naturally occurring experiences in which, for example, younger children will tell an interviewer all of the typical elements in a scripted experience but older children may include some unique elements (e.g., Fivush & Hamond, 1990). There are similar reports for more experimental investigations. For example, Farrar and Goodman (1990, 1992) presented children with four experiences of an initially novel event. Three of the experiences were identical, with one deviating from the rest. They found that 4-year-olds had greater difficulty than 7-year-olds distinguishing between the routine (repeated) aspects of the events and those elements of the events that occurred only once. It was as if the younger children were still extracting the generic representation and the older children had already formed one.

Similarly, Fivush, Kuebli, and Clubb (1992) had 3- and 5-year-olds participate in three types of events: an event that was logical and invariant (making "fundough"), a logical event that varied (shape collage), and an event that was invariant but arbitrarily ordered (sand play). Half the children at each age experienced the events only once, and the other half experienced them four times. With both verbal and nonverbal (behavioral reenactment) recall, Fivush et al. found that performance was better (both quantitatively and qualitatively, as reflected in better organization) for the logical than arbitrary events at both ages. However, 3-year-olds in the single-experience condition recalled less about the variable event than in the two invariant events.

On the basis of findings such as these, several researchers have concluded that young children are still in the process of forming generic representations of everyday experiences and that they therefore do not recall unique or distinctive information about these events (e.g., Bauer, 1995; Farrar & Goodman, 1990, 1992; K. Nelson & Gruendel, 1981). Although the data may be consistent with the former conclusion, they certainly do not support the latter claim that young children do not recall distinctive episodes any better than routine ones. This is because such researchers have failed to provide independent evaluations of the status of the child's knowledge base before presenting the to-be-remembered event. Because researchers do not know what the child already knows about an event (although one might reasonably assume that older children bring more general knowledge to such situations than do younger children), it is difficult to determine what is discrepant from the child's knowledge of that event. At best therefore, like a test of generalization and inference, researchers can treat recall of the presented event as a test of knowledge of that event. What the data show, then, is that for the types of events studied to date, younger children do not have the same generic representations for these events as older children.

However, if experiments were conducted in which researchers knew what generic representations these younger children had, information that is discrepant from them would almost certainly be better remembered. This is analogous to what happened when researchers used lists that were age appropriate, that is, age differences in recall virtually disappeared (see the previous section). Similarly, as seen in chapter 2, infants, once habituating to a particular stimulus, prefer to look at and process stimuli that are novel or discrepant from the standard. There is every reason to expect that this remains unchanged from infancy through the preschool and childhood years. Indeed, as shown in the next two chapters, what children, even 2- and 3-year-olds, remember best about experiences that are emotional are those elements that violate their expectations, ones that are, by definition, based on exceptions to what they already know. In fact, there is a considerable database attesting to the importance of deviations from the expected in young children's retention of naturally occurring events, particularly when that information is salient (e.g., Howe, 1997a). There is also some evidence that 8-year-olds can recall the gist of novel events (e.g., going to the circus) that occurred only once up to 5 years earlier (Fivush & Schwartzmueller, 1998; however, see Howe, 1998b, for a discussion). Thus, these results show that distinctiveness is critical to memory and retention. Unfortunately, however, even if the distinctive or unique character of the information presented in the experiments reviewed earlier was salient to the young children, and it is not clear that it was, not knowing what the status of their knowledge was about these events before the experiment severely constrains any conclusions about their ability to remember (or not remember) distinctive information.

There are additional problems with these earlier studies in the form of stages-of-learning confounds. Confounds of this sort are endemic to much of the literature on the early development of long-term retention (e.g., see Howe & Courage, 1997a; Howe & O'Sullivan, 1997; also see chap. 7 in this book). Specifically, because younger children acquire any information more slowly than older children, perhaps because of differences in their knowledge base, their ability to extract relevant information will be more restricted. What this means is that, after a single presentation of an event (e.g., as in Fivush et al., 1992) or a deviation from a previously repeated event (e.g., as in Farrar & Goodman, 1990, 1992), younger children will have encoded and stored less information than older children. Thus, younger children may provide more generic information in their recall simply because they have not had the same opportunity to encode as much information about these events as older children. It is only when initial encoding (or learning) is equated that valid statements about what is later retained can be made independent of these initial encoding confounds. Moreover, to equate what is in memory, people must either (a) have an independent measure of the background knowledge that exists or (b) ensure that all children, regardless of age, are able to correctly recall the information before the retention interval and subsequent test. It is only when these sorts of controls are in place that researchers will be able to provide a more thorough examination of distinctiveness effects in memory during the preschool years.

Regardless, it does appear that, like many of the other variables examined in this chapter, the effects of distinctiveness and novelty are prevalent early in infancy and continue to influence memory and long-term retention throughout childhood. Clearly, what is needed is a more precise and reliable way of measuring the knowledge that children bring with them to the experimental setting to determine what is distinctive. Once these challenges have been met, researchers will have a clearer idea of exactly what place distinctiveness has in memory development as well as be able to determine its role in what aspects of events will be remembered over the long term. These issues are discussed in the next two chapters.

CONCLUSION

There are several significant developments that occur in memory over the preschool years. For example, not only do true memories of experiences enjoy increased longevity as children get older, so, too, do false memories. Moreover, many of these advances are based on earlier achievements. For example, although infants clearly use spatial location in their memory representations, the use of spatial cues improves over the preschool years. Similarly, early concept formation heralds later conceptual development, including the advent of generic representations, ones that facilitate memory acquisition and long-term retention. Although I have deferred discussion of one of these major achievements, autobiographical memory, until chapter 5, all of these accomplishments can be accounted for parsimoniously as being brought about by changes in the cognitive software that is used to drive basic memory (e.g., encoding, storage, retrieval) functioning. Indeed, it is often through changes in what one knows that memories become reorganized and new memories become easier to establish. As seen in chapter 5, such dynamic reorganization of memory can lead to changes in the accessibility of stored information over time, increasing or decreasing the availability of this information for recall depending on a number of variables. This reorganization in turn begets changes in what type of information is considered unique and distinctive. As shown later, one's first encounter with a car accident as an emergency medical services worker may stand out initially but, after numerous such experiences, these events may no longer be distinctive.

This dynamic model of long-term storage has recently been shown by Howe and O'Sullivan (1997) to account for a large corpus of data. Such data are also consistent with other recent models that emphasize the role of cognitive inhibition as well as more comprehensive approaches such as Brainerd and Reyna's (1998) fuzzy-trace theory. Regardless, the important message is that changes in storage maintenance, brought about in part by corresponding changes in knowledge, is the linchpin of the development of long-term retention skills in almost all domains.

4

LONG-TERM RETENTION OF EMOTIONAL, TRAUMATIC, AND OTHER DISTINCTIVE EVENTS

In the preceding chapters, much of the discussion centered on children's retention of events that were not particularly stressful or traumatic. A question that has emerged in recent years concerns whether events that are traumatic are remembered differently from those that are more mundane and everyday. Although research on this topic is still in its infancy, it has long been believed that trauma is particularly well remembered if not consciously, then at least unconsciously. That is, there is a long-standing belief that traumatic events remain with people for most if not all of their lives and that even if they cannot recall them, people's memories continue to affect them unconsciously. Indeed, this may be particularly true for traumatic events experienced early in life, as it is during this formative time that experiences of all sorts are thought to be crucial (for a recent overview, see Kagan, 1996).

In many ways, this seems to make great intuitive sense. For example, although the forgetting of what one had for today's breakfast might not seem that unusual, forgetting the experience of watching one's classmates and teacher being assassinated by a gunman in school does seem less likely. Being witness to traumatic incidents like this latter situation is not as rare as one might like, even in childhood. For example, this was exactly what

59

happened in 1996 in Dunblane, Scotland, when a former Scout leader walked into the primary school's gym where a class of 5- and 6-year-olds were starting their physical education lesson. Within 2 or 3 minutes, the teacher, 11 girls, and 5 boys were dead or dying and 12 students and 2 other teachers were injured (only 1 member of the class was not physically injured). In 1984 a sniper shot repeatedly at children on an elementary school playground in California. One child and a passerby were killed, and 13 other children and 1 playground attendant were injured (Pynoos & Nader, 1989). In another incident in 1988, a young woman entered the boys' washroom in an upper-middle-class suburban elementary school in California, where she wounded 1 young child and threatened 2 others with one of several handguns. In a second-grade classroom, she killed 1 child and wounded 5 others while classmates observed (E. D. Schwartz & Kowalski, 1991).

Understanding the fate of memories from traumatic experiences such as these is important because it will tell researchers whether such scenes are indelibly etched in memory (conscious or not). For example, many concentration camp survivors claim to have confidence in their memories for the heinous crimes committed at the camps, and for the perpetrators of those crimes. Although survivors often have accurate memories for repeated, routine aspects of the camp (e.g., food, housing), many of the details concerning emotional events are curiously absent or incorrect. This was particularly clear in the statements of 15 witnesses in the trial of suspected war criminal Marinus De Rijke (Wagenaar & Groeneweg, 1990). Some witnesses who had reported deaths, maltreatment, and violent assaults in their statements taken between 1943 and 1948 failed to recall these events in their later statements taken between 1984 and 1988, and some even denied making the earlier statements. As Wagenaar and Groeneweg (1990) pointed out,

> no matter how intense the emotions were felt at the time of encoding, no matter how clearly the images were engraved in the memories of the victims, no matter how certain the survivors were that they would never forget, 40 years of normal life . . . [left] . . . in many cases only the bare backbone of the experience. (pp. 86–87)

What studies like these indicate is that neither the emotional intensity of the experience (although, of course, measures of intensity were not taken at the time of these experiences) nor the individual recaller's level of confidence in their recollection are reliable indexes of recall accuracy. Indeed, as the recent literature (e.g., Bowers & Farvolden, 1996; Brainerd & Reyna, 1996; Brainerd, Reyna, & Brandse, 1995; Ceci, Huffman, Smith, & Loftus, 1994; Conway, Collins, Gathercole, & Anderson, 1996; Garry, Manning, Loftus, & Sherman, 1996; Hyman & Pentland, 1996; Spanos, 1996) and the preceding chapters have indicated, memory, even for traumatic experiences, is reconstructive, is subject to suggestibility, and can involve the construction of false memories.

The following question remains, however: Is it possible that traumatic experiences are etched in storage but simply not retrievable? Answering this question is perhaps not so straightforward, although it is paramount given the claims made by literally thousands of adults that they have remembered traumatic experiences from their childhoods (attributable somehow to the alleged sudden release of retrieval problems that prevented recovery of memories earlier). If it is true that such experiences are "carved" in memory storage for all eternity, this does not necessarily mean that one always has access to these memories because retrieval may be prevented by some (conscious, subconscious, or unconscious) mechanism. For all intents and purposes, such memories would appear to be "forgotten" until they suddenly reappear under more favorable retrieval circumstances (for a recent overview, see Erdelyi, 1996). It is not just these beliefs about adults remembering early traumatic events that need to be evaluated empirically; questions concerning how well children remember horrific crimes that many have claimed were perpetrated against them in their homes and day care centers also must be answered.

In this chapter, I examine the issue of whether memories for traumatic events differ from memories for nontraumatic ones. By the word *nontraumatic*, I do not mean mundane events such as having cereal for breakfast. Rather, I mean other events that have personal importance.

LONG-TERM RETENTION OF TRAUMATIC EXPERIENCES

Here I define *trauma* as physical and sexual abuse, painful and frightening medical procedures, exposure to situations in which violence is perpetrated on another (e.g., homicide of a parent), or involvement in a natural disaster (e.g., a hurricane). Children are all too frequently witness to or the unfortunate victims of traumatic events such as these. Whether children are directly or indirectly involved in these events, the question of what they remember about these incidents and whether these remembrances are different from their memories of other, not so traumatic experiences has not been answered satisfactorily. Adults may experience transient forgetting of experiences that were traumatic in childhood because of so-called "normal forgetting processes" or because intervening events have altered their interpretation of the original experience. This dynamic interplay among age, knowledge, experience, and memory recoding may be important when explaining failures to recall traumatic events. Interestingly, adult recall of traumatic childhood experiences can often appear extraordinary, at least in terms of the durability of such memories, with the majority of individuals recalling being sexually (e.g., Loftus, Polonsky, & Fullilove, 1994; Williams, 1994) or physically (Femina, Yeager, & Lewis, 1990) abused. In a 17-year follow-up study of survivors of a disaster, even those individuals who were 2 years old at the time of the disaster still remembered the event (Green et al., 1994). Although I return to this point later, to establish the reliability of these memories as well as the rate and type of forgetting such memories undergo, one must first establish what children themselves can remember about traumatic events and then track how such events have been reinterpreted during the retention interval and when they are subsequently reported.

Putting aside this methodological issue for now, the questions that need answering are: What is it about traumatic events that children remember, and do these remembrances differ in any way from their memories of other experiences? The evidence is unanimous in its declaration that children can and do recall traumatic experiences over considerable intervals. Even 2- to 3-year-old children can recall single traumatic episodes such as the murder of a parent (e.g., Terr, 1988, 1991). Indeed, these same children not only recall those events, but they may also experience intrusive memories of the episode (Malmquist, 1986; Pynoos & Eth, 1984). Children not only recall unique, one-time events but also, contrary to some speculation (e.g., Terr, 1994), traumatic experiences that are repeated. For example, it has been shown that in a number of high-profile abuse cases, the probability of a survivor remembering the abuse increased as a function of the number of abuse incidents (e.g., Archdiocesan Commission, 1990; Goleman, 1992; Yapko, 1994). Although repeated events may become highly regularized in memory, such generic representations preserve the gist of the experiences, perhaps at the sacrifice of the specific details of each incident. Clearly, severe trauma can be remembered over long intervals regardless of the witnesses' participatory status. This is true from early in life (e.g., 2 years of age), with representations remaining relatively stable over lengthy intervals, even into later adulthood.

Children also remember extreme corporal punishment (e.g., DiTomasso & Routh, 1993). Like other forms of abuse, even though these punishments usually take place in private, the punishments are rarely discussed openly, the punishments are often meted out by caretakers, and children are often motivated to subsequently "forget" the events, such beatings tend to be remembered all too well. Findings such as these run counter to suggestions that selective forgetting might be a mechanism for coping with childhood trauma (e.g., Briere & Conte, 1993). To the contrary, it might be more adaptive for children to understand what contingencies set off abuse and to learn to avoid them in the future. In situations in which there is no discernable rhyme or reason to the abuse and the child remains in the abusive household, it may be adaptive to enhance memory for other, more pleasant events associated with the home or the abuser. Thus, although the child retains memories of the abuse, he or she may attempt to counter such memories by accentuating memories for more pleasant information that are not associated with abuse.

For example, Cloitre, Cancienne, Brodsky, Dulit, and Perry (1996) examined directed forgetting in 24 individuals with borderline personality disorder and early life parental abuse; 24 individuals with borderline personality disorder and no history of parental abuse; and 24 matched, healthy, nonclinical control individuals. All participants were given a list of words to study, some of which were designated "to be remembered" and others "to be forgotten." On the basis of the assumption that individuals with abusive histories are more likely to be better practiced at intentional forgetting than those who have not been abused, as the former are likely to try to forget their abuse, it was hypothesized that they should forget more of the to-be-forgotten items than individuals in the other groups. Contrary to speculation, there were no group differences in the recall of those items designated as to be forgotten. Instead, there were large differences favoring the group with abusive histories in the number of to-be-remembered items that were recalled. In addition, although differences in recall emerged on these explicit (cued recall) memory measures, there were no group differences using implicit (word-stem completion) memory measures.

Despite a number of limitations in the Cloitre et al. (1996) study (e.g., the to-be-remembered/forgotten information consisted of word lists, not personally traumatic experiences), the results suggest a number of interesting possibilities. For example, although victims of abuse may not be any better than other individuals without abusive histories at controlling their forgetting, they do seem to be better at enhancing to-be-remembered information in memory. Thus, it may be that children with abusive histories, particularly young ones, although not having any better directed forgetting skills to help eradicate memories of the abuse, may have better directed remembering skills to help them retain memories for events not associated with the abuse. In this way, the child reduces the cognitive dissonance associated with remaining in an environment that is personally threatening:

> The abused child may not forget instances of abuse, but rather may elaborate in his or her own mind instances of care and loving by the caretaker as a way of preserving the attachment to the caretaker. This interpretation is consistent with the perplexing phenomenon, anecdotally reported by clinicians and potentially exploited in courtrooms, that some abused individuals have heightened memories of positive experiences with their caretakers even though they have acknowledged them as abusive. (Cloitre et al., 1996, p. 209)

The consequences of large-scale natural disasters also have been examined. For example, Parker, Bahrick, Lundy, Fivush, and Levitt (1995; also see Shaw, Applegate, & Schorr, 1996) examined children's reactions to and recollections of the Class IV Hurricane Andrew that created havoc in Homestead, Florida, in August 1992. Like in studies of abuse, the children most affected by the storm tended not to recall many peripheral details (related primarily to the aftermath, including cleanup and repairs), but all of the children who were 3 to 4 years old at the time of the hurricane remembered the event.

To the extent that posttraumatic stress disorder (PTSD) involves the recollection of the target stressful event that precipitated the onset of PTSD (either in terms of conscious recall of the event or the seeming involuntary, unwanted, and intrusive interjection of memories for the incident in daily life), there is evidence that many natural and human-made disasters are remembered throughout one's life span. For instance, although they are young children at the time of the event, many individuals subsequently remember traumatic experiences throughout the ensuing years. Examples include the 1988 Armenian earthquake (e.g., Najarian, Goenjian, Pelcovitz, Mandel, & Najarian, 1996), a fatal bus–train collision in Israel (Tyano et al., 1996), Scud missile attacks during the Gulf War (Laor et al., 1997), and imprisonment in Cambodia (Kinzie, Sack, Angell, Clarke, & Ben, 1989). As seen earlier in the example of memories for concentration camp experiences (Wagenaar & Groeneweg, 1990), these memories, too, have undergone considerable reconstruction. Unfortunately, because initial recollections of these experiences were not available for comparison purposes, one cannot adequately assess the degree of accuracy. It is safe to say, however, that some remnants of the gist of the originally encoded experience remain with these individuals, just as they do with victims of sexual and physical abuse.

A somewhat clearer picture of what is remembered over time comes from the literature on children's memory for medical treatments. Because retention measures are often taken shortly after and at various intervals after the incident, more exact comparisons between reports can be made and changes in memory more precisely evaluated. The incidents that have been studied range from daily injuries (Peterson, Moreno, & Harbeck-Weber, 1993) to anticipated examinations such as the voiding cystourethrogram (VCUG: children are catheterized, their bladder is filled with radioactive fluid, and they are then required to urinate on a table while being X-rayed; e.g., Goodman, Quas, Batterman-Faunce, Riddlesberger, & Kuhn, 1994; Merritt, Ornstein, & Spicker, 1994) to surgical procedures (e.g., Stuber, Nader, Yasuda, Pynoos, & Cohen, 1991) to other serious but unexpected events such as accidents resulting in emergency room treatment (Howe, Courage, & Peterson, 1994a, 1994b, 1995).

Another advantage of these studies is that they serve as analogs to "real-life" abuse traumas. In the case of emergency room treatment, children experience painful and unexpected events. In VCUG studies, children are exposed to anticipated but painful, unwanted, and embarrassing genital contact. In all cases, the reports indicate that children's memory for these events, at least up to 1 year after the event, are generally highly accurate at least for the gist of the experience.

For example, Howe et al. (1994a, 1994b, 1995) reported a series of studies in which children's (aged 18 months to 5 years at the time of the incident) memories for accidents and the subsequent emergency room treatment were examined immediately (within 2 or 3 days), after 6 months, and after 1 year. In the first study, using free- and open-ended cued recall, Howe et al. (1994b) found that although memory for the gist of the event survived reasonably well after 6 months, many of the arguably peripheral details (e.g., whether they received a popsicle or lollipop after treatment) were no longer recalled. This pattern continued over a 1-year interval (Howe et al., 1994a).

Interestingly, Howe et al. (1995) also found that for those children who had subsequent experiences with emergency room treatment (e.g., within the 6-month span from their original to follow-up interview), those experiences became intertwined in their recall narratives. Although these intrusions did not inhibit the recall of the original experience, as it often does in standard retroactive interference experiments with children (e.g., Howe, 1995), a naive interviewer (i.e., one who did not know a priori what the original experience had been) would certainly not have been able to disentangle the "blended" report so as to ascertain an accurate picture of the target event, an issue of considerable concern in courtrooms today. Similar effects have been obtained by Bruck, Ceci, Francoeur, and Barr (1995), who found that young children confused the details of a medical examination (also see Ornstein, Shapiro, Clubb, Follmer, & Baker-Ward, 1997). Indeed, that memories for these events may blend is consistent with what researchers know about the regularization of multiply experienced everyday events (e.g., going to a restaurant) into a single generic representation. As Lindsay and Read (1995) suggested, even memories for corporal punishment become blended, such that although the generic memory for being physically abused is intact, specific memories for the individual incidents may not be. Thus, unlike speculation by some that multiple experiences produce poorer memory (e.g., Terr, 1994), it may simply be that recall of individual episodes is sacrificed for a more general and abstract representation of the abuse scenario.

Children also have enduring memories for painful but anticipated medical procedures such as bone marrow transplants (Stuber et al., 1991). Similar findings have been reported for medical procedures such as the VCUG (e.g., Goodman et al., 1994). Here, like other experiences, many peripheral aspects of the traumatic or painful experience are not well retained but important or central elements of the experience are retained (e.g., Goodman et al., 1994; Merritt et al., 1994). Importantly, it is here that the role of knowledge is critical in modulating what is remembered:

children who are briefed about the procedure before actually being administered the VCUG often remember more about the experience than children who were not as thoroughly informed beforehand (Goodman et al., 1994). As I show later in this chapter, these effects of knowledge may play an important role in modulating stress, thereby improving memory for specific experiences rather than simply acting as a script for encoding and retrieving generic information about the experience.

It is clear that children have memories for physical and sexual abuse, homicides, natural disasters, and expected and unexpected medical procedures and that those memories, at least in terms of the gist of these experiences, are good. That is, the core of an event around which recall is fashioned tends to be well preserved even after considerable delays. Importantly, however, although such memories are durable, they may not be any more detailed than memories for other personally significant events. Thus, although some would argue that traumatic memories are highly detailed (e.g., Terr, 1988), it is not at all clear that such claims are justified. Although traumatic events may be better recalled than what soap one used in the shower 3 weeks ago last Monday, such comparisons are not particularly instructive because the latter event may not be remembered at all. Moreover, as already noted, the relative amount of detail remembered over time is actually unknown in many studies. This is often the case in naturalistic (or humanmade) events in which initial memory assessments often are not available for comparison with subsequent reports. When they are available, as in some of the recent studies concerning memory for medical treatments, some of the reported details are either missing or incorrect (e.g., Howe et al., 1995), or a similar pattern of deterioration of memory is observed for traumatic events as for other event memories (e.g., the gist is remembered but the peripheral details are forgotten; e.g., Howe et al., 1994a, 1994b; Steward et al., 1996). Finally, in most reports, memory for only one type of experience (e.g., traumatic) is assessed. What this means is that any conclusions concerning greater or fewer details being present in memories for different types of experiences must be based on between-studies comparisons. To get a better picture of the durability as well as amount of detail across different memories, within-subjects longitudinal studies are required in which memories for mundane, personally significant, and traumatic events are tracked over time. In this way, not only will researchers be able to assess changes to specific memories over time but also the relative durability and detail of recollections of different types of experiences using each individual as his or her own control. When such studies are conducted (see chap. 5 in this book for an overview of that handful of reports), it often turns out that memories for traumatic experiences behave much like memories for other, less dramatic incidents and that, although certainly durable, they tend not to be any richer in detail.

Another commonality between traumatic and everyday events that determines their memorability concerns the salience of the episode (e.g., see Lindsay & Read, 1995). Not only does salience play a role in remembering events in childhood, but it may also be a powerful determinant of the longevity of memories over time. As already noted in chapter 3, unique experiences tend to be best recalled autobiographically (Linton, 1979), with event uniqueness being the best overall predictor of autobiographical recall (Brewer, 1988). As Brewin, Andrews, and Gotlib (1993) pointed out, when it comes to recalling the core of an experience, adults can recall many "salient factual details of their own childhoods . . . especially concerning experiences that fulfill the criteria of having been unique, consequential, and unexpected" (p. 87).

Perhaps the most intriguing aspect of this suggestion is that trauma per se may not be the variable controlling memorability but the distinctiveness of the event against the background of other experiences. This is not to deny that stress and trauma may lead to well-preserved memories. Rather, they do so because those levels of stress and trauma are unique for that individual. Although I have discussed the distinctiveness or uniqueness hypothesis before in the context of children's memory for traumatic events (e.g., see Howe, 1997a, 1998a), I provide a more extensive discussion of this proposal later in this chapter. Before doing so, however, it is critical to survey the neurobiological impact that stress reactions have on long-term memories. As I point out along the way, the connection between stress and memory is not always simple and, like reactions to novel situations, can be modulated by a number of cognitive and social factors.

THE NEUROSCIENCE OF STRESS

Physiological and psychological stress provoke integrated activity of the neural and neuroendocrine systems. For example, the sympathetic nervous system secretes catecholamines (particularly epinephrine and norepinephrine) and the neuroendocrine component (made up in part by the hypothalamic–pituitary–adrenocortical [HPA] system) contributes glucocorticoids secreted by the adrenal gland. Moreover, there is a nonmonotonic relationship between the degree of catecholamine and glucocorticoid response and memory enhancement, such that memory can be facilitated at low-to-moderate blood levels (or administered dosages) or it can be impaired at high levels (or doses; e.g., see Gold & McCarty, 1995; Izquierdo & Medina, 1997; Korneyev, 1997; McGaugh, 1995). Therefore, as so often happens in empirical reports of the effects of stress on memory, stress can have potentially opposite effects on memory depending on its intensity and chronicity, ones that can be tied to specific experiences (e.g., failures to remember, or enhanced memory, for specific events) or that can have longer lasting structural and functional consequences (e.g., hippocampal cell loss, elevated levels of circulating catecholamines).

Whereas catecholamines do not enter the brain directly, exerting their effects through second-messenger cascades at postsynaptic sites, glucocorticoids directly affect receptors, particularly in the hippocampus, a structure long known to be important in learning and memory (e.g., see chap. 1 in this book). Moreover, the second-messenger effects attributable to catecholamine release occur within seconds, whereas glucocorticoids are secreted over minutes, with their effects taking hours to emerge. Finally, it is thought that stress-induced catecholamine effects primarily involve the amygdaloid complex, whereas glucocorticoid effects are primarily related to changes in the hippocampal complex (McEwen & Sapolsky, 1995). Indeed, there is evidence that the amygdaloid complex plays a central role in modulating memories for stressful experiences (for reviews, see Cahill & McGaugh, 1996; McGaugh, 1995).

Concerning the locus of the stress-induced effects of glucocorticoids, it is well-known that glucocorticoids are involved in neural development, including neurogenesis and neural differentiation (e.g., Bohn, 1980; Yehuda, Fairman, & Meyer, 1989), and that glucocorticoids play an important role in hippocampal development, the brain structure with the highest concentration of corticosteroid receptors (e.g., Agnati et al., 1985; Reul & De Kloet, 1986). Stressful circumstances produce changes in the levels of glucocorticoids in both rats and humans. Moreover, it has been shown that when these changes result in moderate levels of corticosterone (in rats) or cortisol (in humans), memory may actually be enhanced. For example, Pugh, Tremblay, Fleshner, and Rudy (1997) suggested that corticosterone may be selectively involved in promoting neural processes that support the consolidation of memory for contextual elements in fear conditioning of rats. Alternatively, high levels were related to poor memory performance. In fact, Diamond, Fleshner, Ingersoll, and Rose (1996) showed that the poorer memory performance of stressed rats (stress was induced by placing them in an unfamiliar or novel environment) was similar to the memory deficits found in rats with hippocampal damage (e.g., Oades, 1979). These findings are consistent with additional evidence that shows that declarative memory in adult humans is impaired by dexamethasone (a corticosterone receptor agonist; e.g., Newcomer, Craft, Hershey, Askins, & Bardgett, 1994; Wolkowitz et al., 1990).

One way in which both catecholamines and glucocorticoids serve to modulate memory storage is during consolidation (for reviews, see Abel et al., 1995; Cahill & McGaugh, 1996; Izquierdo & Medina, 1997), a process by which memory is transformed from a labile, transient state to a more stable, less volatile form. During the consolidation phase, synaptic connections may be strengthened. Importantly, this consolidation period is roughly equivalent in duration at both the cellular and behavioral levels (for more details, see Abel et al., 1995). Interestingly, it is during consolidation that memories may be the most susceptible to distortion (e.g., interference) from intervening events, although any trace weakening (including long-term residence in storage) is also presumed to be associated with potential for distortion (e.g., Ceci & Bruck, 1995). Although the term *consolidation* is used to refer to two very different events (the stabilization of memory either within the first few hours after encoding or over a few months and may involve the transfer of the memory trace from one brain region, e.g., the hippocampus, to another, e.g., neocortex; e.g., see Squire, Cohen, & Nadel, 1984), the memory-modulating effects of stress would presumably occur early because most of the biochemical cascade effects involve hours, not months (for reviews, see Abel et al., 1995; Izquierdo & Medina, 1997).

The catecholamine-mediated effect of stress on memory may be caused by changes in the delivery of oxygen and glucose to the brain (McEwen & Sapolsky, 1995). Although I do not discuss the effects of glucose in depth, I do point out that the role of glucose in the modulation of memory storage may be specific to the learning situation in which epinephrine is released (Cahill & McGaugh, 1996). When epinephrine is not released during an emotional episode (and therefore glucose levels are not increased), it is likely that beta-adrenergic receptor activation (by norepinephrine) may still produce memory enhancement. The neurotransmitter norepinephrine has been thought to enhance firing in neurons that participate in the encoding of environmentally important information (e.g., Kety, 1970), and recently it has been shown that novelty in the environment is directly linked to norepinephrine release (and enhanced retention) in some animals (e.g., Kitchigina, Vankov, Harley, & Sara, 1997). In humans, blocking norepinephrine reduces the memory enhancing effects of surprise. For example, individuals being treated with beta-blocker antihypertensive medication remembered surprising stories less well than people not on these drugs despite equivalent memory for other events (Cahill, Prins, Weber, & McGaugh, 1994; Nielson & Jensen, 1994). Indeed, Cahill et al. (1994) found that the beta-adrenergic blocking drug propanolol selectively impaired memory for an emotionally arousing story in healthy adults. Ruling out the effects of sedation on attention or reduction in emotional reaction to the story, these findings support the claim that memory modulation attributable to emotional arousal can depend on the activation of these beta-adrenergic receptors even though they may not be critical to the formation of nonemotional memories.

What are the consequences of prolonged exposure to stress? Animal research shows that chronic exposure to stress (glucocorticoids) can lead to morphological changes (e.g., atrophy of dendritic branches in pyramidal neurons of the CA3 region of the hippocampus; Watanabe, Gould, & McEwen, 1992; Wooley, Gould, & McEwen, 1990). Although these changes are sometimes reversible, the loss of neurons does occur with prolonged exposure to glucocorticoids, resulting in irreversible hippocampal damage (Kerr, Campbell, Applegate, Brodish, & Landfield, 1991; Mizoguchi, Kunishita, Chui, & Tabira, 1992; Sapolsky, Krey, & McEwen, 1985; Uno, Ross, Else, Suleman, & Sapolsky, 1989). The finding that chronic stress may have structural and functional consequences does not appear to be species specific, occurring in rats, monkeys, and tree shrews (for a review, see McEwen & Sapolsky, 1995). Studies with humans, although less well controlled, also suggest that hippocampal atrophy can result from sustained glucocorticoid exposure (Axelson et al., 1993; Starkman, Gebarski, Berent, & Schteingart, 1992). Indeed, prolonged exposure to elevated glucocorticoid levels can be accompanied by cognitive impairments (e.g., in declarative memory, as indexed by impaired verbal paired-associates learning and visual episodic memory; see Nasrallah, Coffman, & Olson, 1989) in Cushing's syndrome (Starkman & Schteingart, 1981), some depressive conditions (Wolkowitz et al., 1990), and Alzheimer's conditions in which patients are given high-dose glucocorticoid treatments (Jenike & Albert, 1984; Varney, Alexander, & Macindoe, 1984).

The problem with these sorts of findings is that they are confounded by coincident disease. However, studies with healthy individuals provide a similar pattern of findings. For example, studies with healthy adults have shown a decline in explicit or declarative measures, but not implicit measures, of memory with sustained increases in glucocorticoids (Lupien et al., 1994). Recent magnetic resonance imaging studies of adults who have undergone prolonged stress (e.g., women who have been abused, individuals with combat-related PTSD diagnoses) or who have been exposed to glucocorticoids over prolonged therapeutic intervals show decreased hippocampal volume (for a review, see Howe, 1998a). Although individuals exposed to prolonged stress experience some deficits on explicit or declarative memory tasks, it is not clear that any problems (e.g., transient amnesia) associated with remembering the precipitating event (e.g., sexual abuse, combat) can be directly attributed to prolonged stress (e.g., Howe, 1998a; Schacter, Koutstaal, & Norman, 1996). Nevertheless, there is some evidence that such individuals may experience deficits associated with the recall of autobiographical events (for a review, see Howe, 1998a).

Recall from chapter 1 that experience can alter structure and function even at the cellular level. Consistent with this is evidence that both positive and negative experiences can have long-lasting neurobiological effects that, although not necessarily remembered declaratively, certainly must be considered a memory inasmuch as future behaviors are altered by these earlier experiences (discussed later). For example, animals and humans reared in enriched environments thrive better and this, at least for rats and kittens, results in more synapses per neuron, more and longer dendritic spines and branches, increased glia, and increased capillary branching leading to a better blood supply and greater oxygenation (for a review, see C. A. Nelson & Bloom, 1997). Concerning negative experiences, monkeys exposed to randomly presented loud sounds during the latter half of gestation tend to be jittery and have elevated levels of circulating catecholamines (M. L. Schneider, 1992). Monkeys raised in social isolation show emotional dysfunction and neuroanatomical anomalies (e.g., deficient numbers of particular neurons in areas of the hippocampal formation; Ginsberg, Hof, McKinney, & Morrison, 1993a, 1993b; Siegel et al., 1993). Finally, maternal deprivation in rat pups produces long-term abnormalities in which the behavioral consequences include difficulty coping with stress (Rots et al., 1995; Suchecki, Mozaffarian, Gross, Rosenfeld, & Levine, 1993), a phenomenon that is also being examined in children who are placed in orphanages early in life (e.g., Earls, 1996).

MEASURES OF STRESS

There is little doubt that memory storage is modulated by responses to stress. In fact, "it seems reasonable that the storage of memories should be modulated in some way to enhance the contrast between memories of important events from those of less relevant memories—to enhance the distinction between signal and noise" (Nielson & Jensen, 1994, p. 190). Although memory for low-to-moderately stressful events may be enhanced by biochemical processes during the consolidation period, these same processes may lead to memory storage failures for events that are highly stressful. The question therefore arises: Are there measures of stress that researchers can use to predict the survivability of event memory?

A variety of procedures have been used to measure stress, including subjective rating scales (e.g., self-rated stress levels), behavioral and observational rating scales (i.e., ratings adduced by an objective observer, often a parent), physiological indexes (e.g., heart rate, blood pressure), and neuroendocrine measures (e.g., salivary cortisol). Both Likert-type rating scales of subjective stress and neuroendocrine measures have routinely failed to predict children's retention of stressful events. For example, Howe et al. (1994a, 1994b, 1995) found no association between parent or self-ratings of children's stress and children's recall of emergency room treatment up to 1 year later. Similarly, Goodman and Quas (1997) found no relationship between subjective or behavioral measures of stress and children's correct recall of the VCUG, although these measures were related to children's retention errors. This latter relationship disappeared, however, when parental attachment style was taken into account (see the later discussion of individual differences in stress reactivity). Finally, Merritt et al. (1994) found that behavioral measures of stress (using the Observational Scale of Behavioral Distress; see Elliot, Jay, & Woody, 1987) were negatively related to recall of the VCUG over a 6-week period. Except for this latter scale, subjective and behavioral measures of stress do not correlate well with children's retention of stressful medical events. The absence of an association may arise simply because these psychological measurements of stress are crude and may be insensitive to the underlying physiological changes that are associated with stress responses (Howe, 1997a).

Measures of neuroendocrine responses, at least as reflected in salivary cortisol, have also had limited success. Despite the relationship between levels of glucocorticoids and memory outlined in the preceding section, one that may be confined to therapeutic dosing and immediate retention on episodic list-learning tasks, no relationship has been established between memory for a stressful event (the VCUG) and changes in salivary cortisol (Merritt et al., 1994). Although salivary cortisol levels did rise above control baseline levels during the VCUG procedure, they were not related to variation in children's immediate or 6-week recall of the event. Thus, the effects of glucocorticoids on memory may be restricted to the high levels associated with therapeutic doses, episodic list-learning tasks, immediate retention, or some combination of these three. It would seem, however, that they are absent in children's recall of the VCUG procedure, a naturally occurring event that involves high-stress medical procedures. Before strong conclusions can be made, additional studies should be conducted. Moreover, although variation in cortisol levels may not account for variation in the recall of stressful events, it is possible that such measures may successfully discriminate between memory for stressful experiences per se and those that are not stressful, a comparison that has not been conducted (e.g., Merritt et al., 1994).

Although levels of circulating glucocorticoids may not exceed the threshold necessary for measurable effects at long-term retention, when physiological indicators (e.g., blood pressure, pulse rates) are used instead, there is often a clear, negative association between increasing levels of stress and subsequent memory performance (e.g., Stein & Boyce, 1997). The difference between physiological and neuroendocrine measures of stress and their association with memory may arise because, among other things, physiological measures are based largely on catecholamine release via the sympathetic nervous system. Unfortunately, because this area has received little attention in the literature, more direct analyses of these physiological measures are sorely needed. A number of investigations are under way, ones that are using vagal tone as an index of stress reactivity (for a review of the use of vagal tone as a marker for physiological stress, see Porges, 1992). Howe, Courage, and Harley (1998) have initiated a series of studies linking heart rate variability, norepinephrine, and the sympathetic and parasympathetic systems to changes in long-term memory for distinctive events. Specifically, they are attempting to identify periods of sympathetic activation that will index central norepinephrine activation during novel aspects of events, ones that can be directly associated with corresponding changes in the retention of those experiences. With these newer, more sensitive, and noninvasive indexes of physiological reactivity to novelty and distinctiveness in place, they anticipate that the link between memory performance and underlying neurobiological changes will be found.

INDIVIDUAL DIFFERENCES

Although physiological measures of stress may provide a promising route to understanding the relationship between stress and memory, it is curious that the same does not appear to be true for salivary cortisol, which is, after all, an index activity of the HPA system. One reason why salivary cortisol and memory may not be correlated, at least in studies with children, is that there are marked developmental and individual differences in cortisol responding (for a review, see Gunnar, Tout, de Haan, Pierce, & Stansbury, 1997). Indeed, neuroendocrine reactivity can fluctuate not only with age but also with attachment, temperament, and knowledge. For example, Gunnar and her associates (Gunnar, Brodersen, Krueger, & Rigatuso, 1996; Hertsgaard, Gunnar, Erickson, & Nachmias, 1995; Nachmias, Gunnar, Manglesdorf, Parritz, & Buss, 1996) have found that stress reactivity is modulated by attachment style, such that insecurely, but not securely, attached toddlers exhibit elevated cortisol levels in response to novel or stressful situations. Consistent with these findings, Goodman and Quas (1997) found that anxiously attached children made more errors recalling the VCUG procedure, an indication that attachment was a better predictor of children's memories of the VCUG than behavioral indexes of stress.

Because individual differences in stress reactivity are related to Kagan's recent arguments concerning early differences in temperament (e.g., Boyce, Barr, & Zeltzer, 1992; Kagan, 1994; Kagan, Reznick, Snidman, Gibbons, & Johnson, 1988), differences in memory for traumatic events in childhood (and adulthood) may be traced to differences in the reactivity of the individual to that event. Indeed, differences in adrenocortical activity (indexed by salivary cortisol) as a function of temperament have been observed in 4-month-olds, and these differences tend to remain stable over the first 4 years of life (Schmidt et al., 1997). Even from an early age, then, the same traumatic event may be better remembered by one individual than another depending on reactivity and the associated neuroendocrine response. Individuals whose reactivity is lower (due perhaps to variables such as temperamental predispositions, better coping skills, sensitivity in support from caregivers) may encode and store more about unique and stressful situations than individuals whose reactivity is high.

This is exactly what has been found when individual differences in reactivity have been measured on-line (Goodman & Quas, 1997; Stein & Boyce, 1997).

Although much remains to be evaluated concerning this proposition, it does appear to account for what initially seemed to be contradictory findings concerning the relation between stress and memory. It also alerts researchers to be somewhat judicious in their selection of variables that need to be measured along with salivary cortisol. As Gunnar et al. (1997) remarked, tracking the activity of stress-reactive systems is difficult at the best of times, principally because it varies not only across individuals but also within an individual across stressful occasions. Because stress reactivity is dynamic in this sense, understanding its link to long-term retention requires the concurrent measurement of other modulating social and cognitive factors.

One important factor that determines reactivity is the manner in which an event is appraised cognitively. As seen in chapter 3, people's knowledge base influences subsequent memory. In a similar way, what people already know can influence how they react to a stressful, novel, or traumatic situation and can serve to modulate the neuroendocrine reaction (e.g., Gunnar et al., 1996). For example, knowledge of a medical procedure can modify an individual's reaction to that procedure. Similarly, event memory, including memory for emotional events, depends on how that event was interpreted (e.g., Stein, 1996; Stein & Levine, in press; Stein & Liwag, 1997). Because memory is never an exact copy of experience (i.e., it is interpretive, constructive, and reconstructive), it is, by definition, constrained and influenced throughout its existence (from original encoding and storage, through its residency in storage, and retrieval) by personal knowledge, beliefs, and motivational states. This holds not only for recollections of the event proper but also for the emotions experienced during the event (e.g., Levine, 1997). Because these factors vary across individuals as well as within individuals across time, knowledge, beliefs, and motivational states contribute to individual differences in stress reactivity and hence memory for emotional, stressful, and traumatic experiences.

Simply because these variables are dynamically affiliated with memory does not mean that their contributions cannot be evaluated separately. For example, there is considerable evidence that even the involuntary experience of emotion may be contingent on what people already know. Stein and Levine (in press) have argued that emotion signals that there has been a change in a goal state, one that may indicate that the goal has been attained or that it has been blocked or threatened. Such reactions, which may be involuntary, occur in response to novel aspects of the experience, particularly those that violate expectations based on prior knowledge. Using emotionally laden cues to help children recall events, Stein and Levine found that emotional reactions were related to the child's appraisal of the event, not the event per se.

Knowledge affects the interpretation of and emotional reaction to an event as well as the neuroendocrine response (e.g., Gunnar et al., 1996). Knowledge of a medical procedure can influence an individual's reaction to that procedure. For example, children who are being treated surgically for cancer and who discuss the nature of the surgery not only develop a better understanding of their treatment, but they also may cope better (see Stein, 1996). Goodman, Quas, Batterman-Faunce, Riddlesberger, and Kuhn (1994, 1997) have also shown that a better understanding of the VCUG procedure leads to better memory (e.g., fewer "don't know" responses, more correct responses, fewer commission errors on misleading questions). Although it is true that children's medical knowledge (like their knowledge in general; see chap. 3 in this book) increases with age, there can be substantial variation within age as a function of experience (e.g., children who have vs. those who have not undergone cancer treatment—Bearison & Pacifici, 1989) or education (e.g., children who have vs. those who have not been prepared in advance for day surgery—Atkins, 1987; Lumley, Melamed, & Abeles, 1993; Robinson & Kobayashi, 1991—or emergency medical care—McFarland & Stanton, 1991).

Although knowledge specific to the procedure about to be endured is positively associated with memory for that procedure, it is not clear that such effects are due to the amelioration of stress. For example, McFarland and Stanton (1991) brought kindergarten children to a community hospital, showed them a videotape of Mr. Rogers visiting an emergency room and describing the equipment, and described the treatment of two children, one with a broken arm and one who required stitches. After the video, the children handled the equipment (e.g., thermometer, stethoscope, removable cast), had a snack, and toured an ambulance. Despite the fact that all of the children showed increased medical knowledge and fewer self-reported medical fears immediately and 1 month later, there was little behavioral evidence of reduced stress in children who were high stress reactors to begin with when they underwent a routine physical examination. The absence of stress reduction may have been because the training (emergency room procedures) differed from the follow-up medical procedure (physical examination). Indeed, although there is some evidence that outcomes are better when the training is specific to the procedure they are about to undergo, there is also evidence that such knowledge, although benefiting memory, can have negative consequences for stress reactivity (Howe, 1998a). That is, information may actually heighten arousal, particularly when children are not given the opportunity to practice compensatory responses (e.g., relaxation techniques; for a review, see Melamed, Siegel, & Ridley-Johnson, 1988).

Thus, it is not clear that increased knowledge, even knowledge of the specific procedure, leads to better memory because it reduces stress or simply because, like other knowledge, it serves to aid in the encoding and organization of experiential information in memory storage. It is clear, however, that this knowledge benefits memory for the specific procedure and not simply the generic representation of the medical procedure. For example, Ornstein et al. (1997; also see Baker-Ward, Ornstein, & Principe, 1997) found that prior knowledge of a medical examination was correlated with recall of a specific examination 6 weeks later. To ensure that children's recall was not based on the generic representation of the event, Ornstein et al. (1997) included specific elements in the medical procedure that were unique to that visit to the physician (e.g., having one's picture taken), ones that were recalled by the children in addition to other, more routine aspects of the event (e.g., having one's temperature taken). Goodman et al. (1997), using questioning procedures that elicited specific details of individual experiences as well as monitoring children's spontaneous comments, found that although some of the children's recounting of their VCUG experience could have come from a generic representation, much of the children's recall went well beyond their prior understanding of the procedure.

More important, as seen in the next chapter, cognitive appraisals of events with reference to the self, at least for older (2-year-olds) toddlers, may be critical in predicting memory for such events. The consequences of the event to the individual (something that can vary over time, making this a difficult variable to deal with empirically) have been shown to play an important role not only in establishing memories but also in the longevity of autobiographical experiences in memory (also see Howe & Courage, 1997b). To explore this possibility in more depth, as well as to establish the primacy of novelty or distinctiveness in determining memory regardless of the experience's traumatic status, I return to the issue of children's memory for salient and unique experiences.

THE ROLE OF DISTINCTIVENESS

That emotional events might be well remembered depending to some extent on one's reactivity is consistent with recent claims made by Stein (1996), who found that memories for highly emotional episodes contain information not found in other recall narratives, namely a focus on beliefs that have been violated due to the nature of the event. That is, children (and adults) focus on those aspects of emotional events that are surprising, novel, and unique, ones that often run counter to prior knowledge and the expectations derived from that knowledge (for analogous findings concerning the "disruption effect" in children's story recall, see, e.g., Davidson & Hoe, 1993; Davidson & Jergovic, 1996).

This parallels findings discussed in chapter 3 on distinctiveness effects in memory. In memory for highly emotional or traumatic events, the background that sets the context are personal experiences stored in memory and the expectations they generate for future experiences. The distinctive elements are the violations of those expectations in the current circumstance. Indeed, events can be distinctive regardless of whether their emotional overtone is positive or negative. For example, you are driving to work one morning when you see an airplane fall from the sky. Such an event is clearly unexpected and, although the incident does not involve you directly, it is unpleasant. Alternatively, you are driving to work one morning when an airplane suddenly skywrites someone's name as the winner of $1 million. Again, like the accident, this event is not anticipated. In both cases, even though you were not directly involved in either of the events, you will probably remember both of them largely because they are inconsistent with your expectations for what happens on your drive to work.

These examples illustrate several important points. First, consistent with the proposal of Stein (1996), it is the violation of what is anticipated, or the unique component of the event, that is so compelling. This idea is consistent with the literature reviewed earlier in which stress reactivity is often elicited using a novel situation. For example, in many animal studies of stress, the stressor is actually an unexpected or novel event (e.g., being placed in a new environment, placing a spider in a previously empty location). Repeated experiences with the novel situation (e.g., medical examinations) in which uniqueness gradually dissipates can lead to modulation of stress reactivity (e.g., Gunnar et al., 1996). For example, individuals in emergency response teams may acclimate to scenes of devastation that were once novel and unique. Second, consistent with the findings on children's memory for traumatic experiences, the event need not be participated in directly but can simply be observed (e.g., Bugenthal, Blue, Cortez, Fleck, & Rodriguez, 1992). Third, the event need not be negative. Novelty and surprise occur in a variety of situations and can elicit positive as well as negative emotions. Again, however, it is the distinctiveness that predicts memorability, not necessarily the direction of the emotion.

Although it is not easy to tease apart distinctiveness and emotionality in recall (e.g., see Neisser et al., 1996), there are advantages to conceptualizing memory for traumatic experiences within this broader framework. First, it integrates memory for traumatic events into a larger, established literature on general memory mechanisms. Rather than add yet another memory mechanism to the ever-growing list of specific mechanisms thought to be necessary to account for human memory, integrating traumatic memories with what researchers know about memory in general provides a more parsimonious and grounded perspective, especially in the absence of empirical evidence to the contrary.

Indeed, such a link connects what researchers know about traumatic memories to a vast literature on infants', toddlers', and children's long-term retention of distinctive events reviewed in the previous chapters of this book. As already seen, a variety of procedures have been used to investigate distinctiveness, including deferred imitation (e.g., Meltzoff, 1995), elicited imitation (e.g., Bauer, 1995; Howe & Courage, 1997a), and reenactments of novel events (e.g., Boyer et al., 1994; Fivush & Hamond, 1989; Hudson, 1991; Myers, Perris, & Speaker, 1994). Not only are distinctive events well recalled using these nonverbal procedures, but they have also been seen in older children's recall of one-time events (Fivush & Schwartzmueller, 1998). Indeed, regardless of whether the experience is positive or negative, there is an emerging database consistent with the idea that unique and distinctive experiences are well remembered during early childhood for periods of at least 6 years (also see Howe, 1997a, 1998a; Hudson & Fivush, 1991).

Oftentimes because negative experiences can have the largest impact on people, particularly because the experiences may be self- or life-threatening, the distribution of memories over a life span is thought to be skewed toward unpleasant experiences. However, as seen in the next chapter, a number of recent reports show that positive experiences tend to be recalled more frequently than negative ones over the life span (also see Rubin & Schulkind, 1997). Nevertheless, it can be argued that regardless of the emotional tone of the event (negative or positive), best-remembered experiences are those that are distinctive, unique, and personally consequential (e.g., Brewer, 1986; Conway, 1996).

If one accepts this proposition, then the question of how to relate distinctiveness to long-term retention remains. If people's personal histories provide the background context but these personal histories are constantly changing, altering what people have already stored in memory (e.g., Conway, 1996), previously distinctive experiences may no longer be unique given additional experiences. This problem is particularly vexing because people's interpretations of previously stored experiences may change in light of new knowledge. Such recoding of memories (also see Tulving, 1984) may serve to realign the experience with others or reorganize them along some new dimension of similarity. Indeed, changes such as these may explain why a given individual can recall a distinctive event at one time but fail to do so later. For example, a trip to Walt Disney World may be unique given a single experience but, after repeated visits to similar theme parks, the initial Disney World experience may be realigned with these other experiences. Although such experiences may now be well recalled in generic form, the individual events themselves may no longer be well preserved.

This raises the second question: To understand what would constitute a unique and distinctive experience for a given individual, researchers must somehow evaluate what they already know. As seen in the last chapter, this is no easy task, with both the amount and structure of knowledge playing important roles in memory. Examining distinctiveness in situ, especially with traumatic experiences, is difficult because one must not only measure the knowledge the individual had before the trauma, but one must also measure any changes in that knowledge that have taken place since the event. It is because this knowledge changes dynamically, that what receives distinctive processing varies not only across individuals but also within individuals over the life span. Thus, because distinctiveness exists relative to some background and that background is constantly changing and being modified, including alterations in response to unique and distinctive processing of current experiences, assessment of distinctiveness and its relationship to later retention presents a more complicated measurement problem than many might anticipate. However, these problems are not insurmountable. For example, Levine (1997) was able to evaluate recall of an important event (Ross Perot's decision not to run for the presidency as remembered by his campaign workers) and relate it to individuals' cognitive appraisals of the event at the time it happened as well as at the time of recall. As predicted, recall varied more as a function of the person's current cognitive appraisal. As in all of the literature reviewed in this chapter, a complete picture of what children remember of their emotional experiences, positive or negative, requires the concurrent measurement of a number of physiological, cognitive, and social variables.

CONCLUSION

What can one conclude about children's memory for emotional experiences? First, and perhaps most important, regardless of whether the event has a sudden onset, is a natural disaster, or is an anticipated and patterned form of abuse, children can provide coherent accounts of these experiences over fairly long retention intervals. Although these accounts are often not well adorned with nonessential details and may be subject to intrusions from other like experiences, the gist of the event is well preserved. Such findings are consistent with what researchers know about memory in general. Inasmuch as this similarity holds across experiences, traumatic events seem to adhere to the same principles as memories for other, less salient events.

Second, like other events, memories for emotional events will endure to the extent that they remain unique and distinctive against the background of other experiences. As shown in the next chapter, events that are particularly important or distinctive with reference to the self (e.g.,

Howe & Courage, 1997b) and that are personally significant (e.g., Brewer, 1988; Conway, 1996) can be retained late into adulthood. The problem remains, however, that considerable methodological acumen must be exhibited if researchers are to predict which specific events will be remembered because the background against which distinctiveness is determined is constantly shifting. Such changes not only become appended to one's knowledge base, but they serve to amend memories that are already in storage. Like other dynamic processes, memory for emotional and traumatic events may follow deterministic rules with known variables (e.g., the importance of uniqueness and personal consequentiality) but remain highly unpredictable at an individual level.

Third, although considerable research remains to be done, researchers are beginning to better understand the effects of stress on memory. Although it is possible that extreme stress reactivity may impair memory storage, a variety of individual differences can play an important role in modulating this reactivity. These include constitutional (e.g., temperament), cognitive (e.g., world knowledge), and social (e.g., attachment) factors whose measurement, or lack thereof, across some previous studies may explain the "now-you-see-it/now-you-don't" quality of the effects of stress on memory. Thus, although it can be concluded that special memory mechanisms are not demanded by the data to account for memory for emotional and traumatic events, understanding memories for these events, like understanding memory for most events, requires an understanding of the dynamic interplay among variables that span a number of traditional subdisciplines in psychology and allied sciences, including neuroscience and the cognitive, social, and developmental sciences. This across-discipline integration is not only critical for the understanding of memory for traumatic events but also for the understanding of memory for all autobiographical experiences, a topic I address in the next chapter.

5

DEVELOPMENT OF
AUTOBIOGRAPHICAL MEMORY

Autobiographical memory is, quite simply, "the capacity of people to recollect their lives" (Baddeley, 1992, p. 26). It is often what is meant by the term *memory* in everyday usage and can frequently be characterized as "a recollection of a particular episode from an individual's past" (Brewer, 1986, p. 34). Although the study of autobiographical memory requires the integration of a number of specialist research domains (e.g., social psychology, personality theory, neuroscience, memory), the concern that must be addressed first if researchers are to understand its origins is the extent to which the basic processes that constitute memory functioning are intact early in life. Indeed, this has been the primary purpose of this book up to this point. What the preceding chapters have shown is that the basic encoding, storage, and retrieval processes necessary to memorize and retain information are intact early in life, at least in rudimentary form. Although these processes are operational from birth or before, it also was shown that information stored early in life (e.g., by 2-month-olds) tends to be retained for shorter periods of time than information stored by older infants (e.g., 6-month-olds), especially when additional support (e.g., reactivation) is not provided during the retention period. Indeed, throughout infancy and childhood generally, the ability to maintain information in storage over longer and longer intervals is perhaps one of the single most important achievements in memory development (also see Howe & O'Sullivan,

1997). This accomplishment is brought about, in turn, by changes in the cognitive software that directs encoding, storage, and retrieval processes, with advances in the amount and structure of knowledge being perhaps the single greatest contributor.

What is it about early experiences that is remembered, particularly later in adulthood? Although many experiments on autobiographical memory have shown that most people recall both positive and negative experiences from their childhood, with the former often being more plentiful than the latter (e.g., Betz & Skowronski, 1997; Rubin & Schulkind, 1997), the earliest memories appear to be from the ages of 2 to 3 years (see Eacott & Crawley, 1998; Howe & Courage, 1993, 1997b; Usher & Neisser, 1993). After this period of so-called "infantile amnesia," the number of childhood memories tends to increase with age, with many more experiences being recalled from later childhood years than from earlier years (e.g., Wetzler & Sweeney, 1986).

Curiously, these robust findings, ones that have been well replicated over the past century (e.g., Dudycha & Dudycha, 1941; Waldvogel, 1948), have been challenged in recent years by numerous claims (both in the scientific literature and the popular press) that memories of experiences before the age of 2 years are returning to many individuals. These memories, hitherto unavailable to conscious recollection, are being uncovered at an unprecedented rate, with some people claiming to have remembered experiences from 6 months of age. It is of more than passing interest to note that unlike most of the empirical findings to date, all of these memories concern events that would be considered negative and possibly traumatic (e.g., sexual abuse), and not one has been about a positive experience. Although it is frequently argued that traumatic events should be more memorable and hence this is not at all unusual, there are several points that go against this hypothesis.

First, even if a person experienced sexual abuse at an early age, given the absence of physical distress, such an experience may not have been interpreted as negative or traumatic at the time (i.e., the child might not know what the event was and, unless it was painful, invasive, or uncomfortable, would probably not have encoded it as a negative event). Indeed, it is only later, given that anything was remembered at all, that such an event would be reconstructed at recall as one that was traumatic. Second, had the event been extremely traumatic, the evidence from chapter 4 would suggest that it is unlikely that it would still be in memory as it may not have survived the consolidation period. Third, there are any number of traumatic events that are physically painful during early infancy, including the withdrawal of blood, circumcision, and inoculations. Given that these experiences are not so stressful as to be lost during the consolidation process, it is not clear why these events are not similarly uncovered with the same frequency. Fourth, the evidence reviewed in the earlier chapters of this book suggests that memories for early events, although being available immediately for recall, tend to disappear fairly rapidly and, barring additional reminders, elaboration, or reorganization, are recalled in an extremely fragmentary fashion at a later time. Indeed, often these experiences, although possibly leaving a behavioral residue, are certainly not available for conscious recall and unquestionably do not fulfill the type of detailed autobiographical recollection many claimants have suggested. For example, as already seen, Howe, Courage, and Peterson (1994b) found that one of the 18-month-olds who had gone through a traumatic time while being treated for a fishbone that had been caught in her throat later refused to eat fish and had an extraordinary avoidance reaction to tongue depressors 6 months after this experience despite the fact that she was unable to recall the experience. As already noted, even these behavioral reactions disappeared after another 6 months. Given all of these points and the fact that even at the best of times autobiographical recall is reconstructive, being filtered through one's current beliefs, knowledge, expectations, and motivations, it is unlikely that claims of well-articulated autobiographical memories, even for traumatic events, before the age of 2 years have much merit. If anything, the weight of the evidence indicates that such claims are based on false memories of the sort described earlier in this book (also see Spanos, 1996), a problem that is all too common in autobiographical recall in general (e.g., Conway et al., 1996).

Although the question of "unconscious" and behavioral memories is addressed later (see chap. 6 in this book), there is little evidence to suggest that memories from the first 2 years of life can be later consciously recollected as experiences that happened to "me." To see why this is so, I turn to a discussion of theories of the emergence and development of autobiographical memory and then provide an overview of the relevant empirical phenomenon. I then review a recently proposed theory of autobiographical memory, one that covers both its emergence and development and that shows that autobiographical memory can be subsumed under a single umbrella of what researchers know about memory development in general, providing a unified framework for the development of memory throughout early as well as late childhood.

THE INCEPTION OF AUTOBIOGRAPHICAL MEMORY

Historical Overview

Several theories of the onset of autobiographical memory have been proposed, many of which can be grouped according to whether they emphasize changes in encoding and storage or in retrieval. Historically, memories were thought to consist of permanently stored records of experience, and forgetting was due simply to fluctuations in their retrievability (e.g., Freud, 1914/1938; Hoffding, 1891). For example, Freud (1905/1953, 1916–1917/1963) argued that early autobiographical memories persist and, even if people are unaware of their content, these memories influence their everyday behaviors. Indeed, favorable therapeutic outcomes were often contingent, at least in theory, on the successful retrieval (and resolution) of early childhood experiences. For Freud, then, memory storage was relatively permanent, with the recall of early childhood experiences fluctuating in terms of whether they could be consciously retrieved.

Several other theorists believed that changes in what was stored in memory was at the root of failures to remember early childhood experiences (e.g., Kohler, 1929, 1941). According to Kohler, memory architectures were fluid or dynamic, and memories were subject to change while resident in storage. For example, traces might undergo spontaneous reorganization in accordance with laws similar to those governing perception (e.g., good form, similarity), ones that would metamorphose traces into simple, well-integrated representations (good gestalts) that would be easier to preserve in memory but that would lack specific episodic information. For Kohler (and a number of modern theorists, such as Tulving, 1984), memories did not remain permanently etched in storage but could be altered or recoded.

Still others have claimed that although early experiences may be permanently stored in memory they are inaccessible because they were encoded during infancy and, no longer being infants, adults cannot possibly access those encodings. This argument amounts to encoding specificity in extremis, that is, because the conditions that pertained at encoding (infancy) are so discrepant from the ones in which people are trying to retrieve them (childhood or adulthood), it is impossible to make contact with them (a particularly poignant discussion of this can be found in Nash, 1987). Still other theorists have suggested that early autobiographical events were never properly registered in memory (immature encoding skills) or were rapidly lost from memory. That is, early childhood events were either improperly or poorly encoded in storage to begin with, decayed rapidly, or the memory hardware was too immature to support long-term retention of information (for an overview of these positions, see Kail, 1984). According to this latter reasoning, infantile amnesia (the inability of older children and adults to recall autobiographical events that occurred before the age of 2 or 3 years) is due to the simple fact that such memories no longer exist in the memory system.

Contemporary Theories

Most, if not all, of these early suggestions have failed to provide an answer to the enigma of infantile amnesia for reasons already discussed. For example, if poor encoding and storage, fast decay, or an immature memory system were at the root of infantile amnesia, then researchers should find evidence of this in studies of infant and toddler neurological or perceptual immaturity as well as in their failures to recall much from the events they experienced during this period. As illustrated in chapters 1 and 2, this is far from the truth. Similarly, if retrieval failure of permanently stored traces is at the heart of infantile amnesia, then why is it that older children (e.g., 8-year-olds) can readily recall experiences from when they were younger (2 years old; e.g., Fivush & Schwartzmueller, 1998; also see chaps. 3 and 4 in this book). Certainly the discrepancy between encoding and retrieval contexts is as great in this age span as elsewhere. Simple retrieval failures of intact traces cannot account for this type of forgetting, as there is considerable evidence, already reviewed in this book, that what is stored in memory does not remain there unchanged. Indeed, it has long been known that memories change from a state in which they are highly detailed and elaborate to more gistlike representations over time (e.g., Howe & Brainerd, 1989), can gravitate to new forms that are consistent with new knowledge (e.g., Kohler, 1929, 1941; Liben, 1977; Piaget & Inhelder, 1973; for a review, see Howe & O'Sullivan, 1997), and can be recoded along with incoming information during similar experiences (e.g., as in reinstatement; Howe, Courage, & Bryant-Brown, 1993; Rovee-Collier, 1997) or with information that conflicts with what is in storage (e.g., as in the eyewitness memory literature; Ceci & Bruck, 1995). Thus, "memory is not a repository for experiences that are encoded and recalled one time; rather, meaningful material is subject to continuous reorganization in memory" (Paris & Lindauer, 1977, p. 52).

Because (a) these older theories have failed numerous empirical challenges; (b) memory is viewed as a dynamic, not a static, storage system in which memories can be updated and recoded; and (c) basic memory processes are intact early in infancy and can sustain information for protracted periods of time, newer theories have attempted to account for the infantile amnesia–autobiographical memory shift by focusing on the creation of additional memory systems (e.g., Leichtman & Ceci, 1993; Pillemer & White, 1989), sociolinguistic achievements (Fivush, 1993, 1994; K. Nelson, 1993; Pillemer & White, 1989), developments in children's cognitive sense of self (Howe & Courage, 1993, 1997b), and their own self-awareness or autonoetic consciousness (e.g., Perner & Ruffman, 1995; Wheeler et al., 1997). For example, some have argued that it is not until children are able to reflect on their experiences in the past, present, and future that infantile amnesia will subside (see Perner & Ruffman, 1995). Although conscious awareness of oneself and one's experiences may be a component of episodic memory more generally and may play a role in the accumulation of autobiographical memories throughout childhood, it is apparent that the offset of infantile amnesia and the onset of autobiographical memory (as well as the accumulation of those memories) is contingent on first having a (cognitive) sense of self. Before turning to a theory whose central point is just that, consider some other recent proposals concerning the development of autobiographical memory.

There are several proposals in which autobiographical memory is said to be the result of a late-developing memory system. For example, in contrast to theories that emphasize storage and retrieval difficulties, Pillemer and White (1989) suggested that infantile amnesia could best be understood in terms of the development of two distinct memory systems. The first system, a primitive one present at birth, would store fragmentary information about experiences, emotional associations, learned routines, and generic representations of past experiences. The contents of this system are expressed behaviorally, not verbally, and are elicited by contextual and affective cues. The second system, one that supports autobiographical memories, develops slowly over the preschool years and contains information specific to events (e.g., time and place). These autobiographical memories can be accessed on demand and are communicated verbally. It is because this second system does not come on-line until the preschool years that older children and adults experience infantile amnesia for the first 3 or so years of life. Pillemer and White (1989) further claimed that this second memory system develops with the acquisition of language. That is, when children begin to talk they communicate about personal experiences. Through interchanges with adults, children learn to structure their conversations about the past in more mature ways, enabling them to store more and more information about experiences. It is this verbal exchange with adults in the context of social interaction that is critical to the emergence and development of autobiographical memory.

Other multiple memory system hypotheses have been put forward to explain the beginning and growth of autobiographical memory. For example, Leichtman and Ceci (1993) suggested that fuzzy-trace theory might account for the onset of autobiographical memory inasmuch as verbatim and gist memories may have different developmental courses. Specifically, as argued here, infants and young children may use the same basic encoding, storage, and retrieval processes as adults but, because their representations fall more at the verbatim end of the fuzzy-trace continuum, they may experience rapid forgetting of information. Because verbatim memories may appear earlier in development than gist memories and because they fade more rapidly than gist memories, events that occur before some critical "window" will no longer be available for retrieval. If the shift from primarily verbatim encoding to both verbatim and gist encoding were to occur around the time infantile amnesia waned, then the development of these gist representations alone could be the factor responsible for the appearance of autobiographical memory.

Unfortunately, there is little or no evidence supporting either of these dual-coding theories. As already seen (see chap. 1), there is little direct evidence of any neurological underpinning to support a dual memory system, nor is there any evidence that there is a cataclysmic shift in the ability to remember events around this age that would support the sudden appearance of a new memory system (see chaps. 2–4). Similarly, there is no evidence to suggest that gist-based representations do not come on-line until age 3 and considerable evidence that gistlike recall is the rule rather than the exception, even for toddlers as young as 2 years old (see chap. 2). Whether these dual memory systems are conceived of as independent or interdependent is moot, therefore, because there is little evidence to support the idea (a) that there are separate memory systems or, (b) that they come on-line at different developmental junctures (also see Rovee-Collier, 1997). Indeed, as Polster, Nadel, and Schacter (1991) observed,

> although the evidence for some form of multiple memory systems hypothesis is compelling to many, a number of cognitive psychologists have claimed that it is not necessary to postulate different memory systems, preferring instead the idea of a single but flexible memory system. (p. 110)

Given all the evidence summarized in this book and elsewhere (e.g., Bauer, 1995; Howe & Courage, 1997b) attesting to the overwhelming continuity of memory development from infancy onward, it is perhaps still more parsimonious to view memory as a unitary system that supports a variety of modes of remembering.

Given that researchers accept some version of this last statement, how can they account for the waning of infantile amnesia and the onset of autobiographical memory? That is, how can researchers account for the apparent sudden onset of personalized event memories as well as their accumulation with age over the childhood years? Several authors have suggested that the solution lies in the acquisition of language, much like Pillemer and White (1989), but more particularly in the social interaction that surrounds the retelling of experiences. For example, K. Nelson (1993) and Fivush (1993, 1994; Fivush & Schwartzmueller, 1998) have argued that autobiographical memory starts and infantile amnesia dissipates only when children share their experiences with others linguistically. That is, as young children learn to talk about the past with adults, they begin to organize these events autobiographically in memory. Although such advances may occur as early as 3 to 4 years of age, K. Nelson (1993) maintained that autobiographical memory is late to develop and may be complete only late into the preschool years. According to this sociolinguistic view, then, autobiographical memory is predicated on the development of sophisticated language-based representational skills that do not emerge until the late preschool years. Once these skills are established, memories can be retained and organized around a life history that extends in time.

Because conversations about the past, particularly with parents (especially mothers), are crucial in this conceptualization of the development of autobiographical memories, considerable research has been conducted to evaluate this hypothesis. Unfortunately, little if any support has been found for this viewpoint, particularly the role of conversations about the past. For example, neither Fivush (1994) nor Goodman et al., (1994) found any effects of parental conversations on children's autobiographical memory. Indeed, if anything, it is well-known that verbal rehearsal not only can result in event reinstatement but that it can also lead to a number of errors in recall. More specifically, reconstruction of events through conversations with others can lead to systematic distortions of fact that are congruent with the recaller's and the listener's current beliefs and expectations (e.g., Spence, 1982; Wagenaar, 1988, 1990).

Although language is clearly important, not just to autobiographical memory but to memory in general, particularly as a communicative device (much like gesture, art, mathematics, and music), the evidence does not support the idea that it is the key to the offset of infantile amnesia and the beginning of autobiographical memory. Indeed, there is little evidence to support the claim that memories are even represented linguistically. As the infant memory literature (see chap. 2) illustrates so clearly, language is not necessary for the representation of information in memory. In fact, there is considerable evidence that memory is amodal in newborns (e.g., Kaye & Bower, 1994), older infants (e.g., Kuhl & Meltzoff, 1984; Meltzoff & Borton, 1979; Meltzoff & Moore, 1994), children, and adults (see Howe & Courage, 1997b). Although the exact form in which memories are represented is still at issue—neural nets (e.g., White, 1992), proposition lists (e.g., Anderson, 1978), feature vectors (e.g., Flexser & Tulving, 1978), connectionist networks (e.g., Fodor & Pylyshyn, 1988; Hanson & Burr, 1990), or some other form of distributed memory system (e.g., Murdock, 1982)—it has been apparent for some time that language-based representational units are inappropriate at any age (e.g., see Anderson, 1978, 1979; Palmer, 1978; Pylyshyn, 1979). As several theorists have pointed out (e.g., Karmiloff-Smith, 1992; Mandler, 1992), conceptual representational systems are present, operating, and used for purposes of organizing information in memory well before language is available for the expression of those concepts. Indeed, much of language acquisition is predicated on the child having already formed concepts to which the individual linguistic terms apply (see Mandler, 1992). In essence, then, information that defines concepts represented in memory exists without reference to the modality through which they were experienced or its lexical entry. Thus, although memory representations can be instantiated in a number of ways symbolically at input and output (e.g., verbal, imaginal), these formats should not be confused with how this information is represented in memory.

Given that researchers accept this distinction between symbols and the memorial representations they stand for, what is the role of language in memory, autobiographical and otherwise? What the literature indicates is that language facilitates the organized expression of memories at output (e.g., narrative), much like other avenues of expression do (e.g., gesture, art, music, mathematics) and, as already argued, can be used to reinstate memories. However, that there is a correlation between improvements in autobiographical recall and children's narrative skills should not be taken as evidence that the latter causes the former. Rather, as already shown, children's narrative recall shows improvement in the degree to which memory reports receive elaboration, not in whether the gist of the event is remembered (see chaps. 2–4). Indeed, because verbal recall is so frequently the measure of choice in studies of autobiographical recall it is little wonder that improvements in children's narrative skills could be mistaken for improvements in autobiographical memory itself rather than developments in children's ability to express their memories.

Given that this sociolinguistic hypothesis has been found wanting both empirically and theoretically, what other explanation can there be? As a review of the literature makes clear, it is not a child's ability to remember events that suddenly changes because researchers know that children remember events for long periods of time even before the age of 2 years (see chap. 2). The question is, then, what is it about the memory for these events that changes? What seems to change is the personalization of the event; that is, it is no longer simply something that happened but, something that happened to *me*. A number of years ago, Howe and Courage (1993) suggested that, for events to be personalized, children must acquire a sense of self, an acquisition that is logically before the establishment of autobiographical memory. As noted at that time,

> autobiographical memory, by definition, is memory for information and events pertaining to the self. Therefore, knowledge of the self as an independent entity with characteristics, thoughts, and actions that are separate and distinct from those of others is perhaps the minimum criterion for the existence of autobiographical memory. Without a clear recognition of an independent self, there can be no referent around which personally experienced events can be organized. Prior to articulation of the self, the infant will learn and remember, but these experiences cannot be recognized as specific events, coded with respect to time and place, that happened to a "me." (Howe & Courage, 1993, p. 306)

In what follows, a more detailed accounting of this theory is presented because it is the only one that can simultaneously account for (a) the offset of infantile amnesia and the onset of autobiographical memory, while also acknowledging the possibility that event memory may exist in a nonpersonalized form before the advent of autobiographical memory and (b) the growth in numbers of memories across the childhood to early adult years.

SELF-RECOGNITION AND AUTOBIOGRAPHICAL MEMORY

Essentially, Howe and Courage (1993, 1997b) argued that autobiographical memory begins as a consequence of the development of a new cognitive organizer (or software), namely the cognitive self. Although this cognitive self does not come on-line until about 18 to 24 months of age, and even then it may not be sufficiently fleshed out to support autobiographical encoding, this new self has precursors in developments occurring since birth. Despite disagreement concerning the nature and functioning of the self, there is a growing consensus that at birth, infants are probably unaware of their separateness from the environment and acquire this awareness following a gradual process of individuation, one that likely begins in the early weeks of life (Meltzoff, 1990; Neisser, 1993). There is also agreement that there are at least two fundamental (but complexly interrelated) facets of the self, the "I," a subjective sense of the self as a thinker, knower, and causal agent, and the "me," an objective sense of the self with the unique and recognizable features and characteristics that constitute one's self-concept (however, see Neisser, 1988, for an alternative perspective on the facets of the self that focus on information analysis). The mechanisms and processes underlying the growing awareness of the self in all (both) its aspects are active areas of investigation in both theoretical and empirical spheres (Bullock & Lutkenhaus, 1990; Case, 1991; Cicchetti, 1991; Damon & Hart, 1982, 1988; Emde, Biringen, Clyman, & Oppenheim, 1991; Harter, 1983; Lewis, 1991; Lewis & Brooks-Gunn, 1979; Meltzoff, 1990; Neisser, 1991; Pipp, Fischer, & Jennings, 1987). In particular, this research has focused on visual self-recognition judgments as reflected in infants' reactions to their images in mirrors, photos, and videos. Much of this research has been recently reviewed (Howe & Courage, 1997b), so I restrict my summary to critical features of this work.

Results from numerous studies show that from about 3 months of age, infants are both attentive and affectively positive toward their mirror image and within several months can discriminate their facial features from that of another infant (Fadil, Moss, & Bahrick, 1993). By about 9 months of age, infants are aware of contingency cues provided by tandem movement of the image with themselves, can use these cues for play and imitation, and will turn to locate objects and people they see reflected. Full self-recognition of the mirror image as their own emerges around 18 months of age, when infants first respond to a spot of rouge that has been covertly applied to their noses by touching their own noses rather than the mirror image. Coincident with this behavior, infants begin to show self-consciousness (e.g., shy smiling, gaze aversion, and self-touching) when confronted with their images and by about 22 months of age will correctly label their image. Together, these behaviors provide a consistent picture of an infant who recognizes the mirror image as "me."

This visual self-recognition represents only one facet of the self-concept, one that is relatively easy to operationalize for research with infants. The self-concept (and self-awareness) implies considerably more than recognition of one's physical being and represents a fundamental aspect of social–cognitive development that has incipient roots in the early weeks of life and a continued metamorphosis throughout childhood and adolescence (see Damon & Hart, 1988, for a review). The achievement of self-recognition is thought by many to herald an important developmental milestone during the second year of life (Asendorpf & Baudonniere, 1993; Butterworth, 1990; Kagan, 1981; Lewis, 1986; Meltzoff, 1990; Neisser, 1993), one that represents a pivotal phase in infants' ability to represent themselves as an object of knowledge and imagination and that signals a more pervasive transition in cognitive development (also see Karmiloff-Smith, 1992).

In contrast, empirical work on the self as subject-of-experience (the "I") has lagged behind in large part because it is harder to operationalize. Only recently have researchers designed "self-involvement-in-action" tasks (i.e., those in which the child recognizes the outcome as a product of his or her own participation) that articulate this aspect of the self in terms of a sense of agency more precisely (Bullock & Lutkenhaus, 1990; Meltzoff, 1990; Pipp et al., 1987). Despite the paucity of empirical work, it has been thought that the infant's sense of self-as-subject-of-experience originates well before self-recognition, having its primitive origins in the processes of sensory perception, self-control (e.g., Butterworth, 1990; Neisser, 1993), and imitation (Meltzoff, 1990) in the early weeks and months of life (for reviews, see Howe & Courage, 1997b; Meltzoff, 1990; Neisser, 1988, 1993). In essence, these contemporary theories agree that essential groundwork for the development of the self-as-subject is evident early in infancy, perhaps from birth, that all (both) aspects of the self-system develop in tandem over the first 2 years, and that by the time the infant shows mirror self-recognition, she or he already has a healthy self-awareness (see Butterworth, 1990).

Although how the various facets of the self become integrated into a full self-system developmentally has not been completely articulated, what is critical to Howe and Courage's (1993, 1997b) thesis is that (a) a sense of self is fundamental to the development of autobiographical memory, and (b) by 18–24 months of age infants have a concept of themselves that is sufficiently viable to serve as a referent around which personally experienced events can be organized in memory. Contributors to a special issue of *Developmental Review*, "Development of the Self" (Kopp & Brownell, 1991), concurred that a significant change in one's sense of self occurs at about this time, although the exact nature of this change remains elusive. What is clear, though, is that the self at 18–24 months of age achieves whatever "critical mass" is necessary to serve as an organizer and regulator of experience (also see Emde et al., 1991; Kagan, 1981). That this achievement in self-awareness (recognition) is followed shortly by the onset of autobiographical memory is, according to Howe and Courage (1993, 1997b), more than coincidental.

As noted earlier, the establishment of the cognitive self is no different from the establishment of other conceptual categories or knowledge structures that serve to organize memories. Although the cognitive self permits event memories to become personally organized with respect to "me," this is no different from children's ability to organize information about "rabbits" with memories of other animals. More important, like most other concepts and categories acquired early in life, the self emerges before the use of productive language about that concept. For example, 9-month-old infants acquire the concept of "animal" before having language for that category (e.g., Mandler & McDonough, 1993; Roberts, 1988). More generally, children must already have concepts of objects and events, as well as relational notions about them, for language to be acquired (also see Mandler, 1992; Slobin, 1985). Interestingly, acquisition of any natural language requires a preexisting theory of self (e.g., Bates, 1990), and the self-concept predates any elaboration of the self children might achieve once language facilitates thinking and talking about "I" and "me" (see Howe & Courage, 1993). These linguistic achievements (the emergence of the pronominal references to "I," "me," and "you") appear in a child's productive vocabulary between 22 and 24 months of age (Fenson et al., 1994) about 1 month after the achievement of visual self-recognition (Bertenthal & Fischer, 1978; Bullock & Lutkenhaus, 1990; Lewis & Brooks-Gunn, 1979; Pipp et al., 1987).

REEVALUATING THEORIES

Given this theoretical backdrop, what do the data indicate about the recall of autobiographical events? As noted earlier, toddlers begin to recount their memories of personally experienced (i.e., autobiographical) events as soon as they acquire the rudiments of productive language, even before they have mature use of past-tense markers (e.g., saying "I see big fish" after a trip to the aquarium). One of the earliest studies of toddlers' autobiographical recollections was by Sachs (1983), who reported that Naomi first talked about events in her immediate past when she was 17 months old and was 26 months old when she discussed events from the more distant past. K. Nelson (1989) reported that 21-month-old Emily's spontaneous "narratives from the crib" contained references first to routine events and later, when she was 25 months old, to specific personal events. Miller and Sperry (1988), in a longitudinal study of five toddlers between the ages of 24 and 31 months, noted that not only were all of the children able to recount events that had happened at least one day previously but that over the 7-month period of the study, the rate of talk about personal experiences doubled, production of temporally ordered sequences increased, and toddlers were able to provide more information spontaneously. Critically, these narratives were often about negative events and contained evaluative content (e.g., "Me *big* fall down"), although a substantial portion of this evaluation was conveyed nonverbally through gesture.

As reported in chapter 4, Howe, Courage, and Peterson (1994b) found that 2-year-olds were able to provide coherent and detailed recall of traumatic injuries and their treatment a few days after the experience and that toddlers' recall (at least for the central details of the incidents) was still robust when tested 6 and 12 months later (Howe et al., 1994a, 1994b). Similar findings have been reviewed (see chaps. 2 and 3) for 2.5-year-olds' memories for more positive experiences, particularly for novel events (e.g., a trip to the zoo), that they had experienced either in the recent (less than 3 months) or more distant (more than 3 months) past. Indeed, children's recall was highly accurate for these events, and there were no differences in the amount recalled at the two different times (e.g., Fivush, Gray, & Fromhoff, 1987). Finally, 24- to 30-month-olds can recall specific information about events that occurred up to 10 months previously (e.g., Hudson, 1993). In fact, one 26-month-old child recalled an event she had experienced when she was just 1 year old. These studies (along with those reported throughout this book) provide consistent evidence that toddlers have accurate and durable recall of personally experienced events. Although their reports can be fragmentary and rely heavily on questions and prompts from the listener to elicit additional details, their spontaneous reports are frequently accurate for the gist of what happened.

In contrast, the picture painted for older preschoolers and school-aged children (see chap. 3 in this book) is one in which their narrative recollections about personally experienced events are better structured and more cohesive (i.e., they contain more referential detail, orienting information, evaluative comment, use of temporal markers) than younger children's, and they require less prompting and support from the listener (also see Fivush, 1993; Fivush, Haden, & Adam, 1995). However, as memorial measures are confounded with linguistic proficiency and narrative skill in studies of autobiographical memory, particularly across the preschool years, it may be that older children's narratives of personal events are better articulated and expressed but not necessarily better represented in memory. For example, there was no effect of age (2.5 or 4.5 years) or retention interval (6 months or 18 months) on either the accuracy or amount of children's recall of a trip to Disney World (Hamond & Fivush, 1991), nor was there an effect of age or retention interval on children's recall of the birth of a sibling (e.g., Sheingold & Tenney, 1982). Although some researchers have found developmental differences in the amount, consistency, and durability of information recalled (Fivush, 1993; Howe et al., 1994a, 1994b; Pillemer & White, 1989; Todd & Perlmutter, 1980), few if any differences have been found in accuracy. Thus, the better elaborated narratives of older children may not reflect better memory at all but better language skills to express those memories. Indeed, as far as memory is concerned, deaf and hearing individuals provide remarkably similar autobiographical recollections despite the hearing loss and subsequent language delay experienced by deaf people (West, 1998). On the basis of her findings, West (1998) concluded that "language may not play a strong role in the onset of autobiographical memory" (p. 86). Interestingly, despite debate over whether younger children recall less than older children or simply report less, there is little disagreement that what younger children recall can be highly accurate and durable over considerable periods of time.

With these findings in hand and refreshed in memory, it is time to reconsider the different theoretical positions concerning the emergence of autobiographical memory. First, despite the impressive evidence of young children's recall of personally experienced events, a few theorists maintain that autobiographical memory does not emerge until the late preschool years (K. Nelson, 1989, 1993; Perner & Ruffman, 1995; Pillemer & White, 1989). According to these theories, autobiographical memory undergoes a protracted period of development, either because it is contingent on somewhat protracted developments in the sociolinguistic realm, ones that eventuate in the ability to "use the verbal representation of another person to set up a representation in one's own mental representation system, thus recognizing the verbal account as a reinstatement of one's prior experience" (K. Nelson, 1993, p. 12), or because it is contingent on similarly late-developing phenomena such as the emergence of autonoetic (i.e., self-knowing) consciousness such that "to remember something as experienced requires there to be a mental representation of the fact that the event is known because it has been experienced" (Perner & Ruffman, 1995, p. 543). In the former (social interaction) model, autobiographical memory evolves in the wake of conversational interactions between the child and significant others, something that evolves over the preschool years. In the latter (autonoetic) model, autobiographical memory becomes possible only after achievements in metacognition, in which children are able to have recollective experiences of remembering (as opposed to simply knowing about) past events, experiences that are unlikely to occur before the age of 3–5 years simply because younger children do not understand the relationship between informational access (e.g., seeing) and knowledge. Like the social interaction model, a mother's elaborated talk about past episodes is thought to play a significant role in the evolution of autonoetic consciousness (see Perner & Ruffman, 1995).

Although both of these models may be correct in describing subsequent achievements that may result in increases in the number or duration of autobiographical memories maintained in storage, they fail to account for the age at which the data show that personalized memories begin. Moreover, like the problems noted earlier in the sociolinguistic approach concerning the confusion between growth in linguistic skills as an expressive device for memories with changes in memory per se, it is not clear that autonoetic experience is critical to the establishment of autobiographical memory. That is, although the experience of remembering often accompanies autobiographical recall (e.g., see Conway, 1996), the existence of personalized memories is not contingent on such experiencing.

The data are more consistent with Howe and Courage's (1993, 1997b) argument that the recognition of the cognitive self is the critical event that launches autobiographical memory and that subsequent achievements in productive language provide an expressive outlet for these memories that serve to preserve (through reinstatement) or could potentially alter (through reconstructive processes) memory records of personally experienced events. Of course, language development does not begin with its production in speech but emerges much earlier. There is considerable evidence that infants are (a) receptive to (and can remember) linguistic input from the last trimester of their prenatal life (DeCasper & Spence, 1986) and (b) proficient in the perception and discrimination of speech contrasts and attentive to aspects of language that facilitate subsequent achievements in comprehension and production late in the first postnatal year (Aslin, Pisoni, & Jusczyk, 1983; DeCasper & Spence, 1986; Kuhl, 1987). In many areas of language development, comprehension of words, grammatical forms, and gestures predate their production in speech and action (see Bates, O'Connell, & Shore, 1987, for a review). Given this early predisposition to process and remember linguistic forms, the question arises concerning whether the self might be represented in receptive language or gesture (e.g., self-pointing) before its appearance in visual self-recognition.

In a review of the literature, Howe and Courage (1997b) provided evidence that just as comprehension precedes production in language development in general, comprehension (or receptive understanding) of the sense of self (evidenced in self-pointing and the comprehension of self-referent pronouns), precedes its production in spoken language about the self by several months. At about 8 or 9 months of age infants show comprehension of the meaning of words (Bates et al., 1987; Fenson et al., 1994; Goldin-Meadow, Seligman, & Gelman, 1976; Oviatt, 1985), and by 13 months of age they have a receptive vocabulary of about 17–97 words (however, see Tomasello & Mervis, 1994, for some skepticism). Coincident with this is the use of gestures in intentional communication, where, at about 9 months of age, infants express requests (protoimperatives), showing and giving (protodeclaratives), and by 11 months of age begin to point (Bates, Benigni, Bretherton, Camaioni, & Volterra, 1979; Bates, Camaioni, & Volterra, 1975). By their first birthday infants acquire and express, both in visual recognition and in pointing, new word meanings through instruction (Oviatt, 1985; Reznick & Goldfield, 1992; Woodward, Markman, & Fitzsimmons, 1994). Although parental reports indicate that infants recognize their own names at about 8 months of age (an event that does not in and of itself signal mature self-recognition), there is little evidence that self-referent pronouns are comprehended before about 18 months of age (Fenson et al., 1994). Recent studies of symbolic gesturing (Acredolo & Goodwyn, 1988; Goodwyn & Acredolo, 1993) show that infants' use of gesturing to communicate also expands rapidly in the second postnatal year, when infants use many gesture–referent pairings to denote objects, requests, attributes, replies, and events. Such gestures are used as transitional forms and are replaced by appropriate verbal labels as soon as they can be articulated.

Of particular interest to Howe and Courage's (1993, 1997b) thesis is the finding that infants' comprehension of self-referent pronouns, as well as their use of the gestural mode to communicate, is accompanied by the appearance of another marker of the developing sense of self, namely first-person pointing. Although third-person pointing (i.e., "you") is evident at 9–11 months of age, first-person pointing (i.e., "I" and "me") is not seen before about 18 months of age (Bates et al., 1987; Pettito, 1993). This discontinuity between first- and third-person pointing reflects an underlying uncertainty in the emerging understanding of the self. That is, if third-person pointing indicates that the infant has made a distinction between self *and* object ("I"; H. Werner & Kaplan, 1963), then the delay in first-person pointing might reflect the fact that the cognitively more complex concept of self *as* object ("me") is not in place. Advances in the gestural achievements of self-pointing and self-recognition, as well as in infants' beginning comprehension of self-referent pronouns, all of which emerge when infants are about 18 months old, signal that the infants' sense of self is being consolidated at this age. At the least, the marked discontinuity (at the level of performance) in the onset of first- and third-person referential pointing may well reflect the infant's uncertainty about the nature of the self and the need to sort out "I" and "you" before expressing them some months later in productive language. Such discontinuities are viewed by Goldin-Meadow and her colleagues (Goldin-Meadow, Alibali, & Church, 1993; Morford & Goldin-Meadow, 1992) as being particularly significant developmentally, regarding them as "windows on the mind" of a child in transitional states of knowledge acquisition. That is, when a child is in such a transitional state, knowledge that can be expressed in the gestural mode is still unavailable for (and thus mismatched with) expression in the speech mode. Concerning the development of the concept of the self, it is only after the emergence of the cognitive self as expressed through gestures that infants will be able to consolidate their knowledge about the self and to move on to a new level of competence that will enable them to use self-language and narrative skills to report autobiographical memories in speech.

Thus, according to Howe and Courage (1993, 1997b), infants first reveal their awareness of the cognitive sense of self nonverbally. Beginning at about 18 months of age, they are able to use the gestural mode (i.e., mark-directed behavior to their mirror image, self-referent pointing) to communicate an early awareness of the self that is the cornerstone of autobiographical memory. Also during this time infants begin to understand self-referent pronouns that only later, between about 22 and 24 months, can be expressed in productive language about the self. Of course, it is at this point that autobiographical memories become possible but not necessarily probable. That is, although the onset of the cognitive self defines the lower boundary for the personalization of event memory, it in no way guarantees that such memories will be encrypted as autobiographical. To explain why this is so, I provide an overview of how autobiographical memories are formed and accumulated across the childhood years.

AUTOBIOGRAPHICAL MEMORIES ACROSS CHILDHOOD

It is well documented that childhood memories increase in number after the onset of the self. As already argued, the onset of the cognitive self can explain the origin of autobiographical memory, setting the lower limit for such memories at around 2 years of age, an age that is consistent with many findings (e.g., Eacott & Crawley, 1998; Usher & Neisser, 1993). The following question remains, however: Why is it that adult memories of childhood become more numerous across the early years in childhood (2–3 years of age to 8–10 years of age)? What the evidence shows is that throughout childhood the ability to maintain information in storage increases, not only in autobiographical memory, but also in all of memory (Howe & O'Sullivan, 1997).

I have already reviewed considerable evidence illustrating that even young toddlers can retain information over protracted periods of time and that there are clear age improvements in children's long-term retention performance. Although some of the key factors that contribute to memory development (e.g., changes in strategies, knowledge) are known, it is not clear from a basic-process perspective why such improvements occur. For example, although researchers know that strategic rehearsal can lead to better recall, it is not clear whether these effects arise because the stability of traces in storage increases, the ease of retrieving these traces increases, or both. Similarly, to discover what basic processes mediate these improvements in autobiographical retention, researchers must understand what processes are affected by the self in memory. A number of researchers who have investigated the role of the self in memory have concluded that the self, like any other knowledge structure (e.g., see Bjorklund, 1987), can be used to interpret and organize incoming information (see Greenwald & Banaji, 1989; Klein & Kihlstrom, 1986). In a recent meta-analysis of studies of the self-reference effect in memory, Symons and Johnson (1997) concluded that the self is important not only because of its elaborative and organizational properties but also because it links encoding and test conditions, a phenomenon that facilitates access to memories (e.g., as in encoding-specificity theory; see Tulving, 1984). As seen later in this chapter, the self plays a prominent role in autobiographical recall, particularly at points in time when there are major transitions in the self. The view that the self behaves like any other organizational scheme in memory is consistent with the idea that autobiographical memory is functionally no different from any other "type" of memory.

Howe and Courage (1997b) linked these ideas with the trace-integrity framework, a model recently proposed to account for the development of long-term retention more generally. Briefly, in the trace-integrity framework, storage and retrieval are processes constituting a single continuum in which traces consist of collections of primitive elements (e.g., features). The key to initial acquisition is integrating features into a single, cohesive structure in memory. Following acquisition, traces that are well integrated can undergo disintegration across the long-term retention interval, a process that, like acquisition, has both a storage and a retrieval component. Here, the "glue" that is used to form the original memory trace dissipates, with the result that the memory trace begins to lose its cohesion and distinctiveness, fading into the background noise of other memory traces. Importantly, during the long-term retention test itself, traces can be reintegrated simply as a consequence of the testing situation, a process of trace recovery that can involve both storage and retrieval. This conceptualization of storage and retrieval has gained broad acceptance in the memory development literature and is consistent with other conceptualizations of these processes in other recent models (e.g., see Howe & Courage, 1997b; Howe & O'Sullivan, 1997; W. Schneider & Bjorklund, 1998).

Although a more complete description of this model can be found in Appendix A, the trace-integrity framework is important here because it provides a general context, one that is common to all of long-term memory, in which to situate autobiographical memory. Moreover, it explains the accumulation of autobiographical memories using a simple, basic process mechanism: storage maintenance. Using the same mechanisms to explain autobiographical memory as used to explain other memories and their development, researchers simplify and enhance their understanding of memory development at both specific and global levels. To see how these goals are met, consider first how this system might encode an event both before and after the emergence of the cognitive self. When sampling features to be encoded and stored from an ongoing event (or nominal stimulus), the system often includes interpretive or internal contextual features. It is well-known that only a subset of features that characterize an event (internal and external) are actually encoded, depending on a number of factors (e.g., a feature's salience, the encoder's expectation, attentional factors), and the number of features encoded varies probabilistically. Reminiscent of stimulus sampling theory (e.g., see Hilgard & Bower, 1975; Neimark & Estes, 1967), then, the stored trace of encoded features (the functional stimulus) is extracted and consists of a subset of features from the event itself (the nominal situation) as well as interpretive elements.

Like other categories and concepts, it is not until the self becomes a viable cognitive entity, one with recognizable features, that the encoding of such features into the functional memory trace becomes possible. However, even when the self becomes viable and its features become potentially samplable, like other features in the nominal situation, there is no guarantee that they will be sampled. Indeed, whether self-features are sampled is determined probabilistically and is contingent on the same factors that control sampling probabilities for other features (e.g., salience, attention, the extent to which or centrality of participation by the self in the event). These encoding fluctuations (also see Flexser & Tulving, 1978) may explain variability in the numbers of early autobiographical memories across individuals, as there may be a restricted set of features from which to sample in the first place. As features get added to the "urn," the likelihood that at least some self-features will be sampled and encoded in the functional trace for an event increases. Thus, although there is no chance of encoding self-features before the emergence of a viable cognitive self, this does not mean that events cannot be remembered as events, as attested to by the ever-growing literature reviewed in the earlier chapters of this book. Moreover, even when a viable cognitive self emerges, events can remain depersonalized if features of the self are not sampled and encoded in the stored trace. The effects of this sampling variability should be particularly noticeable early in the establishment of the self because the number of features defining the self may be relatively constrained. As the number of features associated with the self increases, the corresponding likelihood of at least some of these features being sampled increases, with the result that memory for an event now becomes memory for an event that happened to me, a memory that, by definition, is now autobiographical. Thus, having a viable cognitive self sets the bottom limit as to when autobiographical memories can be established; however, this does not guarantee that such memories need be established at that age. As the number of features grow, so, too, does the probability that self-features will be incorporated into the memory trace, transforming simple event memory into memories that are autobiographical. This, added to the growth in storage capacity, can account for the accumulation of autobiographical memories as children grow older. In fact, like other knowledge, the increase in features (knowledge) concerning the self may not only lead to quantitative increases in autobiographical memories but also to more efficient organization of those memories in storage, something that contributes to the increased longevity of those memories.

What do the data indicate about these claims? First, autobiographical memories do increase in both number and longevity in memory as childhood progresses (e.g., Wetzler & Sweeney, 1986). Second, the results of several studies have shown that the best retained memories over the life span are those pertaining to the self. For example, Conway (1996) alerted researchers to the importance of self-transitions in "landmark" memories in one's autobiography. That is, as the self goes through various transitions, events associated with these transition points are well remembered (e.g., Csikszentmihalkyi & Beattie, 1979). Although such findings highlight the importance of changes in the self in autobiographical memories, it is also possible that such transitions represent unique occurrences in one's life. Indeed, Linton (1979) and Brewer (1988) have found that uniqueness of an event is one of the best overall predictors of autobiographical recall. Furthermore, in a recent study of event memory with adults, Betz and Skowronski (1997) found that the best retained events (over the period of an academic semester) were those that pertained to oneself (as opposed to a friend) and that were unique or atypical. Thus, it is clear that events about the self, particularly those that are personally consequential, transition defining, or otherwise distinctive, are best remembered autobiographically.

INDIVIDUAL DIFFERENCES

There is considerable variability across individuals in the age of their first autobiographical memories when, as adults, they are asked to recall their earliest experiences (e.g., Eacott & Crawley, 1998; Usher & Neisser, 1993). One explanation is that there are individual differences in forgetting rates. A more interesting possibility is that these differences are related to individual variation in the age of onset of the cognitive self or the propensity to encode self-relevant features into memory traces for early events. Although this second possibility has already been discussed, it is interesting to note with respect to age of onset that developmental trends in early self-recognition during the second year of life show substantial individual differences in the age of onset of mark-directed behavior (Berenthal & Fischer, 1978; Lewis & Brooks-Gunn, 1979; Lewis, Brooks-Gunn, & Jaskir, 1985; Schneider-Rosen & Cicchetti, 1984, 1991). For example, these studies showed that, whereas about 25% of 15- to 18-month-old infants showed mark-directed behavior to the red spot on their noses, others did not show self-recognition until the end of the second year, at which time about 75% showed mark-directed behavior.

Although these individual differences in the age of onset of visual self-recognition have not been fully explored, there is evidence that they may have their origins in maturational rather than social or experiential factors. According to Lewis and Brooks-Gunn (1979), neither the child's sex nor social experience (as measured by mother's education, family socioeconomic status, birth order, or number of siblings) was related to the onset of self-recognition. Cicchetti and his colleagues (Cicchetti & Beeghly, 1987; Cicchetti & Carlson, 1989; Kaufman & Cicchetti, 1989; Schneider-Rosen & Cicchetti, 1984, 1991) found that maltreated infants whose aberrant caretaking environments resulted in well-documented delays or deviations in their emotional development as it related to the self were not delayed in the onset of mirror self-recognition but that infants who had delayed maturation (e.g., Down's syndrome, familial mental retardation, autism) did show delays in visual self-recognition (Cicchetti, 1991; Hill & Tomlin, 1981; Loveland, 1987, 1993; Mans, Cicchetti, & Sroufe, 1978; Schneider-Rosen & Cicchetti, 1991; Spiker & Ricks, 1984). Interestingly, these latter infants can succeed at the self-recognition task if and when they reach a mental age comparable to that of nondelayed infants who succeed at the task. The almost universal appearance of visual self-recognition among infants who have attained the maturational prerequisites suggests that its emergence is not conspicuously influenced by variations in social or childcare experiences (however, see Lewis et al., 1985, for some evidence to the contrary). This explanation is consistent with Kagan's (1981) argument that the origins of the self-concept are seen in the maturation of the child and that the social environment plays only a minor role in this development. Consistent with Kagan (1981, 1994) and the evidence just reviewed, there are new data that demonstrate a clear link between the early establishment of the self and constitutional factors such as stress reactivity and temperament (DiBiase & Lewis, 1997; Lewis & Ramsey, 1997). For example, DiBiase and Lewis (1997) found that differences in temperament were related to variation in the age at which self-recognition emerged. Moreover, these same differences were predictive of when self-conscious emotions such as embarrassment are expressed (Lewis, Sullivan, Stanger, & Weiss, 1989). That is, infants with a difficult temperament at 5 months of age were more likely to show self-recognition and embarrassment earlier than infants with an easy temperament. Using a longitudinal design, Lewis and Ramsey (1997) found that children with higher stress reactivity (measured both in terms of cortisol levels and behavioral responses to inoculations at 2, 4, 6, and 18 months of age) also had an earlier onset of self-recognition. Thus, self-recognition and self-conscious emotions such as embarrassment are linked to constitutional factors, including temperament and stress reactivity, in which a cognitive sense of self emerges earlier for children who are classified as having a more difficult temperament or whose reactivity to stress is relatively high. Perhaps individual differences in the onset of early autobiographical memories are related to maturational, not social or experiential, factors associated with the emergence of the cognitive self. This hypothesis is in direct contrast to the social-constructivist position (e.g., K. Nelson, 1993), in which the onset of autobiographical memory is said to be directly related to sociolinguistic factors.

Although differences in the onset of autobiographical memory in atypical populations should be directly related to delays in the establishment of the cognitive self and not chronological age, the mirror behavior of children with atypical cognitive development or those with adverse social environments is different from that of normally developing children. Examination of behaviors coincident with visual self-recognition show patterns that may well be linked to differences in social interactional variables. For example, normally developing children as well as those with maturational delays are generally positive in their responses to their self-image (Cicchetti, 1991; Lewis et al., 1989). However, children who have been maltreated show more neutral and negative behavior in response to their mirror images (Cicchetti, Beeghly, Carlson, & Toth, 1990). This raises the interesting possibility that although social and experiential factors may not determine the onset of early autobiographical memory, they may contribute to the contents of these early memories.

CONCLUSION

The data are consistent with the notion that the emergence and subsequent development of autobiographical memory are controlled by the discovery of the cognitive self and increases in the ability to maintain information in memory storage, respectively. Like the development of other knowledge structures in memory, infants acquire a cognitive sense of self, one around which event memories can be personalized and "preserved" as autobiographical. Furthermore, like other structures, categories, and concepts in memory, the cognitive sense of self emerges and is represented nonverbally, only later being expressed, not determined, using language. Thus, the offset of infantile amnesia and the onset of autobiographical memory does not require the appearance of a separate memory system, nor must it await developments in language, autonoetic awareness, or metacognition that occur late in the preschool years. Rather, it is the natural consequence of young toddlers' more general tendency to develop nonverbal representational structures that describe the world around them (e.g., Karmiloff-Smith, 1992; Mandler, 1992).

Because this cognitive sense of self does not emerge until around 24 months of age, personalized memories for experiences are not available before approximately 2 years of age. Although this sets the lower limit for the formation of autobiographical memories, it does not guarantee that such memories will be formed at that age. Indeed, personalized memories may not be formed until sometime later depending on a variety of factors, including the number of features available for encoding and the distribution of sampling probabilities during encoding. The subsequent ability to retain more autobiographical information with age in childhood develops not as a function of advances in narrative skills but as a natural consequence of global improvements in children's general memory abilities, namely the capacity to maintain information in storage over longer and longer intervals. Although a number of skills may be involved in, or at least correlated with, this improvement, including developments in language, strategies, knowledge, and gist extraction, the one common denominator to changes in children's retention over time is the basic ability of keeping information intact in storage.

What happens to event memories that are formed before the cognitive self? Although I discuss the role of consciousness in memory in the next chapter, given the current understanding and the data gathered to date, it seems unlikely that these very early memories persist for a lifetime. Several reasons for this conclusion have already been given, including the fact that even at the best of times early memories appear fragmentary and poorly organized when recalled. Few if any of these memories become verbalizable (see chap. 2 in this book; see also Bauer et al., 1998), even if they were based on traumatic events at the time they were encoded (Howe et al., 1994b). Even though it is possible that memories from one's earliest days could persist behaviorally, what evidence that does exist suggests that such "memories" do not always endure (as in the case of the girl with the fishbone caught in her throat). Although the number of investigations is admittedly small and the evidence often anecdotal, it is unlikely that without an organizer like the (cognitive) self, such events will persist in memory unchanged over a lifetime. Indeed, unless they have been successfully recoded and reorganized, processes afforded the individual by the cognitive self, making them distinctive and meaningful against the background of other memories, it seems unlikely that they will remain intact in storage or will continue to affect the person at the level of behavior. Just as one's earlier concepts and categories become transformed and even supplanted by more mature forms of understanding, so, too, do one's memories of early events. Because storage is dynamic with the information and concepts contained within changing in response to new experiences, it is extremely unlikely that what people remember today of early experiences, especially those not encoded with respect to the self, remains untouched by a lifetime of additional memories and experiences.

6

CONSCIOUSNESS, MEMORY, AND DEVELOPMENT

One of the questions that has been raised a number of times throughout this book in a variety of guises concerns whether early memories can influence later behavior. Clearly, to the extent that such memories can be consciously recollected, there is a potential for them to do so. However, as I discussed, many of these early event memories are fragmentary and tend not to be well recalled until the emergence of the software necessary for the establishment of autobiographical memory. Even then, events can be discarded, modified, or even forgotten over the years. However, assuming that some experiences may survive and are not forgotten but are inaccessible to consciousness, might not this residue of early experience still influence people's behavior in some way?

As I argue, despite a lack of empirical evidence, there are innumerable theories and folk beliefs that either implicitly or explicitly hold that people are inexorably bound by their past, whether they can or cannot consciously remember it. Even at the beginning of this century, psychologists almost canonized the notion that "each mental acquisition leaves its mark. . . . Nothing good or evil is ever lost. . . . Every event of a man's mental life is written indelibly in the brain's archives" (Thorndike, 1905, pp. 330–331). Such ideas were, and still are, popular in the theories of luminaries such as Freud and Erikson, who embedded this fundamental notion in their ideas about the influence of experiences from early development. Indeed, these ideas are still common in the mainstream literature and can be seen in the extraordinary increase in the past decade or so of accounts of memories, particularly ones of abusive experiences, being recovered from the unconscious (e.g., Pope & Brown, 1996). Although the jury may still be out when it comes to the possibility that such recollections of events could occur, the memory evidence is convincing in its indictment of such a possibility (for an overview, see Alpert et al., 1996).

To use a less controversial example, consider Bowlby's (1969) theory of attachment. Here, the importance of early experience is evident in that people's first affective experience, the bond of attachment (also see chap. 4 in this book), is said to evolve from the innumerable hours of interaction between infants and their adult caretakers. The record of these early experiences, consciously recallable or not, is said to be indelibly etched in memory and will persist in its influence on people's attachment relationships with peers and significant others across the life span (e.g., Bretherton & Waters, 1985; Sroufe, 1983) as well as on their psychological well-being in adulthood (e.g., Bowlby, 1980). Although such relationships between early and later experience could occur, there is a scarcity of scientific data to substantiate the extent or the inevitability of such outcomes. For example, although adverse rearing conditions (e.g., insecure attachment, social isolation, institutionalization, chronic abuse) can result in deviant outcomes during infancy in both humans and nonhuman primates (e.g., Harlow & Harlow, 1966; Suomi & Harlow, 1972; also see Kagan, 1996), it has not been established that such behavioral, affective, or cognitive structures necessarily persist or are stable indefinitely. Indeed, the opposite is frequently observed. For example, remarkable resiliency and reversibility of the effects of adverse early experiences are evident in the productive behavior and lifestyles of adults who, as orphans, spent their first few years in concentration camps (Moscovitz, 1983). Similarly, children made homeless by war, who suffered severe malnutrition and emotional distress, can change radically after being adopted by nurturing families (Clarke & Hanisee, 1982; Rathbun, DeVirgilio, & Waldfogel, 1958; Winick, Meyer, & Harris, 1975). Indeed, many researchers and clinicians are astounded by numerous well-documented accounts of resiliency after severe infantile deprivation or trauma (for reviews see, Emde, 1981; Garmezy & Rutter, 1983; Kagan, 1984; Rutter, 1981). Thus, for humans and laboratory animals alike, there is a tendency for the effects of early experiences to diminish and a tendency for the organism to "right itself" in the wake of adversity (Cairns & Hood, 1983; Werner & Smith, 1982; Winick et al., 1975). In fact, contrary to both theory and folk belief, the scientific data overwhelmingly support the conclusion that early experiences do not serve to fix behaviors, attachment, or personality characteristics, especially if alternative caretaking environments foster other adaptive responses.

Clearly, the evidence is inconsistent with the strong version of the early experiential determinism hypothesis (in which early experience "fixes" later behavior) (also see Kagan, 1996), at least in terms of consistencies of behaviors, although it is possible that such memories might persist despite the absence of conspicuous behavioral expression. Moreover, simply because behaviors themselves can change, perhaps in response to new circumstances, does not mean that what they change into is directly determined by the residue of these earlier experiences. Thus, behavioral continuity, although a strong test of the early experiential determinism hypothesis, is not the litmus test of a weaker version of this hypothesis in which early memories can still guide the selection of newer, more adaptive responses. Indeed, continues the argument, if it were not for the residue of these early experiences, perhaps the current behaviors might not have been adopted.

The circularity of such arguments notwithstanding, is there any evidence that despite these changes in behavior there is still a memory for earlier experiences, ones that exert their influence despite people's inability to recall them consciously? The simple answer to this question is no. Of course, this does not mean that because researchers cannot find such memories that they do not exist. Indeed, it could be that researchers have simply not devised a sensitive enough test to detect the presence of these memories. Unfortunately, such arguments often carry little weight because they are ubiquitous, having the advantage of always being in reserve to explain away failures to reject the null hypothesis regardless of the circumstance. This is particularly true when science consistently fails to demonstrate the existence of some phenomenon that is well entrenched in one's intuition or folk belief (e.g., as in the debates concerning recovered memories, UFO abductions, etc.; see Sagan, 1996; Spanos, 1996). Although the failure to confirm a hypothesized phenomenon does not rule out the possibility that it may exist, repeated failures to substantiate it does question its authenticity. Indeed, it is only when concrete, empirical evidence is obtained that the existence of a particular phenomenon can be established and its properties studied. In what follows I provide an overview of the types of tests that are frequently used to evaluate hypotheses on the status of conscious and unconscious memories and examine the evidence concerning what may develop.

TESTS OF CONSCIOUS AND UNCONSCIOUS MEMORY

Surely there must be some evidence that memories can reside in people's unconscious. After all, there is evidence that a number of memory-relevant variables (e.g., similarity, familiarity, distinctiveness) can influence people's performance despite their lack of awareness of those variables. For example, people may vote for a particular candidate whose advertisements they have been exposed to repeatedly even though they have no other particular reason for electing him or her. Indeed, this seemingly unconscious influence of familiarity (in this case, induced through frequency of exposure) can be used to explain a number of similar phenomena, all of which appear, at least on the surface, to be unconscious influences of memory on performance. For example, consider the "sleeper effect." Here, there is an increase over time in the influence of a persuasive message that was previously presented by a source that has been discredited (Pratkanis, Greenwald, Leippe, & Baumgardner, 1988). Similarly, "becoming famous overnight" refers to situations in which a previously nonfamous name, one that is presented during an experimental session, is later but not immediately misidentified as someone who is famous (Jacoby, Kelley, Brown, & Jasechko, 1989). Finally, the "illusory truth effect" refers to the acceptance as true, statements that were earlier identified as false (Begg, Anas, & Farinacci, 1992).

An explanation of these phenomena need not rely on unconscious memory at all. That is, although the influence of variables on people's memory may be outside of their conscious awareness, this does not mean that the memories are also unconscious. Indeed, all of these effects can be explained using a combination of familiarity and misattribution effects. Quite simply, being exposed to material (even once) enhances its familiarity (e.g., it is easier to access in memory than other, less familiar information). After a delay (which all of these effects involve), recollection of the source of the memory (e.g., "it was told to me by an experimenter") is lost. When later asked to use that information in a judgment task (e.g., voting, assessing fame), people can retrieve that piece of information with relative ease (i.e., familiarity), fail to recollect its original context (i.e., source monitoring error), and then attribute the source of the information to themselves (i.e., source misattribution error). Indeed, the effects of familiarity and normal forgetting of the source of information previously acquired conspire to produce a number of effects, including the ubiquitous false memory effect discussed earlier in this book (also see Howe, 1998d). Worse, these effects can even manifest themselves in terms of what is called "unconscious plagiarism," in which someone mistakes another person's phrasing or idea as being his or her own. A wonderful example of this was provided by Ceci (1995) and involves a case of "cryptomnesia," in which Freud (1901/1960) found that he had inadvertently taken credit for a colleague's idea. Freud wrote that during the development of his theory of original bisexuality, a friend reminded him that he had relayed this same idea to Freud several years earlier in a discussion with him:

> One day in the summer of 1901 I remarked to a friend with whom I used at that time to have a lively exchange of scientific ideas: "These problems of the neuroses are only to be solved if we base ourselves wholly and completely on the assumption of the original bisexuality

of the individual." To which he replied: "That's what I told you two and a half years ago at Breslau when we went for that evening walk. But you wouldn't hear of it then." It is painful to be requested in this way to surrender one's originality. (Ceci, 1995, pp. 93–94)

Again, although researchers would like to appeal to the unconscious, it is unnecessary. However, simply because these effects do not require invoking (un)consciousness as an explanation does not mean that there may not be conditions under which memories are unconscious. For example, if researchers define consciousness as wakeful alertness and assume that people's memories are not built anew each morning when they awaken, then, by definition, people's memories must exist in their unconscious, at least during sleep. Although this definition and example may be simpleminded, it does highlight two important issues. First, researchers must be able to provide an adequate definition of what they mean by the term *conscious* and *unconscious* to study whether memories exist in these domains. Second, researchers must then ascertain whether the memories that are in the unconscious are different in any meaningful way from those in consciousness, for if they are not, they may not be intrinsically interesting to study, at least from a memory theorist's point of view.

Concerning the first point, it is not my intention to resolve the issue of what constitutes consciousness and the unconscious. Far more celebrated theorists than I have struggled with this problem for centuries, apparently without agreement on a solution (see Dennett, 1991). However, because my interest here is primarily with memory, the definition I use is the one commonly used in this area: Conscious memories are those associated with explicit recollection (as is usually found in standard recall and recognition tasks), and unconscious memories are those associated with implicit recollection (as is usually found in fragment completion and priming tasks). That is, explicit memory tasks involve not only recollection but also an awareness that recollection has occurred. Implicit memory tasks similarly involve recollection but without the accompanying awareness. Indeed, implicit recollection can be exhibited in a purely behavioral manner, as in using some learned skill (e.g., riding a bicycle, driving a car) as opposed to some verbal response.

For example, consider the Tower of Hanoi problem. In the simplest version, participants try to move three rings arranged by ascending size (diameter) from one of three pegs (e.g., the leftmost one) to another peg (e.g., the rightmost one) subject to the constraints that (a) only one ring can be moved at a time and (b) a larger ring cannot be placed atop a smaller ring. (Note that this same problem can be constructed using coins such as a quarter, nickel, and dime.) For most problem solvers, performance tends to improve across trials (i.e., the number of errors decreases and the time to solve the problem diminishes). Following asymptote, normal participants will be able to explicitly recall having solved the problem, what the goal is, and what constraints are imposed on moves. However, other individuals who have severe anterograde (and retrograde) amnesia (e.g., like the famous case of H.M., whose surgery to control severe epilepsy left him extremely amnesic for events before and after surgery) show similar improvements in performance despite an inability to recall either the problem itself or the rules that must be satisfied to solve the problem. Thus, despite the fact that H.M. could not consciously recollect the problem, having to be reinstructed on the nature of the problem each day, his performance improved steadily over days, a result that, according to some, indicated that even though his explicit memory had been lost during the surgery, his implicit memory was spared. In fact, such a dissociation seemed to provide strong evidence that explicit (conscious) and implicit (unconscious) memories were distinct. I return to this point in the next section after considering how these definitions can be operationalized (e.g., using different tasks or different measures of performance on the same task).

Concerning the second point, having these definitions in hand, I now discuss whether differences exist between memories that are conscious and those that are not. Moreover, I also discuss whether such differences, should they exist, have developmental origins and, if so, whether these differences start early in life. Indeed, there are several models of memory that might lead researchers to believe that conscious and unconscious memories have distinct developmental trajectories.

DISSEVERING CONSCIOUS AND UNCONSCIOUS MEMORIES

Throughout much of this book I have argued that memory consists of unitary trace structures rather than multiple trace structures. Although there may be differences in how well people encode, store, and retrieve information across different types of tasks (e.g., across procedural [implicit] vs. declarative [explicit] memory tasks), these differences are not necessarily due to differences in the types of traces in storage that subserve memory but may simply reflect differences in how well these different task demands engage the basic encoding, storage, and retrieval processes. Indeed, as there is no evidence that leads ineluctably to the conclusion that there is more than a single underlying trace structure, it is more parsimonious to assume that unitary, not multiple, representations provide an adequate account of the data from studies of memory and memory development (also see arguments in Howe & Courage, 1997b).

As already noted, such a conclusion is not without controversy. However, assume for the moment that such a proposition is true. The question then arises as to whether and in what manner conscious memory traces are different from unconscious memory traces. There are a number of theories concerning the unconscious influence of memories on people's (later) behavior and personality. According to those theories, even though people cannot consciously remember a particular event or experience, the residue of that circumstance may still reside in long-term memory's unconscious and may exert a powerful influence on people's behaviors, determine adult personality, and even be at the root of people's current psychological problems (e.g., Freud, 1916–1917/1963).

Can it be that these memories are radically different from people's conscious ones, or is there essentially one memory system in which consciousness is simply that process by which memories enter awareness? In this latter case, memories would simply exist in storage and only those that are being cued or are "in use" are the ones that are "in awareness." Indeed, it is possible that most of what is in memory is not conscious at any one time, although much of it could be available to consciousness (depending on its accessibility which, in turn, depends on a number of storage and retrieval factors already discussed) when required. This is not as strange an idea as it might first appear. There are many aspects of memory traces that are not in consciousness at any one time, with some of those aspects (e.g., how the information is actually represented) perhaps never becoming available to consciousness. Often, conscious recollection is not necessary to use memories effectively. For example, it is not necessary for a well-practiced driver to consciously remember how to apply the brakes in a car to bring it to a stop. Similarly, for someone who knows how to ride a bicycle, it is not necessary to be consciously aware of the memory that generates the relevant behaviors. Although, arguably, these memories may become conscious on "request," the point is that conscious recollection is not necessary to benefit from the memory (e.g., to stop a car or ride a bicycle). It may be, then, that memories "drift" in and out of consciousness depending on current processing demands and the cues available to elicit such memories. Otherwise, these memories, although not disappearing, are not in awareness and may vary in how easily they can be brought to mind (again, depending largely on the cues available to reinstate them).

Again, it would seem that a single trace model can account for what people often observe subjectively. However, consider what scientific evidence exists concerning the differences, if any, between conscious and unconscious memories. Here, too, the field is split, with some taking the side that conscious and unconscious memories differ in type and others assuming that any differences represent variation in processes or uses of traces, not differences among traces (e.g., see discussions in Jacoby, 1991; Roediger, Weldon, & Challis, 1989). As already alluded to, in the scientific literature on memory, conscious recollection has been equated with explicit memory, whereas unconscious familiarity without conscious recollection has been equated with implicit memory. Again, as illustrated earlier, the quintessential example of this dissociation can be found in individuals with amnesia who suffer from profound disruptions in their ability to consciously recollect long-term memories (i.e., failures of the explicit memory type) but who are able to exhibit behavioral improvement on tasks that must, by definition, require memory to perform (i.e., no impairment of memory of the implicit type).

It may be, then, that there are two different memories or at least two different ways of accessing memories, one that results in explicit recollection and the other that results in implicit recollection. The former is associated with the experience of consciously remembering, whereas the other is not. In addition, there exist a variety of means of assessing these different aspects of memory. For example, Tulving (1985) used a remember–know procedure in which participants respond to a standard recognition test in which previously studied items (targets) are to be accepted and unstudied items (distractors) are to be rejected. In addition, for each accepted probe, they are to classify it as "remembered" if they consciously recollect it as having been presented on the previous study list or to classify it as "know" if they recognize it but cannot specifically remember it being presented on the prior list. The proportions of "remember" and "know" responses for accepted targets (i.e., correct recognitions) are taken to be estimates of conscious and unconscious memory, respectively (also see Rajaram, 1996).

Developmentally, only a handful of studies exist, and those studies for the most part have been concerned with fairly circumscribed questions. For example, some researchers have been concerned with whether above-chance performance on unconscious memory tests can be demonstrated by young children after long delays (Bullock Drummey & Newcombe, 1995; Newcombe & Fox, 1994), others with how to dissociate performance on conscious and unconscious memory tests (Newcombe & Lie, 1995), and still others with whether performance on unconscious memory tests varies with age (Russo, Nichelli, Gibertoni, & Cornia, 1995). Here, instead of using remember–know judgments, researchers have focused on measures such as blurred picture identification versus picture recognition (Bullock Drummey & Newcombe, 1995), skin conductance responses to pictures of classmates versus picture recognition (Newcombe & Fox, 1994), covert versus overt recognition (Newcombe & Lie, 1995), and picture completion versus picture recall (Russo et al., 1995) to index unconscious and conscious memory, respectively.

For example, consider the study by Newcombe and Fox (1994). Here, children, now aged 8–11 years old, were shown photographs of their classmates from the preschool they attended from when they were 2–4 years old until they were 5–6 years old. These pictures were converted to slides and were intermixed with pictures of other children with whom they were not familiar. Children were shown this set of slides and asked which pictures they recognized. Actually, there were two measures used in the study, one that was used to index conscious recollection (the overt recognition response) and an index of unconscious memory, namely changes in skin conductance.

The results showed that both conscious and unconscious indexes of memory were produced to faces of old classmates. That is, above-chance levels of recognition and changes in skin conductance were observed to old but not new faces. Although the skin conductance responses were low overall, they occurred for all children regardless of their level of overt recognition. The authors suggested that this result was important because implicit or unconscious memory may still be active when explicit or conscious remembering is low. As illustrated shortly (as well as in chap. 7), although this possibility is intuitively inviting, there are a number of methodological concerns with studies that use different tests to assess conscious and unconscious memory that need to be addressed before such conclusions can be legitimately drawn.

In general, results from studies such as these have produced conflicting findings concerning whether there are developmental differences in conscious and unconscious memory. For example, neither Bullock Drummey and Newcombe (1995) nor Russo et al. (1995) found developmental differences in implicit tasks but did find standard improvements on explicit tasks. These findings are difficult to interpret, however, particularly because ceiling effects (i.e., performance was maximal) were present in the older age groups (5- and 6-year-olds and adults) that may have obscured the detection of age-related changes in implicit memory tasks in these studies. Other studies (e.g., Parkin, 1993) have shown age differences in both implicit and explicit memory tasks. In fact, as discussed later, Brainerd, Stein, and Reyna (1998) found clear developmental improvements in measures of both conscious and unconscious memory processes.

The problem with studies that have used either the two-test (e.g., Tulving, 1985) or task-based (e.g., Newcombe & Fox, 1994) separation methodologies is that neither procedure is completely satisfactory. In the procedures just mentioned, which were used to study developmental issues in conscious and unconscious memories, task was confounded with memory. That is, because different tasks were used to estimate conscious and unconscious memory, it is not clear whether the researchers were measuring different memories or simply different tasks. There is no assurance that the tasks were equivalent on all dimensions except for the one of interest: the type of memory they measured. Because of this, results from these studies are limited, do not provide clear-cut evidence for the existence of dissociable conscious and unconscious memories and, at best, provide some evidence that different tasks may provide different access routes to the same memory traces (also see Brainerd, Stein, & Reyna, 1998; Howe, Rabinowitz, & Grant, 1993).

Similar problems exist with the two-test method used by Tulving (1985). As Jacoby (1991) pointed out, two-test methodologies are inadequate because direct and indirect tests of memory are not pure measures of the different processes they are thought to measure (for a more detailed accounting of the problem of using two simultaneous tests to measure different processes, see Howe & Rabinowitz, 1989, 1991; Howe, Rabinowitz, & Grant, 1993). That is, as Jacoby (1991) showed, measures of conscious recollection (direct tests of memory) are contaminated by unconscious memory, and measures of unconscious memory (indirect tests of memory) are contaminated by conscious memory. Thus, "remember" judgments do not provide pure measures of conscious memory because they can sometimes be based on unconscious memories, and "know" judgments do not provide pure measures of unconscious memory because they can sometimes be based on conscious memories (also see Strack & Forster, 1995).

Even if these measures could be assumed to be pure, there remains a response scaling issue; that is, as seen in chapter 7, there must be an output transformation rule that specifies how conscious and unconscious memories map onto performance (also see Howe, Rabinowitz, & Grant, 1993). This is critical in both the two-test and task-based separation methodologies. Again, as seen earlier, unless these transformations are known or at least specified a priori, the link between differences in performance and differences in type of memories is unknown and uninterpretable.

In a recent study, Brainerd, Stein, and Reyna (1998; also see Brainerd, Reyna, & Wright, 1998) attempted to correct these problems by changing the usual outcome space over which conscious and unconscious memories are defined and by using model-based procedures to specify both the composition rules for how conscious and unconscious memories contribute to performance and how these contributions are output. Although I do not present all the details here, this work is important because it uses the same sorts of solutions to the methodological and modeling problems in the domain of conscious and unconscious memory processes as those used in chapter 7 to resolve initial acquisition and age confounds in other areas of memory research. More specifically, their model eliminates a bias commonly found in the literature on conscious and unconscious memory processing: a dependency between empirical estimates of conscious and unconscious processing. Although the experiments discussed so far have confounded conscious and unconscious processing at the level of the task, some experimenters, despite avoiding these problems by specifying the rules that govern composition and output, have failed to provide estimates of conscious processing that were independent of estimates of unconscious processing. The work by Brainerd and his colleagues avoids all of these problems.

In essence, Brainerd, Stein, and Reyna's (1998) and Brainerd, Reyna, and Wright's (1998) conjoint recognition procedure uses a variant of the standard recognition memory paradigm. Here, for example, children might see a list of categorizable items and later be asked to recognize (say yes to) only those probes that they believed were category names of the studied targets regardless of whether they remembered a specific exemplar that was in the list, accept category names only if they could remember a specific exemplar, or accept all category names except those for which a studied exemplar could be recollected. Using this combination of three conditions, which have a single (recognition) response but different demands on conscious and unconscious processing, a conjoint-recognition model can be derived that permits unbiased measures of the contribution of conscious and unconscious memory processes that combine to produce the recognition response under these different processing demands (see the equations in Brainerd, Reyna, & Wright, 1998). Using procedures like this, ones that deliver independent estimates of developmental trends in conscious and unconscious memory tasks, Brainerd and his colleagues have found separate trends for conscious and unconscious memories. Specifically, for children aged 7–10 years, conscious and unconscious memory tended to increase with age, with the magnitude of the increase in the latter being larger than that in the former. Consistent with the finding that both conscious and unconscious processes develop in tandem, Bullock Drummey and Newcombe (1995) found that 3- to 6-year-olds' conscious and unconscious memory processes tended to increase during childhood. These findings are inconsistent in many ways with the assumption that implicit and explicit tasks tap separate memory systems. In fact, like the other single versus multiple memory controversies discussed in this book, even if separate conscious and unconscious memory streams exist in adulthood, this does not imply that they are distinct in childhood. Indeed, even if they are, they appear to be developing in tandem from the earliest days (also see Rovee-Collier, 1997).

Although differences between implicit and explicit memory may not be as easy to tease apart as first thought, with explicit memory frequently contaminating measures of implicit memory and vice versa, the work of Brainerd and his colleagues shows that under some circumstances, developmental trends in both conscious and unconscious memory processes are robust. This does not mean that these processes constitute distinct memory systems. In fact, in a recent series of experiments with adults in which forgetting was examined across comparable implicit and explicit memory tasks, McBride and Dosher (1997) found no differences in either the form or rate of forgetting. As those authors pointed out, either implicit and explicit tasks use traces from the same memory system or there are different memory systems whose forgetting dynamics are identical. The former conclusion is preferred here not only because it is more parsimonious but also because it is consistent with conclusions from developmental studies. Indeed, contrary to much lore in this area, lore that stipulates that one of the hallmarks of distinct memory systems is differential developmental onsets, it would seem that both conscious and unconscious memory processes are operating from early in life and continue to develop into adulthood. As Rovee-Collier (1997) pointed out, and as I have tried to show throughout this book, young infants display memory performance akin to that of older children and adults, particularly in the sense that they respond in much the same way to experimental manipulations of various independent variables. Indeed, infants' performance on implicit and explicit memory tasks so closely parallel the findings with older children and adults that there is no reason to suspect that there are different memory systems or, at the least, if different memory systems do exist, their appearance is closely linked in time. As reviewed recently by Rovee-Collier (1997), there is no empirical evidence consistent with the claim that there is an implicit memory system that matures early in the first year of life and an explicit memory system that comes on-line at the end of the first year of life. As Rovee-Collier (1997) commented, "This evidence disputes claims that implicit and explicit memory follow different developmental time lines and challenges the utility of conscious recollection as the defining characteristic of explicit memory" (pp. 467–468). Thus, to the extent that the implicit–explicit memory distinction embodies the dichotomy between conscious and unconscious memory processes, the utility of the distinction between conscious–unconscious memory at any age is tenuous at best.

From a more pragmatic standpoint, it is not clear how researchers can test consciousness in preverbal infants or nonverbal animals because it is not apparent what manner of response would be indicative of consciousness. That is, it is not clear how having experienced the past can be tested directly under these circumstances, a problem that vexes researchers who attempt to study the recall of past events early in infancy. Despite this, to the extent that infants', children's, and adults' performance on implicit and explicit memory tasks is analogous, the evidence is clear that conscious and unconscious memory processes must be operating early in life.

If there are no developmental differences in the onset or direction of developmental progression between conscious and unconscious memory processes, it is not clear that there exists a useful dichotomy between these processes, perhaps suggesting that there is no need to postulate separate conscious and unconscious memory systems. As suggested from the outset, perhaps the simplest account is one in which there is a single memory system in which memories are stored and pass in and out of consciousness as a function of need and circumstance. As Neal and Hesketh (1997) suggested with both implicit learning (i.e., learning without awareness) and implicit memory (i.e., recollecting without awareness), perhaps any dissociations that are observed in performance on implicit and explicit tasks "reflect differences in the retrieval cues and processing operations used for the two kinds of tasks, rather than the operation of conscious and unconscious forms of information processing" (p. 34). That is, these differences have more to do with the manner in which people try to access memory traces than with differences between types of memory traces.

CONCLUSION

I began this chapter by inquiring (a) whether memories that were conscious were somehow different from memories that were not; (b) given there is a difference between conscious and unconscious memories, whether these memories have unique developmental trajectories; and (c) whether memories for early experiences could still be influencing people's behavior despite their inability to consciously access them. To answer these questions, I reviewed the literature on the effects of early experience on later development and on separating conscious from unconscious memories. The research on the effects of early experience on subsequent development showed that there need not be a direct association between early and later behaviors. That is, earlier behaviors can be supplanted by other, more adaptive behaviors that are acquired later in childhood. Although this does not rule out the possibility that memories for early experiences that were associated with these behaviors remain in storage, such evidence is not particularly supportive of such claims either.

Similarly, the literature on separating conscious and unconscious memories was found to be fraught with significant methodological problems, many of which are first discussed in chapter 7. Specifically, many experiments in this area relied on two-test or task-based separation methodologies in which neither the composition nor output rules were specified. What this meant was that task (or test) was confounded with memory such that it could not be determined whether different memories or different uses of the same memory were being examined. Thus, demonstration of dissociations between performance on conscious and unconscious memory tasks was not diagnostic of separate memory systems. Furthermore, even if these tasks did discriminate conscious from unconscious memories, because performance differences on these implicit and explicit memory tasks is similar across age from infancy through adulthood, their developmental trajectories would appear not to differ.

Overall, then, there is little evidence to support the claim that there are separate conscious and unconscious memory systems. There is little doubt that memories can be conscious (e.g., as in the recall of some autobiographical event) or that they can be unconscious (e.g., when one is asleep). However, simply because people can distinguish between different functions of memory traces (e.g., recalling past experiences, riding a bicycle, solving crossword puzzles), or between different ways in which they can access these traces, using different tasks does not mean that there somehow exists separable types of conscious and unconscious memory traces. Indeed, it is still more parsimonious to assume a single underlying trace with multiple access routes (conscious or unconscious) to the same information. If this is true, then the finding that conscious and unconscious processing are both available early in infancy is not surprising. Moreover, what this means is that memory traces may be subject to the same "laws" regardless of their status in consciousness and hence all memories undergo the same transformations given additional experiences, growth in knowledge base, strategies, metamemory, and so forth. Although implicit memory tasks may make different demands than explicit memory tasks in terms of trace access, this should not be confused with the establishment of separate memory systems for these different demands.

Thus, according to this reasoning and the scientific evidence on which it is based, there is no reason to accord unconscious memory any special status when it comes to preserving information from experiences, regardless of whether those experiences occur early in life. Because it is the same memory trace that occupies consciousness as occupies unconsciousness, there is little reason to suppose that researchers should observe differences in recoding, forgetting, or reinstatement. Although there may be differences in retrieval demands between conscious and unconscious memory tasks, with traces being more likely at times to be contacted using implicit tasks and at other times using explicit tasks, these differences are not at the level of the type of memory trace but have to do with differences in accessibility.

7

PROBLEMS IN THE MEASUREMENT OF LONG-TERM RETENTION AND ITS DEVELOPMENT

Whenever researchers wish to measure things that are unseen, in this case memory, a number of methodological and measurement issues crop up. For example, the contentious issue of whether there is a single memory system or a number of different systems hinges to a large extent on how memory is measured and the extent to which appropriate tests of independence have been used (e.g., see Howe, Rabinowitz, & Grant, 1993). Until it is clear that what is being measured is in fact different memory systems and not something else, for example, different output mechanisms or input—output correspondences (e.g., Howe & Rabinowitz, 1989; Howe, Rabinowitz, & Grant, 1993), it is more parsimonious to assume the existence of a single underlying memory system (Howe & Courage, 1993, 1997b; Rovee-Collier, 1997).

Similar issues arise when trying to evaluate memory in preverbal participants. Although several behavioral measures have been developed (e.g., imitation, reenactment), it is difficult to use the same sorts of measures in less well-controlled circumstances to derive unambiguous nonverbal indexes of memory. For example, the 18-month-old's aversion to fish after the incident in which the bone was caught in her throat does not constitute unambiguous evidence that the avoidance behavior is a reflection (memory) of that experience. Any number of other things could have given rise to her behavior, including the possibility that she simply took a disliking to fish. Reenacting events related to abuse using various props (e.g., anatomically explicit dolls) is useful in only a limited number of circumstances that depend on a host of factors, not the least of which is age (e.g., Koocher et al., 1995). Indeed, it is the very age group researchers might be particularly interested in using nonverbal measures with (e.g., toddlers whose language skills are still somewhat limited) whose recollections using such props is most unreliable. Importantly, researchers may simply be fooling themselves if they believe that verbal indexes of memory are any better. Indeed, as I have already discussed, these memories may not be any more reliable because they, too, are subject to suggestion, interference, and biasing by personal beliefs and goals. Of course, one would predict that both verbal and nonverbal measures might be similarly (un)reliable, as it is most likely that it is the underlying memory itself that is being affected by these variables, and not the output mechanisms. That is, because memory itself is being altered or adapted to fit the situational demands at output, these changes should be reflected in the recollection regardless of the device or mode used to express that memory (verbal or nonverbal). Although this is not to say that each mode of expression might not bring its own peculiarities or biases to the memory-output table; rather, the variables discussed in this book affect memory per se, and these effects will tend to be observed regardless of which output mode is selected. The problem, then, is to be able to dissever those aspects of the recollection that are "true" or "accurate" from those that are "reconstructed" or "false."

Although there are many problems with measuring memory, retention, and their development, in the remainder of this chapter I focus on three issues that, despite their theoretical and practical importance, have received only limited attention. Specifically, I address the issues of (a) ensuring that developmental differences in performance on tests of long-term retention are not simply the same differences as those measured at acquisition; (b) ensuring that the underlying theoretical processes of interest (e.g., encoding, storage, retrieval) are adequately extricated from empirical observations; and (c) determining what measures are most appropriate when evaluating the accuracy of autobiographical memories. Perhaps the most serious issue concerning research on long-term retention is the measurement (or lack thereof) of the state of to-be-remembered information in memory at the end of initial acquisition of that information. Regardless of whether one is talking about learning in a laboratory setting (e.g., word lists, picture lists, stories, event sequences) or witnessing naturally occurring events (e.g., personally distinctive events, traumatic events), it is essential that researchers be able to evaluate how well learned that information was originally so that their measures at retention are not simple reflections of unfinished processes at acquisition. Clearly, information that is less well learned at acquisition will appear to be less well retained at the time of the retention test than information that was well learned initially. If the goal is to understand retention processes, then such data are fundamentally irrelevant. This is because the measures at retention simply reflect the relative amounts of learning that occurred initially. Thus, it is entirely possible that easier items (e.g., semantically related concepts) will be better remembered at retention than harder items (e.g., unrelated concepts), not because they are necessarily better retained or less susceptible to forgetting but simply because, given equal learning opportunities at acquisition (e.g., a single study trial), more information is encoded and stored around the easier than the harder items.

This issue is problematic at all ages regardless of whether one is talking about infants, toddlers, children, or adults. However, it is worse in developmental studies in which comparisons are conducted between children of different ages. Here, because younger children learn almost anything more slowly than older children, given the same exposure to the to-be-learned information, older children will have better encoded and stored the information than younger children. It should come as no surprise, then, that at the time of retention testing, younger children will appear to have forgotten more information than older children. This, despite the fact that all these data are reflecting are the differences from initial acquisition.

These problems concern much of the research discussed so far in this book. That is, it affects conclusions from the research with infants and toddlers, memory for traumatic events, and general event and autobiographical memory. Although these problems do not necessarily damage the conclusions reached in the preceding chapters, they may limit the sorts of general theoretical statements that can be made about the development of long-term retention and the fate of early memories. Because of this, I discuss these problems in depth in this chapter. I begin by examining problems in the infant memory research and then discuss these issues in the study of the long-term retention of memories established in the laboratory as well as those arising from everyday occurrences.

MEASURING RETENTION INDEPENDENT OF ACQUISITION

As seen earlier in chapter 2, the study of early memory development has escalated in recent years due in large part to concerns about the accuracy and durability of early memories, the central topic of this book. To this end, a vast array of procedures have been developed to study early memory, including novelty preference and the paired-comparisons procedure (Bahrick, Hernandez-Reif, & Pickens, 1997; Bahrick & Pickens, 1995; Courage & Howe, 1998b; DeCasper & Spence, 1986), the mobile conjugate reinforcement paradigm (Rovee-Collier, 1997), deferred (e.g., Meltzoff, 1995) and elicited (Bauer, 1995) imitation, event reenactment (e.g., Fivush & Hamond, 1989; Hudson, 1991; Myers et al., 1994), and recall of traumatic events (Howe, Courage, & Peterson, 1994a, 1994b, 1995). Although researchers have generally been circumspect about drawing inferences about developmental changes in retention on the basis of these studies, some researchers are now extending their conclusions to include inferences about age advances in infants' long-term retention. It has been argued that older infants and toddlers retain more information over longer intervals than younger infants and that forgetting rates decline with age (also see discussions in Bauer, 1995; Fivush, 1994; Rovee-Collier & Shyi, 1992; Sheffield & Hudson, 1994). Although the description of such trends is provocative, the question, from a methodological point of view, is whether they are warranted.

One reason for asking such a question is that the studies on which these inferences are based were not designed to address developmental issues. That is, age comparisons were either not included in the design or were conducted across different materials that were confounded with age. Another reason for worrying about drawing such inferences is that in those studies in which age comparisons were conducted, the procedures used to generate the data contained a potentially serious threat to the validity of those conclusions. Specifically, these designs failed to control for age differences in initial acquisition. Although such research was never directly concerned with the relationship between initial learning and subsequent forgetting rates, conclusions about retention are necessarily contingent on it.

To see why, consider arguments from the classic literature on retention (e.g., Hilgard, 1953; McGeogh, 1942; Underwood, 1954). Here, individual differences in learning rates contribute to individual differences in forgetting rates such that, for example, slower learners may forget more rapidly. Individual differences in developmental studies are also age related, such that younger participants are slower learners. What this implies is that younger children will forget more rapidly simply because they are slower learners, a result that suggests that age differences at retention are fundamentally uninterpretable because they are confounded with differences at learning. Simply put, knowing the status of the information at the end of the acquisition session is critical to the interpretation of outcomes on later tests of long-term retention. This is because any differences that remain at the end of the acquisition phase will be confounded with retention performance (e.g., Gillette, 1936; Howe & Courage, 1997a; Underwood, 1954, 1964).

This learning-retention confound is problematic in almost all of the research in memory development, much of which is discussed in this chapter, including all of the designs used to evaluate infant retention. For example, there are several procedures in which the amount learned after acquisition is not assessed until the retention test is administered. This approach is common in studies in which fetuses or neonates serve as participants (e.g., DeCasper & Spence, 1986; Pascalis, De Schonen, Morton, Deruelle, & Fabre-Grenet, 1995) or in studies of deferred imitation (e.g., Meltzoff, 1988a, 1988b). Unfortunately, the failure to provide an assessment of the state of learning at the end of acquisition practically guarantees that learning and forgetting will be confounded.

Similar problems exist in studies in which acquisition consists of a single learning opportunity, as in deferred imitation studies (e.g., Meltzoff, 1988a, 1988b), and in studies in which the test of retention was an afterthought (e.g., Perris et al., 1990) as well as when a fixed number of trials are administered at acquisition to all participants regardless of their performance. This latter approach typifies research on early event memory in which participants of different ages receive a constant number of exposures to each event (e.g., Fivush & Hamond, 1989; Sheffield & Hudson, 1994). Here, because younger and slower learning infants and toddlers as well as older and faster learning infants and toddlers receive the same fixed number of study opportunities, older children will have acquired more information about the events that are to be remembered than younger children. In these designs, because age and learning rates are confounded at the end of acquisition, any differences in forgetting rates at retention may actually reflect differences in completeness of learning rather than true age differences in forgetting rates.

Finally, there are designs that attempt to correct these problems. For example, Meltzoff (1995) recently used an immediate imitation control group in which the state of information after exposure to an event can be evaluated. By using this approach, considerable control is gained over age differences in information acquisition, especially as critical tests depend on imitation being deferred. However, not all of the problems are eliminated simply because the comparisons are necessarily between subjects. That is, such procedures do not afford the same stringent control over individual differences in learning rate confounds as do within-subjects controls. Within-subjects controls are easier to use and have been used successfully by many researchers in situations in which participants can be required to reach a stringent, performance-based criterion at acquisition. For example, infants must reach a specific level of operant responding (e.g., Myers et al., 1994; Rovee-Collier, 1997), or children must correctly reenact an event (a one-trial success criterion) before learning another event sequence (e.g., Bauer, Hertsgaard, & Dow, 1994; Bauer, Hertsgaard, & Wewerka, 1995). As I discuss in the next section, the use of a criterion performance design, along with some theoretical and mathematical assumptions, can go a long way to ameliorate learning-retention confounds. However, even this approach can create problems simply because age differences in forgetting may be subject to another criticism derived from arguments proferred by Underwood (1954, 1964). In particular, because criterion performance designs almost always require that younger and slower learners receive more learning opportunities to reach the same performance level as older and faster learners, these additional study opportunities could compensate for faster forgetting in the younger and slower learners. That is, because learning opportunities, such as learning rates, are associated with less forgetting over the retention interval (e.g., McGeogh, 1942; Underwood, 1954), younger and slower learners could still have faster forgetting than older learners, but because they are given more study opportunities, their faster forgetting is not observed on later tests of long-term retention. Furthermore, because learning rate and learning opportunities are both related to forgetting and are negatively associated in criterion performance designs, their respective effects may cancel out each other depending on their relative strengths. It is only if learning rates and learning opportunities cancel out each other exactly that there is little to worry about because then researchers should obtain accurate estimates of age differences in forgetting rates. However, if the effects of learning rate are greater than the effects of learning opportunities, criterion designs will provide overestimates of age differences in forgetting rates. Conversely, if the effects of learning rate are smaller than the effects of learning opportunities, then criterion designs will provide underestimates of age differences in forgetting rates. Thus, although both younger and older learners' performance will be equated at the end of acquisition in criterion designs, this design leaves open the possibility that either no age differences or spurious age differences in forgetting rates might be obtained simply because of correlated age differences in learning rates and learning opportunities.

These possibilities were tested in two experiments with infants aged 12, 15, and 18 months (Howe & Courage, 1997a). Infants learned a series of five novel events (e.g., putting a plastic man in the driver's seat of a car and then depressing the man to activate a siren and flashing headlights) to a performance criterion of two consecutive errorless trials. Three months later, infants' retention of the events was tested on four consecutive test trials with no further study opportunities. The findings revealed that despite substantial age differences in learning and forgetting rates, ones that were in the predicted direction (i.e., favoring the older infants), these developmental patterns were independent of each other and were not confounded by the use of a criterion performance design at acquisition. Specifically, using a series of path models to evaluate the various relationships hypothesized between age, learning rate, learning opportunities, and forgetting, Howe and Courage found that the use of criterion performance designs did not bias estimates of forgetting rates. That is, the associations between age and measures of learning (rate and opportunities) were independent of the associations between age and forgetting rate.

In separate analyses, Howe and Courage (1997a) examined whether age differences in forgetting would be related to measures of overlearning. That is, because faster learners may receive more overlearning trials (i.e., the study trials after the first correct response or after the last error on a particular item when the performance criterion is across the entire list), and because overlearning is allegedly related to less forgetting, older infants' diminished rate of forgetting may simply have been an artifact receiving more overlearning opportunities than younger infants. When tested in a series of additional path analyses, age and forgetting rate associations were independent of the associations between age and overlearning. Thus, developmental differences in learning and overlearning rates were independent of, not confounded with, developmental differences in forgetting rates. Importantly, Howe and Courage (1997a) also found that learning and forgetting rates were independent not only at a group level but also at the individual infant level.

Although these results do not address fixed-trials designs, it would seem clear that the accurate assessments of infants' and toddlers' retention can be obtained using criterion performance designs. The question remains, however: How can an appropriate interpretation of the literature that does not use criterion designs be achieved? Before attempting to answer this question, I turn to a more general discussion of the problems inherent in not controlling for performance at the end of acquisition, one that has more traditionally plagued research with older toddlers and children.

SCALING AND MEASUREMENT CONCERNS

Brainerd and Reyna (1990, 1995) conducted a similar series of tests with older children (7- to 11-year-olds) and found, like Howe and Courage (1997a) did with very young children, that for criterion learning designs, developmental differences in learning and overlearning rates were independent of, not confounded with, developmental differences in forgetting rates. Clearly, at least from a methodological standpoint, criterion-based designs appear to be the procedure of choice when studying developmental differences in long-term retention. There are also a number of other, equally important theoretical, statistical, and mathematical reasons, outlined next, why such designs should be preferred when studying the development of long-term retention.

One advantage of criterion performance designs is that the exact state of information in memory can be known. That is, it can be determined precisely whether information has been encoded and stored in memory and the extent to which such information is retrievable. For example, according to most if not all basic process models of memory, acquisition consists of first encoding and storing information in memory and then learning how to retrieve that information (for recent reviews, see Estes, 1997; Howe & O'Sullivan, 1997). Although the exact mechanisms can vary from model to model, all agree that across acquisition trials stored information becomes more stable and retrieval patterns become more reliable and accurate.

The same basic processes affect performance during retention. Here, however, both storage and retrieval processes become less stable across the retention interval, such that retrieval may no longer be as accurate or reliable and storage may deteriorate to the point where the trace fades into the background of other traces. Although there are different conceptualizations, particularly when it comes to the permanence of stored traces, most theorists now acknowledge that changes can occur in both storage and retrieval processes (for reviews, see Howe & Courage, 1997b; Howe & O'Sullivan, 1997).

Despite considerable agreement across models concerning the importance of both storage and retrieval processes in the development of acquisition and retention processes, these formulations are not always consistent on how to measure storage and retrieval. Although a variety of methods exist, the two that have been most frequently used in the area of memory development are what I call the "design-based approach" and the "trace-integrity framework." Because the design-based approach tends to be the default model in this field, one that takes advantage of the more familiar analysis-of-variance methodology, I begin by outlining the process by which researchers using this approach attempt to segregate storage and retrieval. I then illustrate several problems with this approach and show one way these problems can be ameliorated. For ease of exposition, I have consigned the more mathematical and statistical details of these arguments to Appendixes A and B. Appendix A contains more specific details on how storage and retrieval can be separated mathematically at retention using the trace-integrity model. Appendix B contains a worked example of problems with monotonicity assumptions and the design-based separation of storage and retrieval. Although these appendixes provide considerable detail on the issues raised in this part of the chapter, an understanding of these appendixes is not essential to comprehending the points in made this section.

The problem of separating the storage and retrieval components of acquisition and retention performance amounts to extracting theoretical (or unseen) components that drive performance from the performance itself. That is, storage and retrieval, being theoretical entities, cannot be seen directly and must be inferred from participants' memory behavior. To do this, researchers have often resorted to using design-based approaches in which the study phase is associated with storage processes and the test phase is associated with retrieval processes. For instance, when studying the effects of imagery on children's memory, researchers will often assess the impact of imagery manipulations at storage by instructing children to imagine the to-be-remembered objects interacting at the time of study. To assess these effects at retrieval, these same researchers might present children with pictures instead of words as cues at the time of testing (e.g., see Howe, Brainerd, & Kingma, 1985b). Similarly, when evaluating the impact of semantic organization on children's recall, researchers will frequently assess storage effects by blocking the presentation of related items at the time of study and assess retrieval effects by presenting category labels as cues at the time of testing (e.g., see Howe, Brainerd, & Kingma, 1985a).

There are several problems with this approach. First, there is no evidence that children (or adults) do not attempt to develop, test, or modify retrieval processes when information is presented for study. That is, study and storage are not inexorably linked; by studying information people are not simply modifying what is in storage but also amending retrieval processes. Similarly, there is considerable evidence that participants can and do modify traces at the level of storage during testing. Such a phenomenon would be predicted in any theory that embraces the encoding specificity notion that new information can be stored along with, or perhaps lead to the recoding of, the original trace during testing. Like study, then, tests and retrieval are not inexorably linked. Overall, then, what transpires on study trials cannot be uniquely associated with storage processes, and what happens during a memory test cannot be uniquely associated with retrieval processes.

A second important point is that in both of the examples (imagery and semantic organization) just given, the manipulations used during study and at testing were asymmetrical. Thus, not only is timing different but so too is the nature of the manipulation. That is, in the imagery example, the manipulation during study was an instruction to image, whereas the manipulation at testing was cued recall with either pictures or words. For the semantic organization example, the manipulation during study was blocked presentation of categorized list members (all items in one category were presented together and then items from another category were presented together), whereas the manipulation at testing was cuing recall with the category labels. These asymmetries represent what is all too frequently the standard in the literature in which design-based manipulations are used. Indeed, as Howe et al. (1985a) pointed out with respect to the study of organizational factors, manipulations of organization at study trials are frequently not equivalent to manipulations of organization at testing. Of course, even when the manipulations are symmetrical or equivalent, manipulations during study still do not affect only storage processes, just as manipulations at testing do not uniquely affect retrieval processes.

A third problem concerns the sensitivity of the scales used to measure the relative contributions of storage and retrieval. Specifically, these scales are rarely if ever equated in design-based approaches to separating storage and retrieval (also see Chechile, Richman, Topinka, & Ehrensbeck, 1981). Worse, design-based approaches fail to provide even the simplest account of the measurement scales associated with the manipulations used during studying and testing (e.g., Brainerd, 1985). Rather, it is simply assumed, more by default than by anything else, that when storage and retrieval are made easier an item's memory strength should increase faster, something that should lead to improvements in observable performance. What this implies is that, at the least, if there is some monotonic relationship between manipulations during study and storage processes and between manipulations at testing and retrieval process, then there should be coinciding changes in memory strength and therefore in observable performance. For example, concerning semantic organization, blocking during study should improve storage, cuing at testing should improve retrieval, doing both should improve storage and retrieval, all of which should increment memory strength, leading to better memory performance. However, as the worked example in Appendix B illustrates, this simple monotonicity assumption is not always informative. That is, there are any number of conditions in which simple monotonic assumptions (e.g., cuing on tests trials improves retrieval and improved retrieval results in better performance) can be used to construct data and therefore are known to underlie the observed outcomes in a hypothetical experiment. Yet, the outcomes can be much the opposite (e.g., cuing on test trials actually decreases performance). The problem is that the link between outcomes (the data) and the theoretical processes that generate these outcomes are not necessarily monotonic. That is, cuing on test trials might actually improve storage in a linear fashion on early trials, not improve retrieval until later test trials, and affect performance in a logarithmic fashion. Thus, like the problems associated with the noncriterion performance designs discussed earlier, failures to properly consider these scaling and measurement concerns limits the types of theoretical statements researchers can make about storage and retrieval processes based on the outcomes of designed-based studies of children's long-term retention. At this point, it is not clear exactly how serious these errors may be in the understanding of children's memory development. Until the extent of these problems is known, it is at least prudent to be aware of these problems and to use them to temper conclusions accordingly. More important, it is essential that researchers take these methodological shortcomings into account when designing new studies of children's memory and retention and attempt to overcome them by developing a more explicit accounting of these rules regardless of the type of framework that is used.

ASSESSING MEMORY IN
AUTOBIOGRAPHICAL RECOLLECTION

Before concluding this chapter, I consider what additional methodological problems are introduced by studying "real-life" autobiographical memories. Like the problems already discussed, the state of memory at the time the autobiographical memory was formed is frequently unknown. At the time of retention testing, then, it is often unclear whether the inability to recall an event can be attributed to forgetting or to poor initial encoding and storage. Unless original records exist that can be used to adjudicate the veracity of later recollections, little can be said about the accuracy of memory.

Importantly, even when such records are available, it is not clear that failures to report an event are actually instances of forgetting or that misreporting events is actually a case of memory distortion. Indeed, even in cases of documented physical and sexual abuse (e.g., Widom & Morris, 1997; Widom & Shepard, 1996; Williams, 1994), failures to report an event to an interviewer does not constitute unambiguous evidence of forgetting. For example, participants may simply be embarrassed to report such an event (e.g., Widom & Morris, 1997). More important, such an event may not be reported simply because it was not encoded and stored in the first place. Although it may seem unlikely that abusive events do not get encoded, such a finding may not be all that unusual. For example, although an experimenter believes that an event might be important to participants at younger ages (e.g., birth of a sibling), such events may not have been important at all for the participants being tested (e.g., see criticisms of Sheingold & Tenney's, 1982, study). Similarly, as mentioned earlier in this book, experiences that are abusive but are not interpreted as such at the time (e.g., by young toddlers) in situations in which the abuse does not involve threat, fear, or physical discomfort and pain may not be remembered either simply because they were not encoded and stored as being particularly important or personally consequential. Before concluding that an event has been forgotten, it is essential not only that the event be somehow documented but that the documentation include some initial memory assessment. Thus, failing to report an event that has been documented cannot be unambiguously interpreted as a problem with memory unless there is evidence that an earlier memory for that event existed. (Of course, even then, failures to report memories for events may simply index other problems that are at the level of reporting and not memory or may be the result of the loss of episodic information because of the repetition of these events and the formation of a generic representation.)

This is exactly the issue Ross (1997) drew attention to, pointing out that there is a second way in which memory veracity can be examined: whether a later recollection is similar to an initial recounting of the event.

That is, although the courts might be concerned with the relationship between a person's current autobiographical recollection of an event and the event itself, memory theorists must also be concerned with the relationship between the current autobiographical recollection and an earlier recollection of the same event. As discussed earlier, what people encode and store of an event (the functional memory trace) is different from the event itself (the nominal situation). That is, information is not passively "stamped" into people's memories but is "filtered" through their expectations, knowledge, biases, current context, and so forth. Thus, the issue of veracity has two sides: how closely memory corresponds to the event itself and how closely the memories correspond to each other over time.

The problem of accuracy in either sense, particularly in terms of the validity of retrospective reports (see chapters in N. Schwartz & Sudman, 1994), has been a relatively recent one, and it has been only recently that a number of investigators (e.g., Thompson, Skowronski, Larsen, & Betz, 1996) have begun large-scale diary studies. In such studies, participants record events in their lives in a diary, have intermittent retention tests, and complete a final test of autobiographical recollection. In general, although the findings from such studies are preliminary, the correspondence between the event itself and later memory is often weak, even for traumatic experiences (e.g., Wagenaar & Groeneweg, 1990). Although the gist of an experience may not be forgotten, many of the details are, and frequently new details are added to the recollections that are consistent with current beliefs and knowledge. Similar results have been found for initial recollections of events and subsequent recall of the same memory (e.g., Howe et al., 1994a, 1994b, 1995). More important, what is clear in many of these studies is that events that are personally salient and distinctive tend to be the best remembered (e.g., Thompson et al., 1996). What this means is that such memories are more durable and less prone to complete forgetting because less salient events or events that happened to others are often simply not recalled (e.g., Thompson et al., 1996). Of course, even recollections of personally consequential events tend to change over time in a manner consistent with alterations in one's interpretation and understanding of the event as well as one's current needs, goals, and desires (e.g., Levine, 1997).

Perhaps what these studies illustrate is that issues concerning the accuracy of autobiographical memory need to be addressed in a dynamic framework that takes into account (a) the event itself (the nominal situation); (b) the initial encoding and storage of that event with its attendant interpretation and bias (the functional memory trace); (c) changes in what was originally stored due to corresponding alterations in knowledge, additional experience, and so on; and (d) the current context (including motivations) in which autobiographical events are being recollected. Although this is certainly a tall order, it is only when these methodological and measurement issues are taken into account that researchers will be able to say with any degree of certainty how accurate autobiographical memories can be and how the degree of accuracy is affected by these different variables. Indeed, whether researchers are comparing memories with each other across time or memories with the events themselves, the issue is not really one of absolute accuracy but relative accuracy. Because memory is fundamentally reconstructive, no recollection will ever be completely accurate regardless of the baseline with which it is compared.

CONCLUSION

In this chapter I have discussed some of the methodological issues that have been endemic to research in memory development but have received only modest attention in recent years. The issues raised were ones that, if left unattended, complicate the interpretation of much of the data on memory, autobiographical and otherwise, from infancy through childhood (and adulthood). First, I emphasized that knowing what the state of memory is at the end of the acquisition period is critical if the findings obtained at long-term retention are to be independent of any differences obtained at acquisition. This is particularly important developmentally, where younger and older learners differ in their rates of acquisition. Such differences must be removed before tests of long-term retention to ensure that the developmental patterns at long-term retention are not confounded with differences obtained at acquisition.

Second, I discussed the importance of formalizing composition and output transformation rules. I noted that design-based approaches to understanding the link between changes in memory performance and corresponding alterations in the basic theoretical mechanisms that drive those observable changes are inadequate. Instead, I suggested that researchers specify these rules in advance, preferably using formal modeling techniques.

Finally, I addressed issues concerning the accuracy of autobiographical recall, including whether accuracy should be adjudicated on the basis of a comparison between memories for the event and the event itself or simply between different memories of the event across time. In either case, I pointed out that all three measures are relevant (i.e., independent verification of the event, initial recollection of the event, and later recollection of the event) to the issue of accuracy and that perhaps accuracy is best conceived of as relative rather than absolute. Specifically, because memory is often reconstructive and not reproductive, an adequate model of accuracy must take into account dynamic changes in stored representations in response to new knowledge and experiences as well as the context in which autobiographical events are being recalled.

Although there are a number of other important issues that were touched on only briefly (e.g., verbal vs. nonverbal memories, the issue of the role of consciousness and memory, whether there are multiple memory systems or only a single one), ones that I return to at the end of this book, the problems raised here suggest that researchers should be cautious in their theorizing about the development of children's long-term retention. Although the extent of these limitations is not known, perhaps requiring simple fine-tuning of conclusions that already exist rather than a massive revision in thinking, the important point is that these issues are a cause for some concern and need to be taken into account when considering the study of children's memory development. The good news is that in cases in which these limitations have been addressed, the pattern of findings is generally consistent with the conclusions presented in this book (for additional recent overviews, see Brainerd, Howe, & Reyna, in press; Howe & Courage, 1997b; Howe & O'Sullivan, 1997). It may be, then, that when all is said and done, the conclusions outlined in this book will stand the more "stringent" tests that time will provide. Although I am optimistic, I raise these concerns so that all sides of the experimental, methodological, and theoretical issues be known.

8

CONCLUSIONS, SPECULATIONS, AND UNFINISHED BUSINESS

I began this book by discussing the nature of early memory and its development. I also discussed how memories of early experiences were stored and whether these experiences remained in memory for extended periods of time, perhaps even into adulthood. Finally, even if such memories cannot be consciously recollected, I addressed whether some memorial residue of these experiences exist and continue to influence people's behavior unconsciously.

Throughout the book, I have attempted to address (a) these fundamental questions using the scientific data that are available and (b) some of the methodological limitations inherent in the study of memory development in general and early memory and its development in particular. In what follows, I summarize the main points from this review. I then outline a tentative perspective on memory and its development that is preliminary but serves to integrate the research reviewed in this book. Although considerable work remains, this theoretical statement does have the advantage of tying together an extensive literature on memory and its early development. It also has explanatory value inasmuch as it contains several proposals concerning how memory can accommodate both generic and distinctive representations, why consciousness need not be a primary issue in memory development, and under what conditions elements of people's early memories can persist and continue to influence behavior later in life.

Although much of this is speculative, I hope that these ideas provide useful fodder for future research, some of which is alluded to in the final section of this chapter.

WHAT THE EVIDENCE INDICATES ABOUT THE FATE OF EARLY MEMORIES

Synopsis

First, it is clear that the processes necessary for the acquisition and retention of memories (e.g., encoding, storage, retrieval) are operational early in life, if not at birth. Moreover, the evidence is convincing in its demonstration that even very young infants succeed at both implicit (procedural) and explicit (declarative) memory tasks. Although there are clear improvements in memory functioning, some of which (e.g., speed of processing) may correspond to underlying neurological changes (e.g., mylenation), many advances occur at the cognitive, or "software," level. For example, it has been found that as children's knowledge base develops, so, too, does the ability to organize information along more structured lines. These cognitive changes in organization, ones that lead to enhancements in gist extraction (e.g., see Reyna & Brainerd, 1995), facilitate the storage, retention, and subsequent retrieval of information in memory.

Second, the evidence is also clear in its confirmation that young children can remember events over the first few years of life, although intentional recollection is often fragmentary. It is not until the onset of autobiographical memory, an event directly related to the establishment of the cognitive self as a viable entity, that such memories for events become personalized and can be potentially remembered over more extended periods of time. Importantly, a separate memory system need not be invoked to account for autobiographical memories. That is, autobiographical memory is simply the expression of two dynamically emerging elements: the cognitive self and memory for events. Although the self and memory for events are established early, the development of the self does not coalesce into a viable cognitive entity until around 18–24 months of age. It is at this point that features of the self become available for encoding these events, aiding the internal organization of that information and, like other organizing structures, facilitating storage, retention, and subsequent retrieval.

Note that even though these self-features are available for encoding, their availability does not imply that they will necessarily be used (also see Howe & Courage, 1997b). Indeed, it may not be until sometime later, when these features are more abundant, that such memories will emerge in greater numbers, an idea that is consistent with the general growth of storage maintenance that is found throughout early childhood, including autobiographical memory (e.g., see Howe & O'Sullivan, 1997). What makes autobiographical memory so special is that it links events with oneself, imbuing a sense of personal importance to the memory for that event. Indeed, as discussed in several chapters in this book, what tends to be remembered over the life span are those experiences that are personally consequential or distinctive. In addition to specific, distinctive episodes, of course, memories that are consistent with people's generic sense of who they are are also well remembered. However, in this latter case, it is the general sense of the event that will be recalled, not the specific episode. The fate of early memories, then, is contingent on their having some internal cohesion (i.e., they are linked in an enduring cognitive structure such as the cognitive self) and on their consequential or distinctive nature.

Third, that what is in storage represents a balance between the extraction of regularities and the preservation of unique details holds regardless of "type of memory," or better, the type of memory task. That is, regardless of whether the task is implicit or explicit, unconscious or conscious, generic and unique memories tend to be retained over the long haul. This is true for memories of events that are both pleasant and traumatic. In some instances, although physiological factors can serve to enhance or inhibit the establishment of durable memory traces for traumatic or distinctive experiences, the factors that control the durability of these traces are often of the same software variety as those that control the establishment of memories in general. In essence, then, memories of traumatic experiences do and do not have a special status in memory. On one hand, they do not have a special status because they are subject to the same rules as all memories. On the other hand, they do have a special status because they are more likely than many other experiences to be personally consequential and distinctive. However, they have this special status because they are distinctive, not necessarily because they are traumatic.

Fourth, although memories can persist over time, they often undergo substantial modification. That is, the fate of memories not recalled is not one in which they disappear silently into an unconscious void, inhabiting a netherworld where they persist intact and mercilessly continue to exert their influence on people's behavior. In fact, there is little evidence that memories for experiences survive intact for long periods of time regardless of whether they are personally consequential. What is stored in memory is not only an interpreted, nonveridical record of the experience but is subsequently revised, recoded, and reconstructed. There is no scientific evidence to suggest that these processes are somehow confined to memories people consciously recall and that there is another set of laws for memories that cannot be recalled in this way or that reside in people's unconscious. Although links may certainly exist between people's current behaviors and early experience, these links are neither direct nor, strictly speaking, caus-ative. This is because, regardless of whether people are consciously aware of particular memories, what is stored about the past is continually being updated by what is transpiring in the present.

Because there appear to be no special rules for unconscious memories, it is unlikely that early-event memories (ones before the onset of autobi-ographical memory, anyway) survive even at an "unconscious level," un-tainted by subsequent experiences. Although considerable research is still needed in this area, the evidence that does exist is more consistent with the idea that memory, conscious or otherwise, is transformed from the time the original experience occurs and is recoded until the time it is recon-structed at retrieval. The critical task for researchers is to determine the rules that govern the dynamics of these transformations and the extent of the variability or deviation these transformations impose on people's rec-ollections.

Proviso

I am not recommending that people mistrust all their memories, be-cause surely many, particularly the personally consequential ones, must contain a kernel of the original experience (or at least the original encod-ing). On the other hand, people must be cautious of mistaking what they remember for fact. Such a determination cannot be made until researchers have a better appreciation of precisely how and to what extent changes in knowledge, recoding, and reconstruction affect the accuracy of what it is people are remembering. Indeed, perhaps instead of focusing research ef-forts on looking for multiple memory systems, ones that often look more like the performance of a single memory system on different tasks, research-ers' energies might be better devoted to specifying the input composition rules, internal transformation rules, and output reconstruction rules that contribute to long-term retention performance and that determine how memories are potentially alterable, not just from objective experience but also from trace to trace and time to time. Indeed, until researchers under-stand this, they cannot offer much in the way of advice concerning the degree of accuracy of autobiographical recall to those who might seek to know its veracity (e.g., legal personnel including the courts, clinicians). Although researchers know that memories differ from the objective event, that they can be altered without the person being aware of it (e.g., through realignment with new knowledge and experience), and that they can be "filtered" through reconstructive tendencies at recall, it is not clear how different these recollections are from the objective record or originally en-coded trace of the experience. Before discussing ways in which this might be accomplished, I present an integrative theoretical picture of how long-term retention might operate and how it could develop. I do this to organize the information covered in this book and hope that the end product will be beneficial in stimulating some new research on several unanswered questions about what develops in memory.

AN INTEGRATIVE PERSPECTIVE ON MEMORY, RETENTION, AND DEVELOPMENT

Recapitulating the Development of Early Memory

To recap, throughout this book I have argued that memory development consists of both continuities (e.g., at the basic process level, including encoding, storage, and retrieval) and discontinuities (e.g., at the behavioral and software levels). For example, autobiographical memory uses the same basic memory processes as those that are present at birth. The difference between the events that young infants encode, store, and later retrieve is that such events are not personalized until the advent of a viable cognitive self. Thus, at a basic process level, autobiographical memory emerges from three interrelated continuities: fundamental memory processes, processes involved in the formation of categories whose features can be used in the construction of memory traces, and the ongoing development of the self. However, behavioral discontinuities exist and can be seen as memories become expressed as autobiographical (i.e., they are now events that happened to a "me") because of the emergence of a new and viable category, namely the cognitive self.

Of course, this does not mean that early memories are the same as later memories. Indeed, the more features encoded in the memory trace, the more durable that trace will be. Because more features become available as knowledge increases, more durable traces should be laid down as children gain more information about their world. In fact, knowledge not only guides the initial construction of memory traces but also governs the re-coding of traces while resident in memory and the reconstruction processes used during retrieval. Thus, many of the traces laid down early in life tend to be fragmentary and sparse in detail, particularly over long retention intervals, and are subject to the loss of episodic information as they merge to form generic (categorical) representations of events and experiences. With age and, more particularly, with the growth of knowledge, categories, strategies, and metamemory, traces become better fleshed out (i.e., they contain more features) and encoding, storage, and retrieval processes become more fine-tuned so as to pick up and use features that make traces stand out against the background of other memory traces, particularly when those memories are for events that are personally consequential. These refinements provide for changes in memory and memory performance that are relatively automatic and do not require conscious "effort" on the part of children once they have been established. Thus, with age and its attendant changes in knowledge, memories tend to be less fragmentary and more durable because the number of encoded features increases, particularly those associated with the self. It is not just the sheer quantity of features that is important but also how those features are structured. In particular, strong internal coherence within the trace as well as distinctiveness from other traces leads to memories that are more durable.

In terms of autobiographical memories, the more distinctive and personally consequential the memory is at the time of encoding, during any recoding that might occur during the retention interval, and later during attempts to retrieve the information, the more likely it is to be remembered. However, as emphasized several times throughout this book, because storage is a dynamic, not a static, medium, what was encoded as being personally consequential may not be so later at the time information about that experience is being recollected. What this means is that researchers are in the unenviable position of knowing what the general model of early (and later) memory development might look like and even knowing that it is deterministic, but only being able to make general predictions about the operation of retention rather than specific predictions about what will or will not be recalled by a particular individual. Thus, although the importance of personal consequence is well-known in the literature on autobiographical memory, because what is personally consequential is not necessarily the same across individuals or within the same individual over the life span, what particular memories a specific individual will retain may be fundamentally unknowable a priori. Clearly, most researchers would have predicted that concentration camp experiences would be well remembered over a lifetime barring some neurological problem that affected memory. However, as discussed earlier in this book, even critical aspects of these experiences can be forgotten (e.g., Wagenaar & Groeneweg, 1990).

Thus, not only must an experience be encoded as distinctive, but it must also remain so over the long-term retention interval. Again, this brings one back to the problem of knowledge and memory. Recall that even when childhood sexual abuse is the experience to be remembered, not all experiences that were sexually abusive were necessarily understood at the time as being sexual abuse. Indeed, unwanted sexual attention may not be understood as a sexually abusive experience and may not have been encoded (and hence later remembered) as such. Indeed, it may not be until someone points out to the rememberer that such an experience was abusive that the event will be recoded, and subsequently recalled, as such (see Joslyn, Carlin, & Loftus, 1997). Indeed, such an experience might not be remembered at all given it was no longer distinctive against the background of his or her other experiences.

Clearly, understanding what will and what will not be remembered over a person's life span involves several variables that researchers are only beginning to understand. Not only does what is stored in memory change as a function of accretion of knowledge, but it also changes as a function of one's current life circumstances. That is, what is recalled may be a function of one's current needs, desires, and circumstances under which recall is being elicited. Again, much like encoding specificity theory, researchers must somehow be able to track the conditions of encoding, recoding, and recollection to understand, a posteriori, how something was retrieved. To the extent that something that is distinctive remains so, it likely will be recalled if the retrieval circumstances are conducive. However, to the extent that information has become recoded or the retrieval circumstances do not warrant recollection, such information will not be recalled.

Description of This Perspective

In the view espoused here, memory is conceptualized as being fundamentally adaptive in the sense that it seeks to store meanings or the gist of experiences so that the world people live in becomes as knowable and predictable as possible. In essence, memory serves as a record of the meaning of experiences, so that people can not only understand the world but also anticipate and plan for future actions and behaviors. The extraction of this meaning is dynamic in a number of ways but, most importantly, it is in the sense that traces can change in response to the accretion of knowledge. Thus, not only do different experiencers bring distinct points of view to the same nominal event, ones that lead to the extraction of different functional meanings and traces of that experience, but so, too, does each individual over time. That is, not only will there be differences across individuals in their memories for the same event, a phenomenon well-known in the eyewitness memory literature, but there will also be differences within the same individual should they experience the same event repeatedly over time. Interestingly, the variability within an individual may be as great as the variability between individuals over time, although this remains an empirical question.

In essence, then, consistent with Brainerd and Reyna's (1995) fuzzy-trace conceptualization of memory, people extract gist or meaning from experiences and distill it to a point where they can derive a generic representation of how their world operates. This can be seen even in the earliest days of infancy, when regularities are discovered and amalgamated into some form of coherent memory trace that may represent some initial attempt at categorization. Once habituated, infants then turn their attention to novelty to discover the exception to the rules contained in the previously idealized prototype for that (e.g., visual) experience. This in turn may result in the modification of the earlier stored trace or in the storage of a new trace, one whose distinctiveness from the previous experience confers memorability. Thus, memory involves a balance between the old, similar, and predictable (e.g., generic or categorical representation) and the new, distinctive, and unpredictable (e.g., episodic representation of distinctive experiences). As discussed in the chapter on memory for traumatic events, it tends to be those experiences that violate people's expectations (based on previous memory representations) that lead to highly memorable and distinctive traces. Similarly, in autobiographical memory, it tends to be those experiences that violate people's expectations of their conceptualizations of themselves (e.g., experiences that have personal consequences) that tend to be remembered best. Of course, in both cases, what I mean by "being remembered best" is that the specific episodes are remembered best. Equally well remembered are the generic representations of predictable experiences (e.g., who people are, generally speaking; repeated experiences of abuse). Again, from the earliest days of infancy, both predictable and highly regularized aspects of experience and the environment are well remembered as are those particular episodes that are unique or novel and that violate people's expectations based on those generic representations. This makes sense if what people are using memory for is to help predict what will happen in the future, a mechanism that is particularly adaptive, especially if one is trying to forage for food, find shelter, and so on.

Thus, memory can be viewed as a system that attempts to strike a balance between the extraction of regularities (generic representations) that preserve the gist of a class of experiences on the one hand and one that retains more individualized representations that contain information about exceptions or distinct experiences on the other hand. It is this continuous interplay between these opposing tendencies to "normalize" experience and, at the same time, preserving the "variability" of experiences that produce trace updating. The updating process itself, although preserving much of the core of the original trace, also modifies it to bring it in line with the current experience. The overall effect of updating is one in which the memory trace is altered to more closely conform to what all of the experiences in that particular class might mean rather than preserving the meaning of each individual experience. Thus, in a real sense, updating both preserves the past at the same time it refines it in light of current experiences. Indeed, individual experiences may be reasonably well preserved by this process for two reasons: First, if the experience is distinctive or is an exception to the "generic rule," then it is critical that it be remembered because it may serve to augment one's predictions based on that class of experiences. Second, it is also possible that individual experiences may serve as a kind of "exemplar prototype" for the general meaning extracted from that class of experiences. Like categories more generally, then, generic representations may be symbolized by memories of actual experiences rather than by some abstracted prototypical "script" or "schema."

Implications and Future Directions

Given this propensity for change, it may seem remarkable that people remember anything in a way that resembles reality, especially after a long retention interval. However, there are several ways that events can be remembered reasonably accurately. Individual experiences can be preserved if they serve as a prototype for a class of experiences or are distinct in important ways (particularly in personally consequential ways) from those classes of experience. Moreover, to some extent, the past preserves the future in memory. Because what people know guides their current interpretations of experience, updates based on new experiences will be constrained by what is already in memory, a process that restores the past while also updating it. Again, then, memory can be seen as striking a balance between two seemingly opposing forces. On the one hand, using what people know (or have stored in memory) to interpret current experiences serves to preserve what is in memory. On the other hand, because the nominal (objective) and functional (interpreted) event varies from what has transpired in the past, what is already in memory is updated. This updating may sometimes be inconsequential, whereas at other times such updating may involve critical features of the memory for the original experience. The extent of change in what is in memory will be contingent on how extensive the alterations are that are needed to bring the trace in line with experience, something that is contingent on the discrepancy between the original trace and the current encoding. If researchers are to make progress in this area, then, they need to begin to measure the dynamics of this balance between opposing tendencies and determine the conditions under which modest and dramatic alterations are made to memory traces.

Although this account of long-term retention hinges on the idea that there is a unitary structure in memory for an experience, it is entirely possible that models could be derived in which multiple memory structures are used to account for retention. Here, for example, traces might be constructed for each experience, with copies of each stored in memory. Generic representations for experiences could be derived by, for example, taking some weighted average across traces. In this way, generic representations could be updated "automatically" because they would be created anew each time they were needed, taking all of the different experiences into account. Although an interesting possibility, and one that cannot be ruled out by the data, it is somewhat unlikely. That is, there is little evidence to indicate that all instances of a class of experience are remembered and considerable evidence that it is the gist of the class of experiences that is remembered, although certainly some individual experiences are remembered. However, in the vast majority of instances, the generic representation is the one recalled. Indeed, despite the ability of multiple trace models to add assumptions that would produce this result (e.g., only the extracted representation from the individual experiences is consciously accessible), in the absence of incontrovertible evidence to the contrary, it is still more parsimonious to entertain a single, unitary trace hypothesis.

As seen throughout this book, the hardware necessary for many of memory's achievements (including the encoding, storage, and retrieval of event information, accretion of knowledge, etc.) are intact at or just after birth. Indeed, many of the changes witnessed in memory performance during childhood, even those that are apparently discontinuous at the level of behavior, can be accounted for by referring to the continuous changes that occur in underlying cognitive processes (e.g., advances in categorization, knowledge accretion, emergence of the cognitive self). That I have attributed such changes to the continuity of advances in the underlying cognitive software is not simply a matter of preference; rather, it is because there is a large literature that provides direct evidence that gains in memory performance are causally linked to advances in cognitive structures and processes (e.g., Bjorklund, 1995; Flavell, Miller, & Miller, 1993; W. Schneider & Pressley, 1997). This emphasis on software, like that on unitary memory trace structures, does not preclude the potential contribution made by concurrent changes that occur in hardware responsible for memory (see chap. 1 in this book). For example, mylenization and the consequent changes in the rate of neural transmission may well be related to changes in speed of information processing (e.g., see Case, 1995), including rates of encoding, storage, and retrieval. Similarly, neurological development of the frontal lobes has been linked to advances in inhibitory processes that in turn have been associated with increasing proficiency in many areas of cognitive development (see chap. 3 in this book and chapters in Dempster & Brainerd, 1995). Finally, mature neural connectivity is achieved by both progressive dendritic arborization and regressive pruning (e.g., Chugani, Phelps, & Mazziotti, 1987; Huttenlocher & De Courter, 1987), events that are linked to advances in some areas of learning (e.g., Greenough, 1990).

Although these changes in hardware are substantial, direct and causal links have yet to be established between specific changes at the level of hardware and corresponding advances in cognitive performance. Although such links may be forthcoming, their existence in no way diminishes the theories advanced in this book. Rather, there is an even greater need to integrate a number of previously independent areas of research if researchers are to derive a comprehensive theory of long-term retention and its development. What this book reflects is that, at the present time, links between memory performance and changes in cognitive software are better established empirically than those for changes in the neural hardware. Moreover, given the evidence reviewed in various chapters in this book (e.g., chaps. 1 and 3), it seems unlikely that the types of changes observed in the development of long-term retention are mediated by dramatic shifts in neural hardware. This does not mean that there are not neurological incidents (e.g., closed head injuries) and various disease states (e.g., Alzheimer's) that produce amnesias for one's past or that interfere with the establishment of new memories (e.g., see chap. 4 in this book) during childhood and adulthood. All I mean here is that, given a "normal" course of development, there is little empirical evidence that links specific neurological changes to those witnessed in children's advances in the course of memory development.

I argued in chapter 6 that memories operate regardless of consciousness. Memories do not disappear when people fall asleep, a quintessential state (or process) in which individuals are viewed as not being conscious; the memories are simply not in one's conscious awareness. Indeed, memories are useful regardless of whether people can access them consciously or not (e.g., stopping a vehicle when the traffic light turns red does not require conscious awareness that the red light signals "stop"). Although people can become aware of that if necessary (i.e., one's passenger asks why the car was stopped), but this awareness is not required for the memory to serve its adaptive (preventing an accident) function. Similarly, in the absence of total anterograde amnesia, many patients who have amnesia can function well in society without having the conscious experience of remembering. Thus, as noted in the chapter on consciousness, the issue of consciousness may be fundamentally irrelevant to the understanding of the development of early memory because these distinctions may more accurately represent differences in how people access and use memories rather than different types of memory per se.

Finally, what happens to early memories for experiences? Do they persist and continue to influence people's behavior even when they cannot consciously access them (as proposed in several theories outlined in the introductory chapter and the chapter on consciousness), or do they simply fade away? The answer, although somewhat speculative, is both yes and no. On one hand, early memories may "disappear" for all intents and purposes. For example, memories that no longer serve a purpose (e.g., they are useful in generic representations or as exceptions to these representations) may fail to be refreshed and hence may "fade" into the background noise of other, weakened memory traces, where the probability of accessibility may be near zero, particularly in the presence of stronger traces. Whether such traces ever vanish (e.g., whether they become completely unavailable in storage) or simply become inaccessible is not known. On the other hand, early memories may remain in storage. However, the processes involved in maintaining the active status of these traces also involve the modification of these traces so that they are no longer the same as they were originally. That is, by refreshing these traces either in subsequent encounters of similar circumstances or through other means, these traces become updated and modified; in other words, because they have some utility, they are made current by additional experiences and knowledge, a process that, by definition, involves modification of the memory trace for the original experience (a process akin to that used to extract generic representations of experiences). Although there is probably considerably less variability within a trace than between traces even given subsequent modifications, the process itself still involves alterations in the trace from the original. (Much like a pearl that starts from a grain of sand and is modified immediately by the process underlying the formation of pearls, one that continues to alter the pearl by continuing to add layers, memories that persist also undergo transmogrification so that, in a sense, early experience may still be affecting behavior inasmuch as the grain of sand made the pearl.)

Thus, it is not at all clear that early memories remain intact and serve to influence later behavior. Rather, like most memories, those that are functional are so because they have been refreshed and the process of refreshing more often than not leads to change in the original trace. Although models could be constructed in which multiple copies of the traces exist (e.g., the original plus one for each time it has been updated), in all likelihood such models would predict the same outcome. That is, the most recent version of the memory trace should be the first accessed (consciously or otherwise) because it is the most complete, at least in terms of updates, and because it is the strongest, being last accessed and modified. It is more parsimonious to assume a single, unitary trace that contains all of the updated information and relevant modifications and one that can be accessed in a variety of ways, conscious or not. If the tendency is toward "gistification," then it would make sense that a single trace would become transmogrified rather than retain multiple copies of the like traces. In the latter case, there is a greater likelihood of interference among traces. If the goal is to gain quick access to the most recent version, then it is perhaps more economic to retain only that version. Thus, to endure, memories must be refreshed (consciously or not), and it is in the process of refreshing these traces that they become modified. As already noted, storage is a dynamic, not static, medium and changes can be made through recoding or through additional experience with test opportunities or retrievals. It is only because the modified version builds on the prior version that there is greater within-traces than between-traces consistency.

Autobiographical Memory: Not a Different System But No Ordinary Self-Organizing One

Although there is no consensus on exactly what memory traces are made of, many would agree that they can be conceived of as self-organizing structures that are internally cohesive. Much like the early gestalt view of memory, much of the current thinking is consistent with the idea that traces, regardless of content, consist of primitive elements that are bound together by some "glue" (e.g., a similarity relationship of some sort) that integrates these elements into some whole. It is this integrity that leads to a trace's durability and usefulness across tasks. Indeed, the extent to which a trace's internal components are well structured and integrated is related to its durability in memory. Moreover, it is not just its integrity (internal similarity or cohesion) that is critical but its distinctiveness or discriminability from other memory traces that determines its retrievability, particularly the ease with which it can be used given different task (implicit or explicit) demands.

Autobiographical memories are, like other memories, self-organizing. However, they are self-organizing not only in the sense that they can be well-integrated structures that are distinct from other memories but also in that they are organized around the self. These memories not only preserve the self but also participate in changing conceptualizations of the self. These changes can have a ripple effect, such that earlier memories can be modified to be consistent with new conceptualizations of the self. Thus, autobiographical memories are different because they are organized around the self but in all other ways appear to behave much like memories in general, being subject to modification in storage and reconstruction at output.

WHAT'S NEXT?

There are a variety of methodological problems that seriously compromise the integrity of many of the conclusions in this field of memory development. For example, as seen in chapter 7, there are problems interpreting much of the long-term retention data because of failures to control for both individual and age-based differences in initial acquisition. Indeed, in autobiographical memory, this problem was exacerbated by whether one should use the objective experience or the initial encoding of that experience as the comparator for assessing the accuracy of subsequent recall.

In this chapter, I have suggested that memory is self-organizing and consists of a number of opposing tendencies (e.g., generic representations and distinctive representations, maintaining past memories while simultaneously updating memory). Furthermore, because memory is dynamic, changing in time as a function of changes in what has been experienced and the knowledge extracted from those experiences, among other things, no simple model or method of study would seem to suffice in researchers' attempts to understand the development of long-term retention. What these problems have made clear is that new methods and measures need to be derived, ones that are consistent with dynamic modeling in general and memory development in particular. At the least, what is sorely needed are more longitudinal assessments of changes in the contents of memory storage, particularly in autobiographical memory. If researchers can first provide a baseline assessment of the objective event and an evaluation of the contents of the initial encoding and storage for that event, then subsequent tracking of the memory for that event over time and age as well as other changes that are relevant to memory (e.g., shifts in knowledge base and what components are deemed important to the individual, reinstatement opportunities) may indicate what elements of that memory remain preserved.

Such studies would be particularly important for early preverbal experiences. As noted here as well as by Bjorklund (1997), there is little scientific evidence on the long-term influences of early experiences. Perhaps this is because the relevant studies have not been conducted, ones that track the course of memories for events, both nonverbally and verbally. In those few studies in which this type of tracking has been done, the usual length of time has been around only a year or so. Although this is clearly a start in the right direction, longer and more exhaustive studies of this sort are needed if researchers are to understand how such memories influence, if they do, subsequent behavior.

Of course, it is not just the memories themselves that need to be tracked but also the other variables mentioned in this book as being important to how memories are reinterpreted (or recoded). It is clear that modeling efforts along these lines are crucial to theoretical progress. That is, to understand the dynamics of how what is in memory influences what gets into memory and that what gets into memory influences what is already in memory, more complicated and inclusive models of long-term retention and memory development are required. Moreover, such a model also must include parameters that reflect the effects of reinstatement, interference (both retroactive and proactive), intentional and unintentional attempts to forget, and distinctiveness (both locally—i.e., relative to the material being studied—as well as globally—i.e., relative to what is stored in one's knowledge base), among other factors. Indeed, this model must not only specify the composition rules relevant to how memories are formed and reformed but also the rules governing how these memories are output using language or other nonverbal symbols (e.g., pictures, mathematics).

Relative to where researchers began a decade or so ago, when conclusions were much simpler and there seemed to be little of interest for developmental psychologists in the study of long-term retention (for a review, see Howe & Brainerd, 1989), the science of the development of long-term retention in the early years of life is much more complicated. So what has this decade or so of research contributed to the understanding of the fate of early memories? Clearly, although the basic processes controlling memory are robust early in life, it is unlikely that memories formed during this period can be maintained in any autobiographical sense for long periods of time before the age of 2 years. It is certainly possible to have some recollection of events before that, particularly if those events are distinctive, reinstated, or well rehearsed. However, such recollections will be sparse and tend to be fragmentary. Moreover, they would not be, strictly speaking, autobiographical unless they had been rehearsed over time and subsequently linked to some aspect of the self that maintained that memory as one that was personally consequential. Even under such improbable circumstances, the memory would have been transformed by subsequent events and knowledge stored in memory, leaving its veracity, particularly for forensic purposes, highly questionable. Indeed, it is considerably more likely that any memories from these early years would either be highly fragmentary or based on subsequent rehearsal across age. In either case, such reports might be suspect given the highly constructive and reconstructive nature of rehearsal and recollection, particularly when additional experiences and knowledge are added to the mix.

It is also apparent that there are clear developmental trends in retention, ones that appear to be common to all types of memory tasks (implicit, explicit, procedural, declarative, etc.) and ones that involve changes to what is in storage, not just its retrievability. Just how modifiable memories are has perhaps been answered—memories cannot only be altered but new ones can also be created, seemingly out of thin air. What remains to be answered is exactly what conditions promote the modification and creation of memories that are not veridical with experience as well as the conditions that lead to the preservation of accurate memories.

Similarly, it is now clear that memories serve to preserve the gist of experience, particularly for those experiences that are personally consequential. Although what constitutes personal consequentiality varies over time, the fact remains that whatever it is that is personally consequential is likely to be better retained. Although this does not mean that some verbatim aspects of experiences cannot be remembered, the preference in storage is for the retention of the meaning or consequence of experience and not necessarily the particulars of each of the individual experiences.

In a sense, researchers may have come full circle. For many centuries, memory was valued for its gist-, not verbatim-, preserving function as a means of conveying culture and ideas through the medium of storytelling (e.g., Rubin, 1995). These stories conveyed a central meaning or moral but were not expected to be an accurate, word-for-word accounting of what the teller had experienced or been told. Indeed, what was frequently valued in these retellings was the personal embellishment of the story (but not the moral itself) by the reteller using his or her own additional experiences to augment the narrative. Thus, the gist was preserved, but the details were personally adorned or reconstructed according to the speaker's own experiences. This was as understandable then as it is now because our changing world is inherently dynamic and, "in a world of constantly changing environment, literal recall is extraordinarily unimportant" (Bartlett, 1932, p. 204).

Having understood this, future theoretical advances are contingent on providing more developmental (longitudinal) data relevant to all of the variables that influence memory, from the initial objective experience and its encoding, to subsequent encounters with information relevant to what was stored, to changes in the knowledge base that potentially affects memories in storage, to attempts to retrieve that information. It is only when all of these factors have been measured and the combinatorial and output transformation rules specified and tested that researchers will better understand and be able to predict what the influence of memories of early experiences might be on later behavior.

Until then, the bottom line, at least from a scientific perspective, is that although people may have formed memories for many of their early experiences, the memories can change rapidly with additional experience and are less stable in storage than memories formed later in childhood. Moreover, in terms of autobiographical memories, the cognitive organizer necessary for the retention of those experiences is not available until late in the second year of life, and even then it may not be developed enough to sustain many memories for long periods of time. As organizational mechanisms develop, particularly the cognitive self, memories for life's experiences can be better maintained in storage, particularly because they help define who an individual is.

Although clearly more complex, what the data reviewed in this book have also made clear is that early memory development is much more fascinating and intricate than previously thought. That memories can be formed early in life, and that they can be retained over a period of months (e.g., Courage & Howe, 1998b), is remarkable. That preverbal memories can later be verbally recalled (e.g., Bauer et al., 1998) is similarly exceptional. That these memories are also volatile and subject to rapid change under conditions similar to those of older children and adults is also extraordinary. Indeed, there appears to be a high degree of memory continuity from infancy through adulthood because the variables affecting long-term retention in infancy are the same as those affecting retention in later childhood and adulthood. Although there are clear developments in the ability to retain information in memory storage (see Howe & O'Sullivan, 1997), perhaps because of corresponding changes in software used to organize information and experiences in storage, this underlying continuity in encoding, storage, and retrieval is important, at least from a theoretical standpoint.

Thus, as with many things in cognitive development, there is both continuity and apparent discontinuity in the development of long-term retention. I suspect, however, that, like some of the apparent discontinuities discussed in this book (e.g., the offset of infantile amnesia and the onset of autobiographical memory), the remaining discontinuities (e.g., changes in storage maintenance) will turn out to be driven by unseen and continuous changes in basic-level processes. Indeed, as research efforts continue in the development of early retention, many of these changes will be linked to ongoing developments in underlying software processes that drive memory organization. Regardless, the important point is that it is through scientific investigations, the collection of empirical data, and attempts to falsify theoretical speculations such as the ones presented here, that true progress will be made in the understanding of the nature of early memory and its development. As the quote at the beginning of this book suggests, it is only when the data are in that researchers' theories will conform to the facts rather than the facts conforming to their beliefs.

APPENDIX A:
TRACE-INTEGRITY FRAMEWORK

As discussed earlier in this book (particularly in chaps. 5 and 7), the trace-integrity model has provided a much-used and comprehensive framework for understanding the development of children's (and adults') long-term retention. Recall that in this model, storage and retrieval are viewed as lying on a continuum of trace integrity where, at acquisition, elements (e.g., features, nodes) become bound together to form cohesive and distinctive units in memory. Given that a criterion learning design has been used at acquisition, these cohesive units are not only in storage but are also retrievable with a probability of one. Over a retention interval, these units can either remain distinctive in storage and highly retrievable (no storage or retrieval failures), can disintegrate to a point where they are difficult to retrieve (i.e., they undergo retrieval failures), or disintegrate to a point where the "glue" that binds features together no longer does so and the memory trace "fades" into the background noise of other memory traces (i.e., it undergoes both storage and retrieval failures). Notice that storage failure does not mean permanent erasure of the trace and therefore that such traces are potentially recoverable during retention testing. Indeed, during a retention test, all traces are potentially recoverable through reminiscence tendencies that operate at the level of storage and retrieval. Data consistent with these interpretations and the parameter definitions have been reviewed by Howe and O'Sullivan (1997).

The purpose of this appendix is to show the mathematical and statistical machinery used to evaluate the storage and retrieval components of forgetting and the reminiscence processes that make up long-term retention. There are nine parameters in the model: two that measure forgetting, one for storage-based processes (S) and one for retrieval-based processes (R); and seven that measure reminiscence processes, one for restorage (a) and six for retrieval-based reminiscence, three for reminiscence after correct responses (the r_i) and three after errors (the f_i). These parameters are described in Table A1. Before illustrating how these parameters are used to obtain information about the processes they measure, I first show how the parameters map onto empirical outcomes generated using four-trial long-term retention sequences.

The data space from the four-trial retention test is translated into an empirical probability space. That is, the data space in four-trial experiments consists of 16 distinct outcomes: $C_1C_2C_3C_4$, $C_1C_2C_3E_4$, ..., $E_1E_2E_3C_4$, $E_1E_2E_3E_4$, where C denotes a correct response, E denotes an error, and the subscripts 1–4 denote the four retention tests for each item. This data space is converted to an empirical probability space simply by assigning probabilities to each of the outcomes: $p(C_1C_2C_3C_4$; the probability an item is correctly recalled on all four trials), $p(C_1C_2C_3E_4$; the probability an item is correctly recalled on all trials except Trial 4), ..., $p(E_1E_2E_3C_4$; the probability an item is incorrectly recalled on all trials except Trial 4), and $p(E_1E_2E_3E_4$; the probability an item is incorrectly recalled on all trials).

The next step is to convert this empirical probability space to a mathematical space. This is accomplished by expressing each of the 16 empirical probabilities in terms of the model's parameters, a process that yields the expressions shown in Table A2. It is this mapping that allows one to take the (typically) unobservable theoretical events underlying memory perfor-

TABLE A1
Definitions of the Trace-Integrity Model's Parameters

Process and parameter	Description
Trace forgetting	
S	Probability of storage failure
R	Probability of retrieval failure of information in storage
Trace reminiscence	
a	Probability that information not in storage is reintegrated to a level above zero recall
r_1	Probability of two consecutive successes
r_2	Probability of three consecutive successes
r_3	Probability of four consecutive successes
f_1	Probability of a success after one error
f_2	Probability of a success after two consecutive errors
f_3	Probability of a success after three consecutive errors

TABLE A2
The Trace-Integrity Model's Mathematical Expressions
for the Empirical Outcome Space

Outcome	Expression
$p(CCCC)$	$(1 - S)(1 - R)r_1r_2r_3$
$p(CCCE)$	$(1 - S)(1 - R)r_1r_2(1 - r_3)$
$p(CCEC)$	$(1 - S)(1 - R)r_1(1 - r_2)f_1$
$p(CECC)$	$(1 - S)(1 - R)(1 - r_1)f_1r_1$
$p(ECCC)$	$Sa(1 - R)r_1r_2 + (1 - S)Rf_1r_1r_2$
$p(CCEE)$	$(1 - S)(1 - R)r_1(1 - r_2)(1 - f_1)$
$p(CECE)$	$(1 - S)(1 - R)(1 - r_1)f_1(1 - r_1)$
$p(ECCE)$	$Sa(1 - R)r_1(1 - r_2) + (1 - S)Rf_1r_1(1 - r_2)$
$p(CEEC)$	$(1 - S)(1 - R)(1 - r_1)(1 - f_1)f_2$
$p(ECEC)$	$Sa(1 - R)(1 - r_1)f_1 + (1 - S)Rf_1(1 - r_1)f_1$
$p(EECC)$	$S(1 - a)a(1 - R)r_1 + SaRf_1r_1 + (1 - S)R(1 - f_1)f_2r_1$
$p(CEEE)$	$(1 - S)(1 - R)(1 - r_1)(1 - f_1)(1 - f_2)$
$p(ECEE)$	$Sa(1 - R)(1 - r_1)(1 - f_1) + (1 - S)Rf_1(1 - r_1)(1 - f_1)$
$p(EECE)$	$S(1 - a)a(1 - R)(1 - r_1) + SaRf_1(1 - r_1)$ $+ (1 - S)R(1 - f_1)f_2(1 - r_1)$
$p(EEEC)$	$S(1 - a)^2a(1 - R) + S(1 - a)aRf_1 + SaR(1 - f_1)f_2$ $+ (1 - S)R(1 - f_1)(1 - f_2)f_3$
$p(EEEE)$	$S(1 - a)^3 + S(1 - a)^2aR + S(1 - a)aR(1 - f_1)$ $+ SaR(1 - f_1)(1 - f_2) + (1 - S)R(1 - f_1)(1 - f_2)(1 - f_3)$

Note. Each probability in the left column appears in the empirical likelihood function. For the trace-integrity model's mathematical likelihood function, these probabilities are replaced by the corresponding expression in the right column. C = correct response; E = incorrect response; S = storage-based forgetting processes; R = retrieval-based forgetting processes.

mance and make them observable in terms of the empirical events (the 16 error–correct patterns).

To see the association between outcomes and parameters, one should consider a common interpretation of retrieval failures: an item that has been previously recalled (e.g., at the time of acquisition) fails to be recalled later but is subsequently recalled on an even later test. The advantage of a model-based approach is that it also acknowledges the possibility that such patterns in the data can be the result of storage processes. To see how, consider the equations that describe retention performance in Table A2. For example, in the equation for the outcome $p(ECCC)$, the initial error could have been generated by either the unconditional probability of a storage failure (parameter S, as in the first part of the equation) or by the conditional probability of a retrieval failure (the term $[1 - S]R$, as in the second half of the equation). Although most researchers are familiar with this latter possibility, the former event is also possible in this conceptualization, with the subsequent success on Trial 2 therefore being due not to retrieval processes per se (the parameter f_1 in the second part of the equation) but to restorage (parameter a in the first part of the equation). Once recalled, the process is the same regardless of its origin. That is, subsequent successes are generated by the parameters r_1 and r_2.

Notice that in sequences in which a correct response is made on the first trial, storage-based forgetting has not, by definition, occurred (as reflected in the term $[1 - S]$ in the equations in Table A2, in which the event sequence begins with a C). The greater the number of these protocols observed in the outcome space, the lower S will be for that condition. Importantly, the opposite does not hold. That is, although the parameter S is linked to errors that occur on the first retention trial, Table A2 shows that there is also a probability that these errors can arise because of retrieval failures (parameter R). In other words, any error in and of itself is not diagnostic of retrieval or storage failure. Rather, the probability that an error at retention is due to storage or retrieval failure is extracted mathematically across all four trials (i.e., it is the entire pattern of responses that is used to diagnose long-term retention, subject, of course, to the scaling assumptions embodied in the model). Thus, although S is the unconditional probability that an item is unavailable (i.e., it has undergone storage failure), this does not mean that all errors on the first trial are the result of such failures.

To be more concrete, consider the equation describing the probability of the four-trial sequence $EECC$. Here, the first two terms describe this sequence given the initial error was produced by storage failure. However, the third term in the equation (i.e., $[1 - S]R[1 - f_1]f_2r_1$) describes this same sequence given that retrieval failure produced the first error. The term $1 - S$ indicates that the first error was not due to storage-based forgetting and R indicates that it was due to retrieval failure. The remainder of the equation follows, in that $1 - f_1$ indicates that the second error was due to a failure of retrieval-based reminiscence after one error, f_2 signifies that the first correct response was generated by retrieval-based reminiscence after two errors, and r_1 indicates that the last success was due to retrieval-based reminiscence after a single prior success.

Similarly, although a sequence of four consecutive errors might be seen as the prototype for storage failures, such need not be the case. For example, an examination of the equation pertaining to the probability of this outcome ($p[EEEE]$) shows that two of the five possible routes to this outcome involve retrieval, not storage, failure. To illustrate, in the last of these routes, $[(1 - S)R(1 - f_1)(1 - f_2)(1 - f_3)]$, the first error could have been generated by the conditional probability of a retrieval failure, $[(1 - S)R]$, with each subsequent error being generated by continued failures at error-based retrieval reminiscence, $[(1 - f_1)(1 - f_2)(1 - f_3)]$. Other examples can be found in the other equations in Table A2. What this shows is that although the theory and data are linked through the equations in the model, there is not always a simple one-to-one correspondence between the individual parameters (e.g., S and R) and the various outcomes in the experiment.

Interestingly, even if the possibility of retrieval failures occurring on the first test trial was excluded in this model, meaning that all such errors would be those of the storage variety, this definition would not have been that discrepant from current design-based conceptualizations (see chap. 7 in this book). Indeed, in the one-test retention studies typically found in the literature, an error signals forgetting and a success signals remembering. In such cases, there would be no opportunity to tell whether an error was caused by problems at the level of storage, retrieval, or both (because there is no subsequent test, among other things). Despite this, many theorists are not reluctant to conclude that such failures are storage based (i.e., they are attributable to trace blending or overwriting).

Similar reasoning holds for storage-based reminiscence, or restorage (*a*). Indeed, it should already be clear that test trials can affect the quality and retrievability of the trace itself. Whether a single success is due to retrieval- or storage-based reminiscence depends on that item's history. The point is simply that the evaluation of storage and retrieval is not confined to a single measurement but involves the consideration of all of the different possibilities, as embodied in, and extracted using, the mathematical formulation of these processes across at least four test opportunities (see the equations in Table A2).

To use this model to dissever these processes, it is absolutely essential that the goodness-of-fit of the model to the data be evaluated and numerical estimates of the parameters obtained. Fortunately, a well-defined set of procedures is available for these purposes. The process involves the following 5-step sequence.

The first two steps involve translating the data space into a probability space, which is subsequently transformed into a mathematical space (see the above description). Using maximum-likelihood theory, the first transformation results in a function that expresses the a posteriori likelihood of any data sample. The present function has 15 *df*s and takes the following form:

$$\mathbf{L}_{15} = \{ p[C_1C_2C_3C_4]^{N(CCCC)} \times p[C_1C_2C_3E_4]^{N(CCCE)}$$
$$\times \cdots \times p[E_1E_2E_3C_4]^{N(EEEC)} \times p[E_1E_2E_3E_4]^{N(EEEE)} \}. \quad (A1)$$

The second transformation permits derivation of the theoretical likelihood, something that is accomplished by simply substituting the equations in Table A2 (denoted in Equation A2 by the term *h*) for the 16 terms in

Equation A1. This yields a function with 9 *dfs* (because the 16 expressions are based on only nine parameters) and takes the following form:

$$\mathbf{L}_9 = \{h[p(C_1C_2C_3C_4)]^{N(CCCC)} \times h[p(C_1C_2C_3E_4)]^{N(CCCE)} \times \cdots$$

$$\times h[p(E_1E_2E_3C_4)]^{N(EEEC)} \times h[p(E_1E_2E_3E_4)]^{N(EEEE)}\}. \quad (A2)$$

The third step consists of counting the number of times each of the 16 events occurred in the sample data (i.e., summing across both subjects and items within each condition of interest), inserting these numbers into the relevant exponents in Equation A2, and maximizing the function using a standard computer optimization routine (e.g., SIMPLEX). When obtained, the optimal solution yields numerical estimates of the model's nine parameters as well as the value of the likelihood function, $\mathbf{L}_9$. This latter value (which is more commonly estimated using the log transform $-2 \ln \mathbf{L}_9$) can be used to evaluate the model's goodness-of-fit (the fourth step) and to examine hypotheses about between- and within-conditions differences in the numerical estimates of parameters (the fifth step).

The fourth step involves evaluating the fit of the model to the data in hand. This is done by simply maximizing (using the same log transform as above) Equation A1 for the same data as Equation A2, yielding an estimate of the likelihood of the data before the model was imposed (i.e., with all empirical probabilities free to vary, $\mathbf{L}_{15}$). Because Equation A1 exhausts all the information available in the data, the value of $\mathbf{L}_{15}$ will always be the maximum likelihood for that data set. Because the trace-integrity model does not exhaust the available information (having only 9 *dfs*, not 15), the estimated likelihood of Equation A2 will tend to be smaller. Goodness-of-fit is then assessed using likelihood ratio tests that determine whether this difference is statistically reliable. Specifically, this test takes the following form:

$$\chi^2(6) = (-2 \ln \mathbf{L}_9) - (-2 \ln \mathbf{L}_{15}). \quad (A3)$$

This equation evaluates the null hypothesis that the trace-integrity model provides an accurate fit to the data.

Finally, the fifth step involves testing hypotheses about the theoretical processes underlying retention performance by evaluating predictions about the numerical estimates of the model's parameters. Because these parameters are identifiable (see Howe & Brainerd, 1989), they can be used directly in tests of hypotheses concerning between- and within-conditions differences in the rates of forgetting and reminiscence as well as the storage and retrieval loci of these differences. The statistical processes used in hypothesis testing are straightforward and involve a series of likelihood-ratio (chi-square) tests known as an "experimentwise test," "conditionwise tests," and "parameterwise tests." The experimentwise test is much like the omnibus F test, evaluating the null hypothesis that, on average, the model's parameters do not vary between conditions. The exact test is given by

$$\chi^2[k \times (9) - 9] = [(-2 \ln \mathbf{L}_{9i})$$

$$+ (-2 \ln \mathbf{L}_{9i+1}) + \cdots + (-2 \ln \mathbf{L}_{9k})] - (-2 \ln \mathbf{L}_{9\text{pooled}}), \quad \text{(A4)}$$

where the first term represents the summation of the $-2 \ln \mathbf{L}_9$ values for each of the i through k individual conditions in the experiment and the last term represents the single $-2 \ln \mathbf{L}_9$ likelihood value found by pooling the data from all k conditions. Because there are 9 dfs involved in each of the k terms in the first part of the expression, the asymptotic chi-square distribution of the experimentwise test has $k \times (9) - 9$ dfs.

The conditionwise test is much like the t test, evaluating the null hypothesis that, on average, the model's parameters do not vary between specific pairs of conditions. The exact test is given by

$$\chi^2(9) = [(-2 \ln \mathbf{L}_{9i}) + (-2 \ln \mathbf{L}_{9j})] - (-2 \ln \mathbf{L}_{9ij}), \quad \text{(A5)}$$

where the first term represents the summation of the $-2 \ln \mathbf{L}_9$ values for conditions i and j and the final term represents the single $-2 \ln \mathbf{L}_9$ value found by pooling the data for the ij conditions. Because there are always 18 dfs associated with the first term and 9 dfs for the last term, the asymptotic chi-square distribution of the conditionwise test has 9 dfs.

For the pairs of conditions that differ, the parameterwise test evaluates the null hypothesis that the numerical estimate of a specific parameter does not vary between those two conditions. The exact test is given by

$$\chi^2(1) = [(-2 \ln \mathbf{L}_{9i}) + (-2 \ln \mathbf{L}_{9j})] - [(-2 \ln \mathbf{L}'_{9i}) + (-2 \ln \mathbf{L}'_{9j})], \quad \text{(A6)}$$

where the first term is the same as in Equation A5 and the second term represents the joint likelihood of the data from the two conditions (i.e., minimizing $\mathbf{L}'_{9i}$ and $\mathbf{L}'_{9j}$ simultaneously) subject to the single restriction that the parameter being tested (e.g., S) assumes the same value in the two conditions. This restriction results in an asymptotic test statistic of $\chi^2(1)$.

Finally, two types of within-condition hypotheses can be evaluated: numerical equivalences (e.g., $a = 0$; $S = R = .1$; $r_1 = r_2 = 1.0$) and algebraic relationships (e.g., $S > R$; $r_1 < r_3$). Both types of hypotheses can be tested using the following single statistic:

$$\chi^2(1) = (-2 \ln \mathbf{L}_{9i}) - (-2 \ln \mathbf{L}_{8i}), \quad \text{(A7)}$$

where the first term is simply the likelihood value associated with condition i when all of the parameters are free to vary and the last term represents the same condition with a single restriction imposed. Like the between-conditions parameterwise test, this chi-square test has 1 df.

APPENDIX B:
SCALING AND MEASUREMENT
ISSUES

To illustrate the scaling and measurement issues discussed in chapter 7, I offer the following example adapted from Howe and O'Sullivan (1997; also see Brainerd, 1985). Consider two critical scaling assumptions (a) the composition or integration rule and (b) the output transformation or response scale (also see Howe & Rabinowitz, 1989; Howe, Rabinowitz, & Grant, 1993). As already mentioned, storage and retrieval are hypothetical constructs whose combination gives rise to an additional hypothetical construct: memory strength. Because these constructs are hypothetical, they cannot be measured directly but must be extracted from empirical data. Equally important, it is clear that performance on a given memory test is not equivalent to memory strength (e.g., Brainerd, 1985; Howe & O'Sullivan, 1997). It is because of the hypothetical nature of these constructs and the links between them and empirical observations that composition rules and output transformations must be specified precisely so that the hypothetical constructs can be extracted from observable performance. Indeed, regardless of researchers' theoretical definitions of storage, retrieval, and memory strength, they must be able to designate number values to these variables so that variations in storage (Scale S), retrieval (Scale R), and memory strength (Scale M) can be represented. This last variable is, of course, a composite of S and R, in which an item's memory strength increases as its representation becomes more stable in storage and more accurately and reliably retrieved. To specify the exact manner in which changes in an item's status in storage and its retrievability produce changes in its memory strength, a composition rule must be defined, one that describes how values of S and R combine to produce values of M.

For brevity and clarity, I consider only arithmetical composition rules. Given this restriction, I obtain functions such as $S + R = M$, $SR = M$, $aS + bR = M$ (where a and b are constants), and so on. Because design-based strategies for diagnosing the role of storage and retrieval make no scaling assumptions about these variables, the strongest assumption that can be justified is that of monotonicity (e.g., Brainerd, 1985; Krantz & Tversky, 1971), an assumption that is insufficient. Moreover, such an assumption fails to indicate which of the preceding composition rules is correct or even if arithmetical composition rules are the most appropriate. The only information this assumption conveys is that the function cannot be nonmonotonic.

This same imbroglio extends to the problem of determining the correct output transformation rule, one in which a new scale is introduced, namely a performance Scale P. The numbers representing different levels of observable performance (Scale P) on a memory task depend in some manner on the values associated with the memory strength scale (Scale M). An output transformation rule is simply one that states how P and M are related; for example, $P = aM$ (where a is a constant), $P = \ln M$, $P = M^a$ (where a is a constant), and so on. Again, because design-based attempts to measure storage and retrieval fail to specify the output transformation rule, the default assumption must be that P is a monotonic transformation of M.

All of these assumptions can be combined into a single equation in which performance is linked to storage and retrieval by the function,

$$P = f_t[f_c(S, R)], \tag{B1}$$

where f_t is the unknown (but monotonic) output transformation and f_c is the unknown (but monotonic) composition rule. Because the design-based methodologies typically fail to specify the nature of these monotonic functions, the relationship between observable performance and the underlying storage and retrieval processes remains an enigma. It is only when these rules are specified, and their assumptions verified, that measures of the theoretical constructs, storage and retrieval, will be obtained.

To understand what this means, consider a concrete example, taken from Howe and O'Sullivan (1997), in which an experiment on semantic organization is conducted and manipulations are made during study and at testing. To eliminate the problems associated with confounding different manipulations during study and at testing, the example is restricted to the use of cuing manipulations. That is, suppose participants are given a two-category list containing pictures of fruits and furniture and are either given no cues, cues at the time of study that there are both fruits and furniture in the to-be-remembered list, cues at the time of test with the category labels *fruits* and *furniture*, or cues during study and testing. Consistent with much of the literature in this area, assume that organization has a larger effect at retrieval than at storage and that retrieval factors are more important on test trials than study trials. If A and B denote the study and test manipulations respectively in this 2×2 design, consider the following scale values: (a) $S = 6$ and $R = 6$ for A_1B_1 (no cues); (b) $S = 10$ and $R = 8$ for A_2B_1 (cue–no cue); (c) $S = 8$ and $R = 18$ for A_1B_2 (no cue–cue); and (d) $S = 12$ and $R = 18$ for A_2B_2 (cue–cue). These values satisfy the constraint that the cuing manipulation has a larger effect at retrieval than storage because the average between-conditions difference in scale values is 3.33 for S and 7.67 for R. Moreover, these values are consistent with the design-based assumption that retrieval factors are more important on test trials than study trials because the average between-conditions difference in scale values is 2.45 for conditions that have different A treatments but the same B treatment and is 4.22 for conditions that have different B treatments but the same A treatment.

According to design-based separations of storage and retrieval, the cuing manipulation should have a larger effect when manipulated on test trials than study trials. However, what Table B1 shows is that the magnitude of these effects will depend on the nature of the composition rule. Although there are numerous possibilities concerning the nature of both the composition and output rules, I have selected just two of each for my illustration, one that is relatively straightforward and one that is only slightly more complex. Specifically, for the simpler composition rule, I selected one that is strictly additive, $M = S + R$, whereas for the more complicated one, I selected the (natural) log-additive rule, $M = S + \ln R$. Similarly, for the output transformation rules, I selected an equivalence

TABLE B1

Hypothetical Outcomes in an Experiment Where Category Cuing Is Manipulated During Study and at Testing

Composition and output rules	A_1B_1: $S = 6$, $R = 6$	A_2B_1: $S = 10$, $R = 8$	A_1B_2: $S = 8$, $R = 18$	A_2B_2: $S = 12$, $R = 18$
$M = S + R$; $P = M$	12.00	18.00	26.00	30.00
$M = S + R$; $P = \ln M$	2.48	2.89	3.26	3.40
$M = S + \ln R$; $P = M$	7.79	12.08	10.89	14.89
$M = S + \ln R$; $P = \ln M$	2.05	2.49	2.39	2.70

Note. S = storage scale; R = retrieval scale; M = memory strength scale; P = performance scale; ln = natural log.

rule, $P = M$, and a logarithmic rule, $P = \ln M$ (these composition and transformation rules were also selected to be compatible with the examples given in Brainerd, 1985). These rules satisfy the monotonicity constraint already discussed and have been factorially crossed to produce the hypothetical empirical outcomes in Table B1.

It is clear from Table B1 that depending on one's scaling assumptions, organizational cuing can have a larger effect on study trials than on test trials despite the fact that the situation was contrived such that organization had a larger effect at retrieval than at storage, on test trials than study trials, and the composition and transformation rules obey the monotonicity assumption. Specifically, in the first two rows of Table B1, where the composition rule is linear and the transformation rule varies, the observed performance values P are consistent with the predictions. That is, in the first row, the average between-conditions difference with the A treatments varying is 5, whereas with the B treatments varying is 13. Similarly, in the second row these differences are 0.28 and 0.65, respectively, for differing A and B treatments. However, examination of the last two rows shows a different pattern, one that is inconsistent with, and indeed the opposite of, what was predicted. Specifically, in the third row the average A treatment difference is 4.15, but the average B treatment is only 2.96. In the fourth row, the average A treatment difference is 0.38, but the average B treatment difference is only 0.28.

As this example makes clear, unless the composition and transformation rules are made explicit, performance outcomes are not readily interpretable. This is so regardless of whether one is talking about performance on immediate or delayed tests of retention, picture–word effects, and recall-recognition problems (e.g., see Brainerd, 1985). The important point is that formal (mathematical) models make explicit these assumptions and, in the case of the trace-integrity model, provide a statistical methodology for evaluating these assumptions. Because this model has been described elsewhere (e.g., Howe & O'Sullivan, 1997), most readers should be familiar with it by now (see Appendix A). Regardless of whether one agrees with the trace-integrity framework's conceptualization of storage and retrieval processes or the manner in which these processes are mapped onto empirical outcomes (the composition and output transformation rules that form part of Appendix A), the critical point is that meaningful interpretations of the data are seriously constrained when such rules are not specified a priori. As the example in this section makes clear, design-based approaches to separating storage and retrieval processes may be woefully inadequate, largely because they do not contain a properly formalized accounting of these composition and output transformation rules.

REFERENCES

Abel, T., Alberini, C., Ghirardi, M., Huang, Y. -Y., Nguyen, P., & Kandel, E. R. (1995). Steps toward a molecular definition of memory consolidation. In D. L. Schacter, J. T. Coyle, G. D. Fischbach, M. M. Mesulam, & L. E. Sullivan (Eds.), *Memory distortion* (pp. 298–325). Cambridge, MA: Harvard University Press.

Ackerman, B. P. (1984). Item specific and relational encoding effects in children's recall and recognition memory for words. *Journal of Experimental Child Psychology, 37,* 426–450.

Acredolo, L., & Goodwyn, S. (1988). Symbolic gesturing in normal infants. *Child Development, 59,* 450–466.

Adolph, K. E. (1997). Learning in the development of infant locomotion. *Monographs of the Society for Research in Child Development, 62*(3, Serial No. 251).

Aggleton, J. P., & Mishkin, M. (1983). Visual recognition impairment following medial thalamic lesions in monkeys. *Neuropsychologia, 21,* 189–197.

Agnati, K. F., Fuxe, K., Yu, Z. Y., Harfstrand, A., Okret, S., Wikstrom, A. C., Goldstein, M., Zoli, M., Vale, W., & Gustafson, J. A. (1985). Morphometrical analysis of the distribution of corticotropin-releasing factor, glucocorticoid receptor and phenylethanolamine-N-methyltransferase immunoreactive structures in the paraventricular hypothalamic nucleus of the rat. *Neuroscience Letters, 54,* 147–152.

Alexander, J. M., & Schwanenflugel, P. J. (1994). Strategy regulation: The role of intelligence, metacognitive attributes, and knowledge base. *Developmental Psychology, 30,* 709–723.

Alpert, J. L., Brown, L. S., Ceci, S. J., Courtois, C. A., Loftus, E. F., & Ornstein, P. A. (1996). *Final report of the APA working group on investigation of memories of childhood abuse.* Washington, DC: American Psychological Association.

Anderson, J. R. (1978). Arguments concerning representations for mental imagery. *Psychological Review, 85,* 249–277.

Anderson, J. R. (1979). Further arguments concerning representations for mental imagery: A response to Hayes-Roth and Pylyshyn. *Psychological Review, 86,* 395–406.

Anisfeld, M. (1996). Only tongue protrusion modeling is matched by neonates. *Developmental Review, 16,* 149–161.

Archdiocesan Commission. (1990). *The report of the Archdiocesan Commission of inquiry into the sexual abuse of children by members of the clergy.* St. John's, Newfoundland, Canada: Archdiocese of St. John.

Asendorpf, J. B., & Baudonniere, P.-M. (1993). Self-awareness and other-awareness: Mirror self-recognition and synchronic imitation among unfamiliar peers. *Developmental Psychology, 29,* 88–95.

Aslin, R. N. (1987). Visual and auditory development in infancy. In J. D. Osofsky (Ed.), *Handbook of infant development* (2nd ed., pp. 5–97). New York: Wiley.

163

Aslin, R. N., Pisoni, D. B., & Jusczyk, P. W. (1983). Auditory development and speech perception in infancy. In M. M. Haith & J. J. Campos (Eds.), *Handbook of child psychology: Vol. II. Infancy and developmental psychobiology* (pp. 573–687). New York: Wiley.

Atkins, D. M. (1987). Evaluation of pediatric preparation program for short-stay surgical patients. *Journal of Pediatric Psychology, 12,* 285–290.

Axelson, D., Doraiswamy, P., McDonald, W., Boyko, O., Typler, L., Patterson, L., Nemeroff, C., Ellinwood, E., & Krishnan, K. (1993). Hypercortisolemia and hippocampal changes in depression. *Psychiatry Research, 47,* 163–173.

Bachevalier, J., Brickson, M., & Hagger, C. (1993). Limbic-dependent recognition memory in monkeys develops early in infancy. *NeuroReport, 4,* 77–80.

Bachevalier, J., & Mishkin, M. (1984). An early and late developing system for learning and retention in infant monkeys. *Behavioral Neuroscience, 98,* 770–778.

Baddeley, A. D. (1992). What is autobiographical memory? In M. A. Conway, D. C. Rubin, H. Spinnler, & W. A. Wagenaar (Eds.), *Theoretical perspectives on autobiographical memory* (pp. 13–29). Dordrecht, The Netherlands: Kluwer Academic.

Bahrick, L. E., Hernandez-Reif, M., & Pickens, J. N. (1997). The effect of retrieval cues on visual preferences and memory in infancy: Evidence for a four-phase attention function. *Journal of Experimental Child Psychology, 67,* 1–20.

Bahrick, L. E., & Pickens, J. N. (1995). Infant memory for object motion across a period of three months: Implications for a four-phase attention function. *Journal of Experimental Child Psychology, 59,* 343–371.

Baker-Ward, L., Ornstein, P. A., & Principe, G. F. A. (1997). Revealing the representation: Evidence from children's reports of events. In P. van den Broek, P. J. Bauer, & T. Bourg (Eds.), *Developmental spans in event comprehension and representation: Bridging fictional and actual events* (pp. 65–95). Mahwah, NJ: Erlbaum.

Banks, M. S., & Ginsberg, A. P. (1985). Early visual preferences: A review and new theoretical treatment. *Advances in Child Development and Behavior, 19,* 207–246.

Banks, M. S., & Salapatek, P. (1983). Infant visual perception. In M. M. Haith & J. J. Campos (Eds.), *Handbook of child psychology: Vol. II. Infancy and developmental psychobiology* (pp. 435–571). New York: Wiley.

Barnat, S. B., Klein, P. J., & Meltzoff, A. N. (1996). Deferred imitation across changes in context and object: Memory and generalization in 14-month-old infants. *Infant Behavior and Development, 19,* 241–251.

Barr, R., Dowden, A., & Hayne, H. (1996). Developmental changes in deferred imitation by 6- to 24-month-old infants. *Infant Behavior and Development, 19,* 159–170.

Barr, R., & Hayne, H. (1996a). The effect of event structure on imitation in infancy: Practice makes perfect? *Infant Behavior and Development, 19,* 253–257.

Barr, R., & Hayne, H. (1996b, April). *The effects of live and videotaped models on imitation in infancy.* Paper presented at the Biennial International Conference on Infant Studies, Providence, RI.

Bartlett, F. C. (1932). *Remembering: A study in experimental and social psychology.* Cambridge, England: Cambridge University Press.

Bass, E., & Davis, L. (1988). *The courage to heal: A guide for women survivors of child sexual abuse.* New York: Harper & Row.

Bates, E. (1990). Language about me and you: Pronominal reference and the emerging concept of self. In D. Cicchetti & M. Beeghly (Eds.), *The self in transition: Infancy to childhood* (pp. 165–192). Chicago: University of Chicago Press.

Bates, E., Benigni, L., Bretherton, I., Camaioni, L., & Volterra, V. (1979). *The emergence of symbols: Cognition and communication in infancy.* New York: Academic Press.

Bates, E., Camaioni, L., & Volterra, V. (1975). The acquisition of performatives prior to speech. *Merrill-Palmer Quarterly, 21,* 205–226.

Bates, E., & Carnevale, G. F. (1993). New directions in research on language development. *Developmental Review, 13,* 436–470.

Bates, E., O'Connell, B., & Shore, C. (1987). Language and communication in infancy. In J. Osofsky (Ed.), *Handbook of infant development* (2nd ed., pp. 149–203). New York: Wiley.

Bauer, P. J. (1995). Recalling past events: From infancy to early childhood. *Annals of Child Development, 11,* 25–71.

Bauer, P. J. (1996). What do infants recall of their lives? Memory for specific events by one- and two-year-olds. *American Psychologist, 51,* 29–41.

Bauer, P. J., & Dow, G. A. (1994). Episodic memory in 16- and 20-month-old children: Specifics are generalized, but not forgotten. *Developmental Psychology, 30,* 403–417.

Bauer, P. J., & Hertsgaard, L. A. (1993). Increasing steps in recall of events: Factors facilitating immediate and long-term memory in 13.5- and 16.5-month-old children. *Child Development, 64,* 1204–1223.

Bauer, P. J., Hertsgaard, L. A., & Dow, G. A. (1994). After 8 months have passed: Long-term recall of events by 1- to 2-year-old children. *Memory, 2,* 353–382.

Bauer, P. J., Hertsgaard, L. A., & Wewerka, S. S. (1995). Effects of experience and reminding on long-term recall in infancy: Remembering not to forget. *Journal of Experimental Child Psychology, 59,* 260–298.

Bauer, P. J., Kroupina, M. G., Schwade, J. A., Dropik, P., & Wewerka, S. (1998). If memory serves, will language? Later verbal accessibility of early memories. *Development and Psychopathology, 10,* 655–679.

Bauer, P. J., & Mandler, J. M. (1989). One thing follows another: Effects of temporal structure on 1- and 2-year-olds' recall of events. *Developmental Psychology, 25,* 197–206.

Bauer, P. J., & Mandler, J. M. (1992). Putting the cart before the horse: The use of temporal order in recall of events by one-year-old children. *Developmental Psychology, 28,* 441–452.

Bauer, P. J., & Shore, C. M. (1987). Making a memorable event: Effects of familiarity and organization of young children's recall of action sequences. *Cognitive Development, 2,* 327–338.

Bauer, P. J., & Thal, D. J. (1990). Scripts or scraps: Reconsidering the development of sequential understanding. *Journal of Experimental Child Psychology, 50,* 287–304.

Bauer, P. J., & Travis, L. L. (1993). The fabric of an event: Different sources of temporal invariance differentially affect 24-month-olds' recall. *Cognitive Development, 8,* 319–341.

Bearison, D. J., & Pacifici, C. (1989). Children's event knowledge of cancer treatment. *Journal of Applied Developmental Psychology, 10,* 469–486.

Begg, I., Anas, A., & Farinacci, S. (1992). Dissociation of processes in belief: Source recollection, statement familiarity, and the illusion of truth. *Journal of Experimental Psychology: General, 121,* 446–458.

Berger, B., & Alvarez, C. (1994). Neurochemical development of the hippocampal region in the fetal monkey: II. Immunocytochemistry of peptides, calcium-binding proteins, DARPP-32, and monoamine innervation in the entorhinal cortex by the end of gestation. *Hippocampus, 4,* 84–114.

Bertenthal, B. I., Campos, J. J., & Barrett, K. C. (1984). Self-produced locomotion: An organizer of emotional, cognitive, and social development in infancy. In R. N. Emde & R. J. Harmon (Eds.), *Continuities and discontinuities in development* (pp. 175–210). New York: Plenum.

Bertenthal, B. I., Campos, J. J., & Haith, M. M. (1980). Development of visual organization: Perception of substantive contours. *Child Development, 51,* 1072–1080.

Bertenthal, B. I., & Fischer, K. (1978). Development of self-recognition in the infant. *Developmental Psychology, 14,* 44–50.

Betz, A. L., & Skowronski, J. J. (1997). Self-events and other-events: Temporal dating and event memory. *Memory & Cognition, 25,* 701–714.

Bjork, R. A. (1972). Theoretical implications of directed forgetting. In A. W. Melton & E. Martin (Eds.), *Coding processes in human memory* (pp. 217–235). Washington, DC: Winston.

Bjork, R. A. (1989). Retrieval inhibition as an adaptive mechanism in human memory. In H. L. Roediger III & F. I. M. Craik (Eds.), *Varieties of memory and consciousness* (pp. 309–330). Hillsdale, NJ: Erlbaum.

Bjorklund, D. F. (1987). How age changes in knowledge base contribute to the development of organization in children's memory: An interpretive review. *Developmental Review, 7,* 93–130.

Bjorklund, D. F. (1995). *Children's thinking: Developmental function and individual differences* (2nd ed.). Belmont, CA: Brooks/Cole.

Bjorklund, D. F. (1997). The role of immaturity in human development. *Psychological Bulletin, 122,* 153–169.

Bjorklund, D. F., & Bjorklund, B. R. (1985). Organization versus item effects of an elaborated knowledge base on children's memory. *Developmental Psychology, 21*, 1120–1131.

Bjorklund, D. F., & Harnishfeger, K. K. (1995). The evolution of inhibition mechanisms and their role in human cognition and behavior. In F. N. Dempster & C. J. Brainerd (Eds.), *Interference and inhibition in cognition* (pp. 141–173). San Diego, CA: Academic Press.

Bjorklund, D. F., & Schneider, W. (in press). The interaction of knowledge, aptitude, and strategies in children's memory performance. In H. W. Reese (Ed.), *Advances in Child Development and Behavior.* San Diego, CA: Academic Press.

Bohn, M. C. (1980). Granule cell genesis in the hippocampus of rats treated neonatally with hydrocortisone. *Neuroscience, 5*, 2003–2012.

Boller, K., Rovee-Collier, C., Gulya, M., & Prete, K. (1996). Infants' memory for context: Timing effects of postevent information. *Journal of Experimental Child Psychology, 63*, 583–602.

Bower, G. H., & Mann, T. (1992). Improving recall by recoding interfering material at the time of retrieval. *Journal of Experimental Psychology: Learning, Memory, and Cognition, 18*, 1310–1320.

Bowers, K. S., & Farvolden, P. (1996). Revisiting a century-old Freudian slip: From suggestion disavowed to the truth repressed. *Psychological Bulletin, 119*, 355–380.

Bowlby, J. (1969). *Attachment and loss* (Vol. 1). New York: Basic Books.

Bowlby, J. (1980). *Attachment and loss* (Vol. 3). New York: Basic Books.

Boyce, W. T., Barr, R. G., & Zeltzer, L. K. (1992). Temperament and the psychobiology of childhood stress. *Pediatrics, 90*, 483–486.

Boyer, M. E., Barron, K. L., & Farrar, M. L. (1994). Three-year-olds remember a novel event from 20 months: Evidence for long-term memory in children? *Memory, 2*, 417–445.

Bradley, R. M. (1972). Development of the taste bud and gustatory papillae in human fetuses. In J. Bosma (Ed.), *The Third Symposium on Oral Sensation and Perception: The mouth of the infant* (pp. 137–162). Springfield, IL: Charles C Thomas.

Brainerd, C. J. (1985). Model-based approaches to storage and retrieval development. In C. J. Brainerd & M. Pressley (Eds.), *Basic processes in memory development* (pp. 143–208). New York: Springer-Verlag.

Brainerd, C. J., Howe, M. L., & Reyna, V. F. (in press). Fuzzy-trace theory and the development of recall. *Psychological Review.*

Brainerd, C. J., & Reyna, V. F. (1990). Can Age × Learnability interactions explain the development of forgetting? *Developmental Psychology, 26*, 194–203.

Brainerd, C. J., & Reyna, V. F. (1995). Learning rate, learning opportunities, and the development of forgetting. *Developmental Psychology, 31*, 251–262.

Brainerd, C. J., & Reyna, V. F. (1996). Mere memory testing creates false memories in children. *Developmental Psychology, 32*, 467–478.

Brainerd, C. J., & Reyna, V. F. (1998). Fuzzy-trace theory and children's false memories. *Journal of Experimental Child Psychology, 71*, 89–129.

Brainerd, C. J., Reyna, V. F., & Brandse, E. (1995). Are children's false memories more persistent than their true memories? *Psychological Science, 6*, 359–364.

Brainerd, C. J., Reyna, V. F., & Wright, R. (1998). *Eliminating estimation bias in dual-memory models*. Manuscript submitted for publication.

Brainerd, C. J., Stein, L., & Reyna, V. F. (1998). On the development of conscious and unconscious memory. *Developmental Psychology, 34*, 342–357.

Bretherton, I., & Waters, E. (Eds.). (1985). Growing points of attachment theory and research. *Monographs of the Society for Research in Child Development, 50*(1–2, Serial No. 209).

Brewer, W. F. (1986). What is autobiographical memory? In D. C. Rubin (Ed.), *Autobiographical memory* (pp. 25–49). Cambridge, England: Cambridge University Press.

Brewer, W. F. (1988). Memory for randomly sampled autobiographical events. In U. Neisser & E. Winograd (Eds.), *Remembering reconsidered: Ecological and traditional approaches to the study of memory* (pp. 21–90). New York: Cambridge University Press.

Brewin, C. R., Andrews, B., & Gotlib, I. H. (1993). Psychopathology and early experience: A reappraisal of retrospective reports. *Psychological Bulletin, 113*, 82–98.

Briere, J. N., & Conte, J. (1993). Self-reported amnesia for abuse in adults molested as children. *Journal of Traumatic Stress, 6*, 21–31.

Bronson, G. W. (1991). Infant differences in rate of visual encoding. *Child Development, 45*, 873–890.

Bruck, M., Ceci, S. J., Francoeur, E., & Barr, R. (1995). "I hardly cried when I got my shot!" Influencing children's reports about a visit to their pediatrician. *Child Development, 66*, 193–208.

Bugenthal, D. B., Blue, J., Cortez, V., Fleck, K., & Rodriguez, A. (1992). Influences of witnessed affect on information processing in children. *Child Development, 63*, 774–786.

Bullock, M., & Lutkenhaus, P. (1990). Who am I? Self-understanding in toddlers. *Merrill-Palmer Quarterly, 36*, 217–238.

Bullock Drummey, A., & Newcombe, N. (1995). Remembering versus knowing the past: Children's explicit and implicit memories for pictures. *Journal of Experimental Child Psychology, 59*, 549–565.

Butterworth, G. (1990). Self-perception in infancy. In D. Cicchetti & M. Beeghly (Eds.), *The self in transition: Infancy to childhood* (pp. 119–137). Chicago: University of Chicago Press.

Cahill, L., & McGaugh, J. L. (1996). Modulation of memory storage. *Current Opinion in Neurobiology, 6*, 237–242.

Cahill, L., Prins, B., Weber, M., & McGaugh, J. L. (1994). β-adrenergic activation and memory for emotional events. *Nature, 371*, 702–704.

Cairns, R. B., & Hood, K. E. (1983). Continuity in social development. In P. Baltes & O. G. Brim (Eds.), *Life span development* (Vol. 5, pp. 301–358). New York: Academic Press.

Campos, J. J., Bertenthal, B. I., & Kermoian, R. (1992). Early experience and emotional development: The emergence of wariness of heights. *Psychological Science, 3,* 61–64.

Case, R. (1991). Stages in the development of the young child's first sense of self. *Developmental Review, 11,* 210–230.

Case, R. (1995). Capacity-based explanations of working memory growth: A brief history and reevaluation. In F. E. Weinert & W. Schneider (Eds.), *Memory performance and competencies: Issues of growth and development* (pp. 23–44). Hillsdale, NJ: Erlbaum.

Ceci, S. J. (1995). False beliefs: Some developmental and clinical considerations. In D. L. Schacter (Ed.), *Memory distortion* (pp. 91–125). Cambridge, MA: Harvard University Press.

Ceci, S. J., & Bruck, M. (1995). *Jeopardy in the courtroom: A scientific analysis of children's testimony.* Washington, DC: American Psychological Association.

Ceci, S. J., Huffman, M. L. C., Smith, E., & Loftus, E. F. (1994). Repeatedly thinking about a nonevent: Source misattributions among preschoolers. *Consciousness and Cognition, 3,* 388–407.

Ceci, S. J., Loftus, E. F., Leichtman, M. D., & Bruck, M. (1994). The possible role of source misattributions in the creation of false beliefs among preschoolers. *International Journal of Clinical and Experimental Hypnosis, 42,* 304–320.

Cernoch, J. M., & Porter, R. H. (1985). Recognition of maternal axillary odors by infants. *Child Development, 56,* 1593–1598.

Chechile, R. A., & Richman, C. L. (1982). The interaction of semantic memory with storage and retrieval processes. *Developmental Review, 2,* 237–250.

Chechile, R. A., Richman, C. L., Topinka, C., & Ehrensbeck, K. (1981). A developmental study of the storage and retrieval of information. *Child Development, 52,* 251–259.

Chi, M. T. H., & Ceci, S. J. (1987). Content knowledge: Its role, representation, and restructuring in memory development. *Advances in Child Development and Behavior, 20,* 91–142.

Chi, M. T. H., & Koeske, R. D. (1983). Network representation of a child's dinosaur knowledge. *Developmental Psychology, 19,* 29–39.

Chugani, H. T. (1994). Development of regional brain glucose metabolism in relation to behavior and plasticity. In G. Dawson & K. Fischer (Eds.), *Human behavior and the developing brain* (pp. 153–175). New York: Guilford Press.

Chugani, H. T., & Phelps, M. E. (1986). Maturational changes in cerebral function in infants determined by [18]FDG positron emission tomography. *Science, 231,* 840–843.

Chugani, H. T., Phelps, M. E., & Mazziotti, J. C. (1987). Positron emission tomography study of human brain functional development. *Annals of Neurology, 22,* 487–497.

Cicchetti, D. (1991). Fractures in the crystal: Developmental psychopathology and the emergence of the self. *Developmental Review, 11*, 271–287.

Cicchetti, D., & Beeghly, M. (1987). Symbolic development in maltreated youngsters: An organizational perspective. *New Directions for Child Development, 36*, 5–29.

Cicchetti, D., Beeghly, M., Carlson, V., & Toth, S. (1990). The emergence of the self in atypical populations. In D. Cicchetti & M. Beeghly (Eds.), *The self in transition: Infancy to childhood* (pp. 309–344). Chicago: University of Chicago Press.

Cicchetti, D., & Carlson, V. (1989). *Child maltreatment: Theory and research on the causes and consequences of child abuse and neglect.* New York: Cambridge University Press.

Clark, S. L. (1993). *Knowledge base and children's long-term retention.* Unpublished doctoral dissertation, Memorial University of Newfoundland, St. John's, Newfoundland, Canada.

Clark, S. L., & Howe, M. L. (1990, May). *Do differences in knowledge base alleviate forgetting?* Paper presented at the University of Waterloo Conference on Child Development, Waterloo, Ontario, Canada.

Clarke, E. A., & Hanisee, J. (1982). Intellectual and adaptive performance of Asian children in adoptive American settings. *Child Development, 53*, 595–599.

Cloitre, M., Cancienne, J., Brodsky, B., Dulit, R., & Perry, S. W. (1996). Memory performance among women with parental abuse histories: Enhanced directed forgetting or directed remembering? *Journal of Abnormal Psychology, 105*, 204–211.

Cohen, L. B., DeLoache, J. S., & Pearl, R. A. (1977). An examination of interference effects in infants' memory for faces. *Child Development, 48*, 88–96.

Cohen, L. B., & Salapatek, P. (Eds.). (1987). *Handbook of infant perception: From sensation to perception* (Vol. 1). New York: Academic Press.

Cohen, N. J., & Squire, L. R. (1980). Preserved learning and retention of pattern-analyzing skill in amnesia: Dissociation of knowing how and knowing that. *Science, 210*, 207–210.

Conway, M. A. (1996). Autobiographical knowledge and autobiographical memories. In D. Rubin (Ed.), *Remembering our past: Studies in autobiographical memory* (pp. 67–93). New York: Cambridge University Press.

Conway, M. A., Collins, A. F., Gathercole, S. E., & Anderson, S. J. (1996). Recollections of true and false autobiographical memories. *Journal of Experimental Psychology: General, 125*, 69–95.

Courage, M. L., & Howe, M. L. (1998a). *From infant to child: The foundation of cognitive achievements in the second year of life.* Manuscript submitted for publication.

Courage, M. L., & Howe, M. L. (1998b). The ebb and flow of infant attentional preferences: Evidence for long-term recognition memory in 3-month-olds. *Journal of Experimental Child Psychology, 70*, 26–53.

Crook, C. (1987). Taste and olfaction. In P. Salapatek & L. Cohen (Eds.), *Handbook of infant perception: Vol. 1: From sensation to perception* (pp. 237–264). New York: Academic Press.

Csikszentmihalkyi, M., & Beattie, O. V. (1979). Life themes: A theoretical and empirical exploration of their origins and effects. *Journal of Humanistic Psychology, 19,* 45–63.

Damon, W., & Hart, D. (1982). The development of self-understanding from infancy through adolescence. *Child Development, 53,* 841–864.

Damon, W., & Hart, D. (1988). *Self-understanding in childhood and adolescence.* Cambridge, England: Cambridge University Press.

Davidson, D., & Hoe, S. (1993). Children's recall and recognition for typical and atypical actions in script-based stories. *Journal of Experimental Child Psychology, 55,* 104–126.

Davidson, D., & Jergovic, D. (1996). Children's memory for atypical actions in script-based stories: An examination of the disruption effect. *Journal of Experimental Child Psychology, 61,* 134–152.

Dawson, G., & Fischer, K. W. (Eds.). (1994). *Human behavior and the developing brain.* New York: Guilford Press.

DeCasper, A. J., & Fifer, W. P. (1980). Of human bonding: Newborns prefer their mothers' voices. *Science, 208,* 1174–1176.

DeCasper, A. J., Lecanuet, J., Busnel, M., Granier-Deferre, C., & Maugeais, R. (1994). Fetal reactions to recurrent maternal speech. *Infant Behavior and Development, 17,* 159–164.

DeCasper, A. J., & Prescott, P. A. (1984). Human newborns' perception of male voices: Preference, discrimination, and reinforcing value. *Developmental Psychobiology, 17,* 481–491.

DeCasper, A. J., & Spence, M. J. (1986). Prenatal maternal speech influences newborns' perception of speech sounds. *Infant Behavior and Development, 9,* 133–150.

DeCasper, A. J., & Spence, M. J. (1991). Auditory mediated behavior during the prenatal period: A cognitive view. In M. Weiss & P. Zelazo (Eds.), *Newborn attention: Biological constraints and the influence of experience* (pp. 142–176). Norwood, NJ: Ablex.

DeLoache, J. S., & Brown, A. L. (1983). Very young children's memory for the location of objects in a large-scale environment. *Child Development, 54,* 888–897.

DeLoache, J. S., & Todd, C. M. (1988). Young children's use of spatial categorization as a mnemonic strategy. *Journal of Experimental Child Psychology, 46,* 1–20.

Dempster, F. N. (1978). Memory span and short-term memory capacity: A developmental study. *Journal of Experimental Child Psychology, 26,* 419–431.

Dempster, F. N. (1988). The spacing effect: A case study in the failure to apply the results of psychological research. *American Psychologist, 43,* 627–634.

Dempster, F. N. (1993). Resistance to interference: Developmental changes in a basic processing mechanism. In M. L. Howe & R. Pasnak (Eds.), *Emerging themes in cognitive development: Vol. 1. Foundations* (pp. 3–27). New York: Springer-Verlag.

Dempster, F. N., & Brainerd, C. J. (Eds.). (1995). *Interference and inhibition in cognition*. San Diego, CA: Academic Press.

Dennett, D. C. (1991). *Consciousness explained*. Boston: Little, Brown.

Diamond, A. (1988). Abilities and neural mechanisms underlying A not B performance. *Child Development, 59,* 523–527.

Diamond, A. (1990a). Rate of maturation of the hippocampus and the developmental progression of children's performance on the delayed non-matching to sample and visual paired comparison tasks. *Annals of the New York Academy of Sciences, 608,* 394–426.

Diamond, A. (1990b). The development and neural bases of memory functions as indexed by the AB and delayed response tasks in human infants and infant monkeys. *Annals of the New York Academy of Sciences, 608,* 267–309.

Diamond, A. (1991). Frontal lobe involvement in cognitive changes during the first year of life. In K. Gibson & A. C. Petersen (Eds.), *Brain maturation and cognitive development: Comparative and cross-cultural perspectives* (pp. 127–180). New York: Aldine de Gruyter.

Diamond, D. M., Fleshner, M., Ingersoll, N., & Rose, G. M. (1996). Psychological stress impairs spatial working memory: Relevance to electrophysiological studies of hippocampal function. *Behavioral Neuroscience, 110,* 661–672.

DiBiase, R., & Lewis, M. (1997). The relation between temperament and embarrassment. *Cognition and Emotion, 11,* 259–271.

DiTomasso, M. J., & Routh, D. K. (1993). Recall of abuse in childhood and three measures of dissociation. *Child Abuse and Neglect, 17,* 477–485.

Dudycha, G. J., & Dudycha, M. M. (1941). Childhood memories: A review of the literature. *Psychological Bulletin, 38,* 668–682.

Eacott, M. J., & Crawley, R. A. (1998). The offset of childhood amnesia: Memory for events that occurred before age 3. *Journal of Experimental Psychology: General, 127,* 22–33.

Earls, F. (1996, May). *Recovery from profound early social deprivation*. Paper presented at the meeting Advancing Research on Developmental Plasticity: Integrating the Behavioral Science and the Neuroscience of Mental Health, Washington, DC.

Eimas, P. D., Siqueland, E. R., Jusczyk, P., & Vigorito, J. (1971). Speech perception in infants. *Science, 171,* 303–306.

Elliot, C. H., Jay, S. M., & Woody, P. (1987). An observational scale for measuring children's distress during medical procedures. *Journal of Pediatric Psychology, 12,* 543–551.

Elman, J. L., Bates, E. A., Johnson, M. H., Karmiloff-Smith, A., Parisi, D., & Plunkett, K. (1996). *Rethinking innateness: A connectionist perspective on development*. Cambridge, MA: MIT Press.

Emde, R. N. (1981). Changing models of infancy and the nature of early development: Re-modeling the foundation. *Journal of the American Psychoanalytic Association, 29,* 179–219.

Emde, R. N., Biringen, Z., Clyman, R. B., & Oppenheim, D. (1991). The moral self of infancy: Affective core and procedural knowledge. *Developmental Review, 11,* 251–270.

Enright, M. K., Rovee-Collier, C., Fagen, J. W., & Caniglia, K. (1983). The effects of distributed training on retention of operant conditioning in human infants. *Journal of Experimental Child Psychology, 36,* 209–225.

Erdelyi, M. H. (1996). *The recovery of unconscious memories: Hypermnesia and reminiscence.* Chicago: University of Chicago Press.

Estes, W. K. (1997). Processes of memory loss, recovery, and distortion. *Psychological Review, 104,* 148–169.

Fadil, L., Moss, L., & Bahrick, L. (1993, March). *Infants' visual recognition of their own faces.* Paper presented at the biennial meeting of the Society for Research in Child Development, New Orleans, LA.

Falmange, J. Claude, & Doignon, J. P. (1988). A Markovian procedure for assessing the state of a system. *Journal of Mathematical Psychology, 32,* 232–258.

Farrar, M. J., & Goodman, G. S. (1990). Developmental differences in the relation between scripts and episodic memory: Do they exist? In R. Fivush & J. A. Hudson (Eds.), *Knowing and remembering in young children* (pp. 30–64). New York: Cambridge University Press.

Farrar, M. J., & Goodman, G. S. (1992). Developmental changes in event memory. *Child Development, 63,* 173–187.

Femina, D. D., Yeager, C. A., & Lewis, D. O. (1990). Child abuse: Adolescent records vs. adult recall. *Child Abuse and Neglect, 14,* 227–231.

Fenson, L., Dale, P. S., Reznick, J. S., Bates, E., Thal, D., & Pethick, S. (1994). Variability in early communicative development. *Monographs of the Society for Research in Child Development, 59*(5, Serial No. 242).

Fernald, A. (1985). Four-month-old infants prefer to listen to "motherese." *Infant Behavior and Development, 8,* 181–195.

Fernald, A. (1992). Human maternal vocalization to infants as biologically relevant signals: An evolutionary perspective. In J. Barkow, L. Cosmides, & J. Tooby (Eds.), *The adaptive mind: Evolutionary psychology and the generation of culture* (pp. 391–428). New York: Oxford University Press.

Finlay, D., & Ivinskis, A. (1987). Cardiac change responses and attentional mechanisms in infants. In B. McKenzie & R. Day (Eds.), *Perceptual development in early infancy: Problems and issues* (pp. 45–63). Hillsdale, NJ: Erlbaum.

Fivush, R. (1984). Learning about school: The development of kindergartners' school scripts. *Child Development, 55,* 1697–1709.

Fivush, R. (1993). Developmental perspectives on autobiographical recall. In G. S. Goodman & B. L. Bottoms (Eds.), *Understanding and improving children's testimony* (pp. 1–24). New York: Guilford Press.

Fivush, R. (1994). Young children's event recall: Are memories constructed through discourse? *Consciousness and Cognition, 3,* 356–373.

Fivush, R., Gray, J. T., & Fromhoff, F. A. (1987). Two-year-olds talk about the past. *Cognitive Development, 2,* 393–409.

Fivush, R., Haden, C., & Adam, S. (1995). Structure and coherence of preschoolers' personal narratives over time: Implications for childhood amnesia. *Journal of Experimental Child Psychology, 60,* 32–56.

Fivush, R., & Hamond, N. R. (1989). Time and again: Effects of repetition and retention interval on 2-year-olds' event recall. *Journal of Experimental Child Psychology, 47,* 259–273.

Fivush, R., & Hamond, N. R. (1990). Autobiographical memory across the preschool years: Toward conceptualizing childhood amnesia. In R. Fivush & J. A. Hudson (Eds.), *Knowing and remembering in young children* (pp. 223–248). New York: Cambridge University Press.

Fivush, R., & Hudson, J. A. (Eds.). (1990). *Knowing and remembering in young children.* New York: Cambridge University Press.

Fivush, R., Kuebli, J., & Clubb, P. A. (1992). The structure of event representations: A developmental analysis. *Child Development, 63,* 188–201.

Fivush, R., & Mandler, J. M. (1985). Developmental changes in the understanding of temporal sequence. *Child Development, 56,* 1437–1446.

Fivush, R., & Schwartzmueller, A. (1998). Children remember childhood: Implications for childhood amnesia. *Applied Cognitive Psychology, 12,* 455–473.

Flavell, J. H., Miller, P. H., & Miller, S. A. (1993). *Cognitive development* (3rd ed.). Englewood Cliffs, NJ; Prentice Hall.

Flexser, A. J., & Tulving, E. (1978). Retrieval independence on recognition and recall. *Psychological Review, 85,* 153–171.

Fodor, J. A., & Pylyshyn, Z. W. (1988). Connectionism and cognitive architecture: A critical analysis. *Cognition, 28,* 3–71.

Freud, S. (1938). The psychopathology of everyday life. In A. A. Brill (Ed.), *The writings of Sigmund Freud* (pp. 35–178). New York: Modern Library. (Original work published 1914)

Freud, S. (1953). Three essays on the theory of sexuality. In J. Strachey (Ed.), *The standard edition of the complete psychological works of Sigmund Freud* (Vol. 7, pp. 135–243). London: Hogarth Press. (Original work published 1905)

Freud, S. (1960). The psychopathology of everyday life. In J. Strachey (Ed.), *The standard edition of the complete psychological works of Sigmund Freud* (Vol. 6, pp. 26–159). London: Hogarth Press. (Original work published 1901)

Freud, S. (1963). Introductory lectures on psychoanalysis. In J. Strachey (Ed.), *The standard edition of the complete psychological works of Sigmund Freud* (Vols. 15–16, pp. 243–496). London: Hogarth Press. (Original work published 1916–1917)

Fuster, J. M. (1980). *The prefrontal cortex: Anatomy, physiology, and neuropsychology of the frontal lobe.* New York: Raven Press.

Fuster, J. M. (1984). The prefrontal cortex and temporal integration. In A. Peters & E. G. Jones (Eds.), *Cerebral cortex: Vol. 4. Association and auditory cortices* (pp. 151–177). New York: Plenum.

Fuster, J. M. (1989). *The prefrontal cortex: Anatomy, physiology, and neuropsychology of the frontal lobe* (2nd ed.). New York: Raven Press.

Garmezy, N., & Rutter, M. (Eds.). (1983). *Stress, coping, and development in children.* New York: McGraw-Hill.

Garry, M., Manning, C. G., Loftus, E. F., & Sherman, S. J. (1996). Imagination inflation: Imagining a childhood event inflates confidence that it occurred. *Psychonomic Bulletin and Review, 3,* 208–214.

Gaultney, J. F., Bjorklund, D. F., & Schneider, W. (1992). The role of children's expertise in a strategic memory task. *Contemporary Educational Psychology, 17,* 244–257.

Gelman, S. A., & Gottfried, G. M. (1996). Children's causal explanations of animate and inanimate motion. *Child Development, 67,* 1970–1987.

Ghatala, E. S. (1984). Developmental changes in incidental memory as a function of meaningfulness and encoding condition. *Developmental Psychology, 20,* 208–211.

Gillette, A. L. (1936). Learning and retention: A comparison of three experimental procedures. *Archives of Psychology, 28*(Serial No. 198).

Ginsberg, S. D., Hof, P. R., McKinney, W. T., & Morrison, J. H. (1993a). Quantitative analysis of tuberoinfundibular tyrosine hydroxylase- and corticotropin-releasing factor-immunoreactive neurons in monkeys raised with differential rearing conditions. *Experimental Neurology, 120,* 95–105.

Ginsberg, S. D., Hof, P. R., McKinney, W. T., & Morrison, J. H. (1993b). The noradrenergic innervation density of the monkey paraventricular nucleus is not altered by early social deprivation. *Neuroscience Letters, 158,* 130–134.

Gold, P. E., & McCarty, R. C. (1995). Stress regulation of memory processes: Role of peripheral catecholamines and glucose. In M. J. Friedman, D. S. Charney, & A. Y. Deutch (Eds.), *Neurobiological and clinical consequences of stress* (pp. 151–162). Philadelphia: Lippincott-Raven.

Goldin-Meadow, S., Alibali, M. W., & Church, R. B. (1993). Transitions in concept acquisition: Using the hand to read the mind. *Psychological Review, 100,* 279–297.

Goldin-Meadow, S., Seligman, M., & Gelman, R. (1976). Language in the two-year-old. *Cognition, 4,* 189–202.

Golding, J. M., & MacLeod, C. M. (Eds.). (1998). *Intentional forgetting: Interdisciplinary approaches.* Mahwah, NJ: Erlbaum.

Goleman, D. (1992, July 21). Childhood trauma: Memory or invention? *New York Times,* p. B5.

Goodman, G. S., & Quas, J. A. (1997). Trauma and memory: Individual differences in children's recounting of a stressful experience. In N. Stein, P. A. Ornstein, C. J. B. Tversky, & C. J. Brainerd (Eds.), *Memory for everyday and emotional events* (pp. 267–294). Mahwah, NJ: Erlbaum.

Goodman, G. S., Quas, J. A., Batterman-Faunce, J. M., Riddlesberger, M. M., & Kuhn, J. (1994). Predictors of accurate and inaccurate memories of traumatic events experienced in childhood. *Consciousness and Cognition, 3,* 269–294.

Goodman, G. S., Quas, J. A., Batterman-Faunce, J. M., Riddlesberger, M. M., & Kuhn, J. (1997). Children's reactions to and memory for a stressful event: Influences of age, anatomical dolls, knowledge, and parental attachment. *Applied Developmental Science*, *1*, 54–75.

Goodwyn, S., & Acredolo, L. (1993). Symbolic gesture versus word: Is there a modality advantage for the inset of symbol use? *Child development*, *64*, 688–701.

Greco, C., Hayne, H., & Rovee-Collier, C. (1990). The roles of function, reminding, and variability in categorization by 3-month-old infants. *Journal of Experimental Psychology: Learning, Memory, and Cognition*, *16*, 617–633.

Greco, C., Rovee-Collier, C., Hayne, H., Griesler, P., & Early, L. A. (1986). Ontogeny of early event memory: I. Forgetting and retrieval by 2- and 3-month-olds. *Infant Behavior and Development*, *9*, 441–460.

Green, B. L., Grace, M. C., Vary, M. G., Kramer, T. L., Cleser, G. C., & Leonard, A. C. (1994). Children of disaster in the second decade: A 17-year follow-up of Buffalo Creek survivors. *Journal of the Academy of Child and Adolescent Psychiatry*, *33*, 71–79.

Greenough, W. T. (1990). Brain adaptation to experience: An update. In M. H. Johnson (Ed.), *Brain development and cognition: A reader* (pp. 319–322). Cambridge, MA: Blackwell.

Greenough, W. T., & Bailey, C. H. (1988). The anatomy of a memory: Convergence of results across a diversity of tests. *Trends in Neuroscience*, *11*, 142–147.

Greenough, W. T., & Black, J. E. (1992). Induction of brain structure by experience: Substrates for cognitive development. In M. Gunnar & C. A. Nelson (Eds.), *Minnesota Symposium on Child Psychology: Vol. 25. Developmental behavioral neuroscience* (pp. 155–200). Hillsdale, NJ: Erlbaum.

Greenough, W. T., Black, J. E., & Wallace, C. S. (1987). Experience and brain development. *Child Development*, *58*, 539–559.

Greenwald, A. G., & Banaji, M. R. (1989). The self as a memory system: Powerful, but ordinary. *Journal of Personality and Social Psychology*, *57*, 41–54.

Gribbin, J., & Gribbin, M. (1997). *Richard Feynman: A life in science*. New York: Dutton.

Gunnar, M. R., Brodersen, L., Krueger, K., & Rigatuso, J. (1996). Dampening of adrenocortical responses during infancy: Normative changes and individual differences. *Child Development*, *67*, 877–889.

Gunnar, M. R., Tout, K., de Haan, M., Pierce, S., & Stansbury, K. (1997). Temperament, social competence, and adrenocortical activity in preschoolers. *Developmental Psychobiology*, *31*, 65–85.

Haith, M. M. (1980). *Rules that babies look by*. Hillsdale, NJ: Erlbaum.

Haith, M. M., Hazan, C., & Goodman, G. S. (1988). Expectation and anticipation of dynamic visual events by 3.5-month-old babies. *Child Development*, *59*, 467–479.

Hamann, S. B., & Squire, L. R. (1995). On the acquisition of new declarative knowledge in amnesia. *Behavioral Neuroscience, 109,* 1027–1044.

Hamond, N. R., & Fivush, R. (1991). Memories of Mickey Mouse: Young children recount their trip to Disneyworld. *Cognitive Development, 6,* 433–448.

Hanson, S. J., & Burr, D. J. (1990). What connectionist models learn: Learning and representation in connectionist networks. *Behavioral and Brain Sciences, 13,* 471–518.

Harlow, H. F., & Harlow, M. K. (1966). Learning to love. *American Scientist, 54,* 244–272.

Harnishfeger, K. K. (1995). The development of cognitive inhibition: Theories, definitions, and research evidence. In F. N. Dempster & C. J. Brainerd (Eds.), *Interference and inhibition in cognition* (pp. 175–204). San Diego, CA: Academic Press.

Harnishfeger, K. K., & Bjorklund, D. F. (1993). The ontogeny of inhibition mechanisms: A renewed approach to cognitive development. In M. L. Howe & R. Pasnak (Eds.), *Emerging themes in cognitive development: Vol. 1. Foundations* (pp. 28–49). New York: Springer-Verlag.

Harnishfeger, K. K., & Pope, R. S. (1996). Intending to forget: The development of cognitive inhibition in directed forgetting. *Journal of Experimental Child Psychology, 62,* 292–315.

Harris, P. L. (1987). The development of search. In P. Salapatek & L. Cohen (Eds.), *Handbook of infant perception: Vol. 2. From perception to cognition* (pp. 155–207). New York: Academic Press.

Harter, S. (1983). Developmental perspectives on the self-system. In E. M. Hetherington (Ed.), *Handbook of child psychology: Vol. 4. Social and personality development* (pp. 275–385). New York: Wiley.

Hartshorn, K., & Rovee-Collier, C. (1997). Infant learning and long-term memory at 6 months: A confirming analysis. *Developmental Psychobiology, 30,* 71–85.

Hasher, L., Stoltzfus, E. R., Zacks, R. T., & Rypma, B. (1991). Age and inhibition. *Journal of Experimental Psychology: Learning, Memory, and Cognition, 17,* 163–169.

Hasher, L., & Zacks, R. T. (1988). Working memory, comprehension, and aging: A review and a new view. *Psychology of Learning and Motivation: Advances in Research and Theory, 22,* 193–225.

Hasselhorn, M. (1992). Task dependency and the role of category typicality and metamemory in the development of an organizational strategy. *Child Development, 63,* 202–214.

Hayne, H., Greco, C., Early, L. A., Griesler, P., & Rovee-Collier, C. (1986). Ontogeny of early event memory: II. Encoding and retrieval by 2- and 3-month-olds. *Infant Behavior and Development, 9,* 461–472.

Hayne, H., Greco-Vigorito, C., & Rovee-Collier, C. (1993). Forming contextual categories in infancy. *Cognitive Development, 8,* 63–82.

Hazen, N. L., & Volk-Hudson, S. (1984). The effect of spatial context on young children's recall. *Child Development, 55,* 1835–1844.

Hertsgaard, L., Gunnar, M., Erickson, M. F., & Nachmias, M. (1995). Adreno-cortical responses to the Strange Situation in infants with disorganized/disoriented attachment relationships. *Child Development, 66,* 1100–1106.

Herz, R. S. (1997). The effects of cue distinctiveness on odor-based context-dependent memory. *Memory & Cognition, 25,* 375–380.

Herz, R. S., & Cupchik, G. C. (1995). The emotional distinctiveness of odor-evoked memories. *Chemical Senses, 20,* 517–520.

Hickey, T. L., & Peduzzi, J. D. (1987). Structure and development of the visual system. In P. Salapatek & L. Cohen (Eds.), *Handbook of infant perception* (Vol. 1, pp. 1–42). San Diego, CA: Academic Press.

Hickling, A. K., & Gelman, S. A. (1995). How does your garden grow? Early conceptualizations of seeds and their place in the plant growth cycle. *Child Development, 66,* 856–876.

Hilgard, E. R. (1953). *Introduction to psychology.* New York: Harcourt Brace.

Hilgard, E. R., & Bower, G. H. (1975). *Theories of learning* (4th ed.). Englewood Cliffs, NJ: Prentice Hall.

Hill, S., & Tomlin, C. (1981). Self recognition in retarded children. *Child Development, 52,* 145–150.

Hill, W. L., Borovsky, D., & Rovee-Collier, C. (1988). Continuities in infant memory development. *Developmental Psychobiology, 21,* 43–62.

Hoffding, H. (1891). *Outlines of psychology.* New York: Macmillan.

Howe, M. L. (1995). Interference effects in young children's long-term retention. *Developmental Psychology, 31,* 579–596.

Howe, M. L. (1997a). Children's memory for traumatic experiences. *Learning and Individual Differences, 9,* 153–174.

Howe, M. L. (1997b, November). *Directed forgetting in preschoolers: Release from retroactive interference when induced at acquisition but not retention.* Paper presented at the annual meeting of the Psychonomic Society, Philadelphia.

Howe, M. L. (1998a). Individual differences in factors that modulate storage and retrieval of traumatic memories. *Development and Psychopathology, 10,* 681–698.

Howe, M. L. (1998b). Language is never enough: Memories are more than words reveal. *Applied Cognitive Psychology, 12,* 475–481.

Howe, M. L. (1998c). *Reducing interference effects in children's long-term retention: I. The role of directed forgetting.* Manuscript submitted for publication.

Howe, M. L. (1998d). When distinctiveness fails, false memories prevail. *Journal of Experimental Child Psychology, 71,* 170–177.

Howe, M. L., & Brainerd, C. J. (1989). Development of children's long-term retention. *Developmental Review, 9,* 301–340.

Howe, M. L., Brainerd, C. J., & Kingma, J. (1985a). Development of organization in recall: A stages-of-learning analysis. *Journal of Experimental Child Psychology, 39,* 230–251.

Howe, M. L., Brainerd, C. J., & Kingma, J. (1985b). Storage-retrieval processes of normal and learning-disabled children: A stages-of-learning analysis of picture-word effects. *Child Development, 56,* 1120–1133.

Howe, M. L., & Courage, M. L. (1993). On resolving the enigma of infantile amnesia. *Psychological Bulletin, 113,* 305–326.

Howe, M. L., & Courage, M. L. (1997a). Independent paths in the development of infant learning and forgetting. *Journal of Experimental Child Psychology, 67,* 131–163.

Howe, M. L., & Courage, M. L. (1997b). The emergence and early development of autobiographical memory. *Psychological Review, 104,* 499–523.

Howe, M. L., Courage, M. L., & Bryant-Brown, L. (1993). Reinstating preschoolers' memories. *Developmental Psychology, 29,* 854–869.

Howe, M. L., Courage, M. L., & Harley, C. (1998). *Using heart-rate variability to map the relationship between neurological and behavioral indices of long-term memory*, technical research report, Memorial University, St. John's, Newfoundland, Canada.

Howe, M. L., Courage, M. L., & Peterson, C. (1994a). *Children's memories of traumatic events*. Paper presented at the annual meeting of the Psychonomic Society, St. Louis, MO.

Howe, M. L., Courage, M. L., & Peterson, C. (1994b). How can I remember when "I" wasn't there: Long-term retention of traumatic experiences and emergence of the cognitive self. *Consciousness and Cognition, 3,* 327–355.

Howe, M. L., Courage, M. L., & Peterson, C. (1995). Intrusions in preschoolers' recall of traumatic childhood events. *Psychonomic Bulletin and Review, 2,* 130–134.

Howe, M. L., & O'Sullivan, J. T. (1997). What children's memories tell us about recalling our childhoods: A review of storage and retrieval processes in the development of long-term retention. *Developmental Review, 17,* 148–204.

Howe, M. L., Peddle, J., & Wadwahan, S. (1999). *Reducing retroactive interference in children's long-term retention: II. The role of recoding.* Manuscript in preparation.

Howe, M. L., & Rabinowitz, F. M. (1989). On the uninterpretability of dual-task performance. *Journal of Experimental Child Psychology, 47,* 32–38.

Howe, M. L., & Rabinowitz, F. M. (1991). Gist another panacea? Or just the illusion of inclusion. *Developmental Review, 11,* 305–316.

Howe, M. L., Rabinowitz, F. M., & Grant, M. J. (1993). On measuring (in)dependence of cognitive processes. *Psychological Review, 100,* 737–747.

Hudson, J. A. (1986). Memories are made of this: General event knowledge and development of autobiographical memory. In K. Nelson (Ed.), *Event knowledge: Structure and function in development* (pp. 97–118). Hillsdale, NJ: Erlbaum.

Hudson, J. A. (1990). Constructive processing in children's event memory. *Developmental Psychology, 26,* 180–187.

Hudson, J. A. (1991, April). *Effects of re-enactment on toddlers' memory for a novel event*. Paper presented at the biennial meeting of the Society for Research in Child Development, Seattle, WA.

Hudson, J. A. (1993). Reminiscing with mothers and others: Autobiographical memory in young two-year-olds. *Journal of Narrative and Life History*, 3, 1–32.

Hudson, J. A., & Fivush, R. (1991). As time goes by: Sixth graders remember a kindergarten experience. *Applied Cognitive Psychology*, 5, 347–360.

Huffman, M. L., Crossman, A., & Ceci, S. J. (1996, March). *An investigation of the long-term effects of source misattribution error: Are false memories permanent?* Poster presented at the meeting of the American Psychology-Law Society, Hilton Head, SC.

Hunt, R. R. (1995). The subtlety of distinctiveness: What von Restorff really did. *Psychonomic Bulletin and Review*, 2, 105–112.

Hunter, M. A., & Ames, E. (1988). A multifactor model of infant preferences for novel and familiar stimuli. *Advances in Infancy Research*, 5, 69–95.

Huttenlocher, P. R., & DeCourter, C. (1987). The development of synapses in striate cortex of man. *Human Neurobiology*, 6, 1–9.

Hyman, I. E., & Pentland, J. (1996). The role of mental imagery in the creation of false childhood memories. *Journal of Memory and Language*, 35, 101–117.

Izquierdo, I., & Medina, J. H. (1997). The biochemistry of memory formation and its regulation by hormones and neuromodulators. *Psychobiology*, 25, 1–9.

Jacoby, L. L. (1991). A process dissociation framework: Separating automatic from intentional uses of memory. *Journal of Memory and Language*, 30, 513–541.

Jacoby, L. L., Kelley, C., Brown, J., & Jasechko, J. (1989). Becoming famous overnight: Limits on the ability to avoid unconscious influences of the past. *Journal of Personality and Social Psychology*, 56, 326–338.

Jenike, M., & Albert, M. (1984). The dexamethasone suppression test in patients with presenile and senile dementia of the Alzheimer's type. *Journal of the American Geriatric Society*, 32, 441–447.

Johnson, H. M. (1994). Processes of successful intention forgetting. *Psychological Bulletin*, 116, 274–292.

Johnson, M. H., Posner, M. I., & Rothbart, M. K. (1991). Components of visual orienting in early infancy: Contingency learning, anticipatory, looking, and disengaging. *Journal of Cognitive Neuroscience*, 3, 335–344.

Johnson, M. K., Hashtroudi, S., & Lindsay, D. S. (1993). Source monitoring. *Psychological Bulletin*, 114, 3–28.

Jones, D. C., Swift, D. J., & Johnson, M. A. (1988). Nondeliberate memory for a novel event among preschoolers. *Developmental Psychology*, 24, 641–645.

Joslyn, S., Carlin, L., & Loftus, E. F. (1997). Remembering and forgetting childhood sexual abuse. *Memory*, 5, 703–724.

Kagan, J. (1981). *The second year: The emergence of self-awareness*. Cambridge, MA: Harvard University Press.

Kagan, J. (1984). Continuity and change in the opening years of life. In R. N.

Emde & R. J. Harmon (Eds.), *Continuities and discontinuities in development* (pp. 15–39). New York: Plenum.

Kagan, J. (1994). *Galen's prophecy: Temperment in human nature.* New York: Basic Books.

Kagan, J. (1996). Three pleasing ideas. *American Psychologist, 51,* 901–908.

Kagan, J., Reznick, S., Snidman, N., Gibbons, J., & Johnson, M. O. (1988). Childhood derivatives of inhibition and lack of inhibition to the unfamiliar. *Child Development, 59,* 1–9.

Kail, R. (1984). *The development of memory in children* (2nd ed.). New York: Freeman.

Kapur, S., Craik, F. I. M., Tulving, E., Wilson, A. A., Houle, S., & Brown, G. M. (1994). Neuroanatomical correlates of encoding in episodic memory: Levels of processing effect. *Proceedings of the National Academy of Sciences USA, 91,* 2008–2011.

Karmiloff-Smith, A. (1992). *Beyond modularity: A developmental perspective on cognitive science.* Cambridge, MA: MIT Press.

Kaufman, J., & Cicchetti, D. (1989). Effects of maltreatment on school-age children's socioemotional development: Assessments in a day-camp setting. *Developmental Psychology, 25,* 516–524.

Kaye, K. L., & Bower, T. G. R. (1994). Learning and intermodal transfer of information in newborns. *Psychological Science, 5,* 286–288.

Kerr, D., Campbell, L., Applegate, M., Brodish, A., & Landfield, P. (1991). Chronic stress-induced acceleration of electrophysiologic and morphometric biomarkers of hippocampal aging. *Journal of Neuroscience, 11,* 1316–1322.

Kety, S. S. (1970). The biogenic amines in the central nervous system: Their possible role in arousal, emotion, and learning. In F. O. Schmitt (Ed.), *The neurosciences: Second study program* (pp. 324–336). New York: Rockefeller University Press.

Kinzie, J. D., Sack, W., Angell, R., Clarke, G., & Ben, R. (1989). A three-year follow-up of Cambodian young people traumatized as children. *Journal of the American Academy of Child and Adolescent Psychiatry, 28,* 501–504.

Kitchigina, V., Vankov, A., Harley, C., & Sara, S. J. (1997). Novelty-elicited, noradrenaline-dependent enhancement of excitability in the dentate gyrus. *European Journal of Neuroscience, 9,* 41–47.

Klein, S. B., & Kihlstrom, J. F. (1986). Elaboration, organization, and the self-reference effect in memory. *Journal of Experimental Psychology: General, 115,* 26–38.

Kohler, W. (1929). *Gestalt psychology.* New York: Liveright.

Kohler, W. (1941). On the nature of associations. *Proceedings of the American Philosophical Society, 84,* 489–502.

Koocher, G. P., Goodman, G. S., White, C. S., Friedrich, W. N., Sivan, A. B., & Reynolds, C. R. (1995). Psychological science and the use of anatomically detailed dolls in child sexual-abuse assessments. *Psychological Bulletin, 118,* 199–222.

Kopp, C. B., & Brownell, C. A. (Eds.). (1991). The development of the self: The first three years [Special issue]. *Developmental Review, 11*(3).

Korneyev, A. Y. (1997). The role of the hypothalamic-pituitary-adrenocortical axis in memory-related effects of anxiolytics. *Neurobiology of Learning and Memory, 67,* 1–13.

Krantz, D. H., & Tversky, A. (1971). Conjoint-measurement analysis of composition rules in psychology. *Psychological Review, 78,* 151–169.

Kretschmann, J. J., Kammradt, G., Krauthausen, I., Sauer, B., & Wingert, F. (1986). Growth of the hippocampal formation in man. *Bibliotheca Anatomica, 28,* 27–52.

Kuhl, P. K. (1987). Perception of speech and sound in early infancy. In P. Salapatek & L. Cohen (Eds.), *Handbook of infant perception: Vol. 2. From perception to cognition* (pp. 275–382). San Diego, CA: Academic Press.

Kuhl, P. K., & Meltzoff, A. N. (1984). The intermodal representation of speech in infants. *Infant Behavior and Development, 7,* 361–381.

Laor, N., Wolmer, L., Mayes, L. C., Gershon, A., Weizman, R., & Cohen, D. J. (1997). Israeli preschool children under Scuds: A 30-month follow-up. *Journal of the American Academy of Child and Adolescent Psychiatry, 36,* 349–356.

Lehman, E. B., & Bovasso, M. (1993). Development of intentional forgetting in children. In M. L. Howe & R. Pasnak (Eds.), *Emerging themes in cognitive development: Vol. 1. Foundations* (pp. 214–233). New York: Springer-Verlag.

Lehman, E. B., McKinley-Pace, M. J., Wilson, J. A., Slavsky, M. D., & Woodson, M. E. (1997). Direct and indirect measures of intentional forgetting in children and adults: Evidence for retrieval inhibition and reinstatement. *Journal of Experimental Child Psychology, 64,* 295–316.

Lehman, E. B., Morath, R., Franklin, K., & Elbaz, V. (1998). Knowing what to remember and forget: A developmental study of cue memory in intentional forgetting. *Memory & Cognition, 26,* 860–868.

Leichtman, M. D., & Ceci, S. J. (1993). The problem of infantile amnesia: Lessons from fuzzy-trace theory. In M. L. Howe & R. Pasnak (Eds.), *Emerging themes in cognitive development: Vol. 1. Foundations* (pp. 195–213). New York: Springer-Verlag.

Levine, L. J. (1997). Reconstructing memory for emotions. *Journal of Experimental Psychology: General, 126,* 165–177.

Lewis, M. (1986). Origins of self-knowledge and individual differences in early self-recognition. In A. Greenwald & J. Suls (Eds.), *Psychological perspectives on the self* (Vol. 3, pp. 55–78). Hillsdale, NJ: Erlbaum.

Lewis, M. (1991). Ways of knowing: Objective self-awareness or consciousness. *Developmental Review, 11,* 231–243.

Lewis, M., & Brooks-Gunn, J. (1979). *Social cognition and the acquisition of self.* New York: Plenum.

Lewis, M., Brooks-Gunn, J., & Jaskir, J. (1985). Individual differences in early visual self-recognition. *Developmental Psychology, 21,* 1181–1187.

Lewis, M., & Ramsey, D. S. (1997). Stress reactivity and self-recognition. *Child Development*, 68, 621–629.

Lewis, M., Sullivan, M., Stanger, C., & Weiss, M. (1989). Self-development and self-conscious emotions. *Child Development*, 60, 146–156.

Liben, L. S. (1977). Memory in the context of cognitive development: The Piagetian approach. In R. Kail & J. Hagen (Eds.), *Perspectives on the development of memory and cognition* (pp. 297–331). Hillsdale, NJ: Erlbaum.

Lindsay, D. S., & Read, J. D. (1995). "Memorywork" and recovered memories of childhood sexual abuse: Scientific evidence and public, professional, and personal issues. *Psychology, Public Policy, and Law*, 1, 846–908.

Linton, M. (1979). Real-world memory after six years: An in vivo study of very long term memory. In M. M. Gruneberg, P. E. Morris, & R. N. Sykes (Eds.), *Practical aspects of memory* (pp. 69–76). New York: Academic Press.

Loftus, E. F. (1993). The reality of repressed memories. *American Psychologist*, 48, 518–537.

Loftus, E. F., & Ketcham, K. (1994). *The myth of repressed memory: False memories and allegations of sexual abuse*. New York: St. Martin's Press.

Loftus, E. F., Polonsky, S., & Fullilove, M. T. (1994). Memories of childhood sexual abuse: Remembering and repressing. *Psychology of Women Quarterly*, 18, 67–84.

Loveland, K. (1987). Behavior of young children with Down syndrome before the mirror: Finding things reflected. *Child Development*, 58, 928–936.

Loveland, K. (1993). Autism, affordances, and the self. In U. Neisser (Ed.), *The perceived self* (pp. 237–253). New York: Cambridge University Press.

Lumley, M. A., Melamed, B. G., & Abeles, L. A. (1993). Predicting children's presurgical anxiety and subsequent behavior changes. *Journal of Pediatric Psychology*, 18, 481–497.

Lupien, S., Lecours, A., Lussier, I., Schwartz, G., Nair, N., & Meaney, M. (1994). Basalcortisol levels and cognitive deficits in human aging. *Journal of Neuroscience*, 14, 2893–2903.

Luria, A. R. (1961). *The role of speech in the regulation of normal and abnormal behavior*. New York: Liveright.

Luria, A. R. (1973). *The working brain*. New York: Basic Books.

MacFarlane, A. (1975). Olfaction in the development of social preferences in the human neonate. *Ciba Foundation Symposium*, 33, 103–117.

Malamut, B., Saunders, R., & Mishkin, M. (1984). Monkeys with combined amygdala-hippocampal lesions succeed in object discrimination learning despite 24-hour retention intervals. *Behavioral Neuroscience*, 98, 759–769.

Malloy, P. (1987). Frontal lobe dysfunction in obsessive-compulsive disorder. In E. Perecman (Ed.), *The frontal lobes revisited* (pp. 207–223). New York: IRBN Press.

Malmquist, C. P. (1986). Children who witness parental murder: Post-traumatic aspects. *Journal of the American Academy of Child Psychiatry*, 25, 320–325.

Mandler, J. M. (1992). How to build a baby: 2. Conceptual primitives. *Psychological Review, 99,* 587–604.

Mandler, J. M., Fivush, R., & Reznick, J. S. (1987). The development of contextual categories. *Cognitive Development, 2,* 339–354.

Mandler, J. M., & McDonough, L. (1993). Concept formation in infancy. *Cognitive Development, 8,* 291–318.

Mandler, J. M., & McDonough, L. (1995). Long-term recall of event sequences in infancy. *Journal of Experimental Child Psychology, 59,* 457–474.

Mandler, J. M., & McDonough, L. (1996). Drinking and driving don't mix: Inductive generalization in infancy. *Cognition, 59,* 307–335.

Mandler, J. M., & McDonough, L. (1997). Nonverbal recall. In N. L. Stein, P. A. Ornstein, B. Tversky, & C. J. Brainerd (Eds.), *Memory for everyday and emotional events* (pp. 141–164). Mahwah, NJ: Erlbaum.

Mans, L., Cicchetti, D., & Sroufe, L. A. (1978). Mirror reaction of Down's syndrome infants and toddlers: Cognitive underpinnings of self-recognition. *Child Development, 49,* 1247–1250.

Maurer, D. (1983). The scanning of compound figures by young infants. *Journal of Experimental Child Psychology, 35,* 437–448.

McBride, D. M., & Dosher, B. A. (1997). A comparison of forgetting in an implicit and explicit memory task. *Journal of Experimental Psychology: General, 126,* 371–392.

McCall, R. B., & Carriger, M. (1993). A meta-analysis of infant habituation and recognition memory performance as predictors of later IQ. *Child Development, 64,* 57–79.

McDonough, L., & Mandler, J. M. (1994). Very long-term recall in infants: Infantile amnesia reconsidered. *Memory, 2,* 339–352.

McDonough, L., Mandler, J. M., McKee, R. D., & Squire, L. R. (1995). The deferred imitation task as a nonverbal measure of declarative memory. *Proceedings of the National Academy of Science USA, 92,* 7580–7584.

McDowd, J. M., Oseas-Kreger, D. M., & Filion, D. L. (1995). Inhibitory processes in cognition and aging. In F. N. Dempster & C. J. Brainerd (Eds.), *Interference and inhibition in cognition* (pp. 363–400). San Diego, CA: Academic Press.

McEwen, B. S., & Sapolsky, R. M. (1995). Stress and cognitive function. *Current Opinion in Neurobiology, 5,* 205–216.

McFarland, P. H., & Stanton, A. L. (1991). Preparation of children for emergency medical care: A primary prevention approach. *Journal of Pediatric Psychology, 16,* 489–504.

McGaugh, J. L. (1995). Emotional activation, neuromodulatory systems, and memory. In D. L. Schacter, J. T. Coyle, G. D. Fischbach, M. M. Mesulam, & L. E. Sullivan (Eds.), *Memory distortion* (pp. 255–273). Cambridge, MA: Harvard University Press.

McGeogh, J. A. (1942). *The psychology of human learning.* New York: Longmans, Green.

McKee, R. D., & Squire, L. R. (1993). On the development of declarative memory. *Journal of Experimental Psychology: Learning, Memory, and Cognition, 19,* 397–404.

Medin, D. L., Goldstone, R. L., & Gentner, D. (1993). Respects for similarity. *Psychological Review, 100,* 254–278.

Melamed, B. G., Siegel, L. J., & Ridley-Johnson, R. (1988). Coping behaviors in children facing medical stress. In T. Field, P. McCabe, & N. Schneidermann (Eds.), *Stress and coping across development* (pp. 115–137). Hillsdale, NJ: Erlbaum.

Meltzoff, A. N. (1985). Immediate and deferred imitation in fourteen- and twenty-four-month-old infants. *Child Development, 56,* 62–73.

Meltzoff, A. N. (1988a). Infant imitation after a 1-week delay: Long-term memory for novel acts and multiple stimuli. *Developmental Psychology, 24,* 470–476.

Meltzoff, A. N. (1988b). Infant imitation and memory: Nine-month-olds in immediate and deferred tests. *Child Development, 59,* 217–225.

Meltzoff, A. N. (1990). Towards a developmental cognitive science: The implications of cross-modal matching and imitation for the development of representation and memory in infancy. *Annals of the New York Academy of Sciences, 608,* 1–37.

Meltzoff, A. N. (1995). What infant memory tells us about infantile amnesia: Long-term recall and deferred imitation. *Journal of Experimental Child Psychology, 59,* 497–515.

Meltzoff, A. N., & Borton, R. W. (1979). Intermodal matching by human neonates. *Nature, 282,* 403–404.

Meltzoff, A. N., & Moore, M. K. (1994). Imitation, memory, and the representation of persons. *Infant Behavior and Development, 17,* 83–99.

Merritt, K. A., Ornstein, P. A., & Spicker, B. (1994). Children's memory for a salient medical procedure: Implications for testimony. *Pediatrics, 94,* 17–23.

Meyers, N. A., Perris, E. E., & Speaker, C. J. (1994). Fifty months of memory: A longitudinal study in early childhood. *Memory, 2,* 383–415.

Millar, W. S. (1972). A study of operant conditioning under delayed reinforcement in early infancy. *Monographs of the Society for Research in Child Development, 37*(2, Serial No. 147).

Millar, W. S., & Schaffer, H. R. (1972). The influence of spatially displaced feedback on infant operant conditioning. *Journal of Experimental Child Psychology, 14,* 442–453.

Miller, P. J., & Sperry, L. L. (1988). Early talk about the past: The origins of conversational stories about personal experiences. *Journal of Child Language, 15,* 293–315.

Mischel, W., Shoda, Y., & Rodriguez, M. L. (1989). Delay of gratification in children. *Science, 244,* 933–938.

Mishkin, M., Malamut, B., & Bachevalier, J. (1984). Memories and habits: Two neural systems. In G. Lynch, J. McGaugh, & N. Weinberger (Eds.), *Neurobiology of learning and memory* (pp. 65–77). New York: Guilford Press.

Mishkin, M., Spiegler, B. J., Saunders, R. C., & Malamut, B. L. (1982). An animal model of global amnesia. *Alzheimer's Disease: A Report in Progress, 19,* 235–247.

Mizoguchi, K., Kunishita, T., Chui, D., & Tabira, T. (1992). Stress induces neuronal death in the hippocampus of castrated rats. *Neuroscience Letters, 138,* 157–164.

Morford, M., & Goldin-Meadow, S. (1992). Comprehension and production of gesture in combination with speech in one-word speakers. *Journal of Child Language, 19,* 559–580.

Morrongiello, B. A. (1988). Infants' localization of sounds along two spatial dimensions: Horizontal and vertical axes. *Infant Behavior and Development, 11,* 127–143.

Moscovitz, S. (1983). *Love despite hate.* New York: Schocken Books.

Muir, D., & Clifton, R. K. (1985). Infants' orientation to the location of sound sources. In G. Gottlieb & N. A. Krasnegor (Eds.), *The measurement of vision and audition in the first year of postnatal life* (pp. 171–195). Norwood, NJ: Ablex.

Murdock, B. B., Jr. (1982). A theory for the storage and retrieval of item and associative information. *Psychological Review, 89,* 609–626.

Myers, N. A., Perris, E. E., & Speaker, C. J. (1994). Fifty months of memory: A longitudinal study in early childhood. *Memory, 2,* 383–415.

Myles-Worsley, M., Cromer, C. C., & Dodd, D. H. (1986). Children's preschool script reconstruction: Reliance on general knowledge as memory fades. *Developmental Psychology, 22,* 22–30.

Nachmias, M., Gunnar, M., Mangelsdorf, S., Parritz, R. H., & Buss, K. (1996). Behavioral inhibition and stress reactivity: The moderating role of attachment security. *Child Development, 67,* 508–522.

Nadel, L., & Zola-Morgan, S. (1984). Infantile amnesia: A neurobiological perspective. In M. Moscovitch (Ed.), *Advances in the study of communication and affect: Vol. 9. Infant memory* (pp. 145–172). New York: Plenum.

Najarian, L. M., Goenjian, A. K., Pelcovitz, D., Mandel, F., & Najarian, B. (1996). Relocation after a disaster: Posttraumatic stress disorder in Armenia after the earthquake. *Journal of the American Academy of Child and Adolescent Psychiatry, 35,* 374–383.

Nash, M. (1987). What, if anything, is regressed about hypnotic age regression? A review of the empirical literature. *Psychological Bulletin, 102,* 42–52.

Nasrallah, H., Coffman, J., & Olson, S. (1989). Structural brain-imaging findings in affective disorders: An overview. *Journal of Neuropsychiatry and Clinical Neuroscience, 1,* 21–32.

Neal, A., & Hesketh, B. (1997). Episodic knowledge and implicit learning. *Psychonomic Bulletin & Review, 4,* 24–37.

Neimark, E. D., & Estes, W. K. (1967). *Stimulus sampling theory.* San Francisco: Holden-Day.

Neisser, U. (1988). Five kinds of self knowledge. *Philosophical Psychology, 1,* 35–59.

Neisser, U. (1991). Two perceptually given aspects of the self and their development. *Developmental Review, 11,* 197–209.

Neisser, U. (Ed.). (1993). *The perceived self.* New York: Cambridge University Press.

Neisser, U., Winograd, E., Bergman, E. T., Schreiber, C. A., Palmer, S. E., & Weldon, M. S. (1996). Remembering the earthquake: Direct experience vs. hearing the news. *Memory, 4,* 337–357.

Nelson, C. A. (1995). The ontogeny of human memory: A cognitive neuroscience perspective. *Developmental Psychology, 31,* 723–738.

Nelson, C. A., & Bloom, F. E. (1997). Child development and neuroscience. *Child Development, 68,* 970–987.

Nelson, K. (Ed.). (1989). *Narratives from the crib.* Cambridge, MA: Harvard University Press.

Nelson, K. (1993). The psychological and social origins of autobiographical memory. *Psychological Science, 4,* 7–14.

Nelson, K., & Gruendel, J. M. (1981). Generalized event representations: Basic building blocks of cognitive development. *Advances in Developmental Psychology, 1,* 131–158.

Newcombe, N., & Fox, N. (1994). Infantile amnesia: Through a glass darkly. *Child Development, 65,* 31–40.

Newcombe, N., & Lie, E. (1995). Overt and covert recognition of faces in children and adults. *Psychological Science, 6,* 241–245.

Newcomer, J. W., Craft, S., Hershey, T., Askins, K., & Bardgett, M. E. (1994). Glucocorticoid-induced impairment in declarative memory performance in adult humans. *Journal of Neuroscience, 14,* 2047–2053.

Nielson, K. A., & Jensen, R. A. (1994). Beta-adrenergic receptor antagonist antihypertensive medications impair arousal-induced modulation of working memory in elderly humans. *Behavioral and Neural Biology, 62,* 190–200.

Nyberg, L., Cabeza, R., & Tulving, E. (1996). PET studies of encoding and retrieval: The HERA model. *Psychonomic Bulletin & Review, 2,* 134–147.

Oades, R. D. (1979). Search and attention: Interactions of the hippocampal-septal axis, adrenalcortical, and gonadal hormones. *Neuroscience and Biobehavioral Reviews, 3,* 31–48.

Oakes, L. M., & Tellinghuisen, D. J. (1994). Examining in infancy: Does it reflect active processing? *Developmental Psychology, 30,* 748–756.

Ohr, P. S., Fagen, J. W., Rovee-Collier, C., Hayne, H., & Vander Linde, E. (1989). Amount of training and retention by infants. *Developmental Psychobiology, 22,* 69–80.

Olsho, W. D. (1984). Infant frequency discrimination. *Infant Behavior and Development, 7,* 27–35.

Olson, G. M., & Sherman, T. (1983). Attention, learning, and memory in infants.

In M. M. Haith & J. J. Campos (Vol. Eds.), *Infancy and developmental psychobiology* (Vol. 2, pp. 1001–1080). New York: Wiley.

O'Neil, J. B., Friedman, D. P., Bachevalier, J., & Ungerleider, L. G. (1986). Distribution of muscarinic receptors in the brain of the newborn rhesus monkey. *Society for Neuroscience Abstracts, 12,* 809.

Ornstein, P. A., Shapiro, L. R., Clubb, P. A., Follmer, A., & Baker-Ward, L. (1997). The influence of prior knowledge on children's memory for salient medical experiences. In N. L. Stein, P. A. Ornstein, B. Tversky, & C. J. Brainerd (Eds.), *Memory for everyday and emotional events* (pp. 83–112). Mahwah, NJ: Erlbaum.

O'Sullivan, J. T., & Howe, M. L. (1998). A different view of metamemory with illustrations from children's beliefs about long-term retention. *European Journal of Psychology of Education, 8,* 9–28.

Oviatt, S. L. (1985). Tracing developmental changes in language comprehension ability before twelve months of age. *Papers and Reports on Child Language and Development, 24,* 87–94.

Palmer, S. E. (1978). Fundamental aspects of cognitive representation. In E. Rosch & B. Lloyd (Eds.), *Cognition and categorization* (pp. 259–303). Hillsdale, NJ: Erlbaum.

Paris, S. G., & Lindauer, B. K. (1977). Constructive aspects of children's comprehension and memory. In R. Kail & J. Hagen (Eds.), *Perspectives on the development of memory and cognition* (pp. 35–60). Hillsdale, NJ: Erlbaum.

Parker, J. F., Bahrick, L., Lundy, B., Fivush, R., & Levitt, M. (1995). *Children's memory for a natural disaster: Effects of stress.* Paper presented at the Society for Applied Research in Memory and Cognition Conference, Vancouver, British Columbia, Canada.

Parkin, A. J. (1993). Implicit memory across the lifespan. In P. Graf & M. E. J. Masson (Eds.), *Implicit memory* (pp. 191–207). Hillsdale, NJ: Erlbaum.

Parmelee, A. H., & Sigman, M. D. (1983). Perinatal brain development and behavior. In M. M. Haith & J. J. Campos (Eds.), *Handbook of child psychology: Vol. II. Infancy and developmental psychobiology* (pp. 95–155). New York: Wiley.

Pascalis, O., De Schonen, S., Morton, J., Deruelle, C., & Fabre-Grenet, M. (1995). Mothers' face recognition by neonates: A replication and extension. *Infant Behavior and Development, 18,* 79–86.

Perner, J., & Ruffman, T. (1995). Episodic memory and autonoetic consciousness: Developmental evidence and a theory of childhood amnesia. *Journal of Experimental Child Psychology, 59,* 516–548.

Perris, E. E., Myers, N. A., & Clifton, R. K. (1990). Long-term memory for a single infancy experience. *Child Development, 61,* 1796–1807.

Peterson, L., Moreno, A., & Harbeck-Weber, C. (1993). "And then it started bleeding": Children's and mothers' perceptions and recollections of daily injury event. *Journal of Clinical Child Psychology, 22,* 345–354.

Pettito, A. (1993). On the ontogenetic requirements for early language acquisition.

In B. de Boysson-Bardies, S. de Schonen, P. Jusczyk, P. McNeilage, & J. Morton (Eds.), *Developmental neurocognition: Speech and face processing in the first year of life* (pp. 365–383). Ultrecht, The Netherlands: Kluwer Academic.

Pezdek, K., & Banks, W. P. (Eds.). (1996). *The recovered memory/false memory debate*. San Diego, CA: Academic Press.

Piaget, J., & Inhelder, B. (1973). *Memory and intelligence*. New York: Basic Books.

Pillemer, D. B., & White, S. H. (1989). Childhood events recalled by children and adults. *Advances in Child Development and Behavior, 21*, 297–340.

Pipp, S., Fischer, K., & Jennings, S. (1987). Acquisition of self- and mother-knowledge in infancy. *Developmental Psychology, 23*, 86–96.

Polster, M. R., Nadel, L., & Schacter, D. (1991). Cognitive neuroscience analysis of memory: A historical perspective. *Journal of Cognitive Neuroscience, 3*, 95–116.

Pope, K. S., & Brown, L. S. (1996). *Recovered memories of abuse: Assessment, therapy, forensics*. Washington, DC: American Psychological Association.

Porges, S. W. (1992). Vagal tone: A physiological marker of stress vulnerability. *Pediatrics, 90*, 498–504.

Postman, L., & Knecht, K. (1983). Encoding variability and retention. *Journal of Verbal Learning and Verbal Behavior, 22*, 133–152.

Pratkanis, A. R., Greenwald, A. G., Leippe, M. R., & Baumgardner, M. H. (1988). In search of reliable persuasion effects: III—The sleeper effect is dead: Long live the sleeper effect. *Journal of Personality and Social Psychology, 54*, 203–218.

Pugh, C. R., Tremblay, D., Fleshner, M., & Rudy, J. W. (1997). A selective role for corticosterone in contextual-fear conditioning. *Behavioral Neuroscience, 111*, 503–511.

Pylyshyn, Z. W. (1979). Validating computational models: A critique of Anderson's indeterminacy of representation claim. *Psychological Review, 86*, 383–394.

Pynoos, R. S., & Eth, S. (1984). The child as witness to homicide. *Journal of Social Issues, 2*, 87–108.

Pynoos, R. S., & Nader, K. (1989). Children's memory and proximity to violence. *Journal of the American Academy of Child and Adolescent Psychiatry, 28*, 236–241.

Rabinowitz, F. M., & Andrews, S. R. (1973). Intentional and incidental learning in children and the von Restorff effect. *Journal of Experimental Psychology, 100*, 315–318.

Rajaram, S. (1996). Perceptual effects on remembering: Recollective processes in picture recognition. *Journal of Experimental Psychology: Learning, Memory, and Cognition, 22*, 365–377.

Ramey, C. T., & Ourth, L. L. (1971). Delayed reinforcement and vocalization rates of infants. *Child Development, 42*, 291–297.

Rathburn, C., DeVirgilio, L., & Waldfogel, S. (1958). A restituted process in children following radical separation from family and culture. *American Journal of Orthopsychiatry, 28,* 408–415.

Ratner, H. H., & Myers, N. A. (1981). Long-term memory and retrieval at ages 2, 3, 4. *Journal of Experimental Child Psychology, 31,* 365–386.

Reul, J. M. H. M., & De Kloet, E. R. (1986). Anatomical resolution of two types of corticosterone receptor sites in rat brain with in vitro autoradiography and computerized image analysis. *Journal of Steroid Biochemistry, 24,* 269–272.

Reyna, V. F., & Brainerd, C. J. (1995). Fuzzy-trace theory: An interim synthesis. *Learning and Individual Differences, 7,* 1–75.

Reyna, V. F., & Lloyd, F. (1997). Theories of false memory in children and adults. *Learning and Individual Differences, 9,* 95–124.

Reznick, J. S., & Goldfield, B. A. (1992). Rapid change in lexical development in comprehension and production. *Developmental Psychology, 28,* 406–413.

Richardson, R., Riccio, D. C., & McKenney, M. (1988). Stimulus attributes of reactivated memory: Alleviation of ontogenetic forgetting in rats is context specific. *Developmental Psychobiology, 21,* 135–143.

Richman, C. L., Nida, S., & Pittman, L. (1976). Effects of meaningfulness on children's free-recall learning. *Developmental Psychology, 12,* 460–465.

Roberts, K. (1988). Retrieval of basic-level category in prelinguistic infants. *Developmental Psychology, 24,* 21–27.

Robinson, P. J., & Kobayashi, K. (1991). Development and evaluation of a pre-surgical preparation program. *Journal of Pediatric Psychology, 16,* 193–212.

Roediger, H. L. III, Rajaram, S., & Srinvas, K. (1990). Specifying criteria for postulating memory systems. *Annals of the New York Academy of Sciences, 608,* 572–595.

Roediger, H. L. III, Weldon, M. S., & Challis, B. H. (1989). Explaining dissociations between implicit and explicit measures of retention: A processing account. In H. L. Roediger & F. I. M. Craik (Eds.), *Varieties of memory and consciousness: Essays in honor of Endel Tulving* (pp. 3–41). Hillsdale, NJ: Erlbaum.

Rose, S. A., Gottfried, A. W., & Bridger, W. H. (1979). Effects of haptic cues on visual recognition memory in fullterm and preterm infants. *Infant Behavior and Development, 2,* 55–67.

Rosengren, K. S., Gelman, S. A., Kalish, C. W., & McCormick, M. (1991). As time goes by: Children's early understanding of growth in animals. *Child Development, 62,* 1302–1320.

Rosenstein, D., & Oster, H. (1988). Differential facial responses to four basic tastes in newborns. *Child Development, 59,* 1555–1568.

Ross, M. (1997). Validating memories. In N. L. Stein, P. A. Ornstein, B. Tversky, & C. J. Brainerd (Eds.), *Memory for everyday and emotional events* (pp. 49–82). Mahwah, NJ: Erlbaum.

Rots, N. Y., Workerl, J. O., Sutanto, W., Cools, A. R., Levine, S., de Kloet, E. R., & Oitzl, M. S. (1995). Maternal deprivation results in an enhanced pituitary-adrenal activity and an increased dopamine susceptibility at adulthood. *Society for Neuroscience Abstracts, 21,* 524.

Rovee-Collier, C. (1990). The "memory system" of prelinguistic infants. *Annals of the New York Academy of Sciences, 608,* 517–542.

Rovee-Collier, C. (1997). Dissociations in infant memory: Rethinking the development of implicit and explicit memory. *Psychological Review, 104,* 467–498.

Rovee-Collier, C., & Bhatt, R. S. (1993). Evidence of long-term memory in infancy. *Annals of Child Development, 9,* 1–45.

Rovee-Collier, C., & Boller, K. (1995). Interference or facilitation in infant memory? In F. N. Dempster & C. J. Brainerd (Eds.), *Interference and inhibition in cognition* (pp. 61–104). San Diego, CA: Academic Press.

Rovee-Collier, C., Greco-Vigorito, C., & Hayne, H. (1993). The time window hypothesis: Implications for categorization and memory modification. *Infant Behavior Development, 16,* 149–176.

Rovee-Collier, C., Early, L., & Stafford, S. (1989). Ontogeny of early event memory: III. Attentional determinants of retrieval at 2 and 3 months. *Infant Behavior and Development, 12,* 147–161.

Rovee-Collier, C., & Hayne, H. (1987). Reactivation of infant memory: Implications for cognitive development. *Advances in Child Development and Behavior, 20,* 185–238.

Rovee-Collier, C., & Shyi, G. (1992). A functional and cognitive analysis of infant long-term retention. In M. L. Howe, C. J. Brainerd, & V. F. Reyna (Eds.), *Development of long-term retention* (pp. 3–55). New York: Springer-Verlag.

Rubin, D. C. (1995). *Memory in oral traditions.* New York: Oxford University Press.

Rubin, D. C., & Schulkind, M. D. (1997). Distribution of important and word-cued autobiographical memories in 20-, 35-, and 70-year-olds adults. *Psychology and Aging, 12,* 524–535.

Ruff, H. A. (1986). Components of attention during infants' manipulative exploration. *Child Development, 57,* 105–114.

Ruff, H. A., & Rothbart, M. K. (1996). *Attention in early development: Themes and variations.* New York: Oxford University Press.

Russo, R., Nichelli, P., Gibertoni, M., & Cornia, C. (1995). Developmental trends in implicit and explicit memory: A picture completion study. *Journal of Experimental Child Psychology, 59,* 566–578.

Rutter, M. (1981). *Maternal deprivation reassessed.* New York: Penguin Books.

Sachs, J. (1983). Talking about the there and then: The emergence of displaced reference in parent-child discourse. In K. Nelson (Ed.), *Children's language* (Vol. 4, pp. 1–28). New York: Gardner Press.

Sagan, C. (1996). *The demon-haunted world: Science as a candle in the dark.* New York: Random House.

Salapatek, P. (1975). Pattern perception in early infancy. In L. B. Cohen & P. Salapatek (Eds.), *Infant perception: From sensation to cognition* (Vol. 1, pp. 133–248). New York: Academic Press.

Salmon, K., Bidrose, S., & Pipe, M.-E. (1995). Providing props to facilitate children's event reports: A comparison of toys and real items. *Journal of Experimental Child Psychology, 60*, 174–194.

Salmon, K., & Pipe, M.-E. (1997). Props and children's event reports: The impact of a 1-year delay. *Journal of Experimental Child Psychology, 65*, 261–292.

Sapolsky, R., Krey, L., & McEwen, B. S. (1985). Prolonged glucocorticoid exposure reduces hippocampal neuron number: Implications for aging. *Journal of Neuroscience, 5*, 1121–1127.

Sarnat, H. B. (1978). Olfactory reflexes in the newborn infant. *Journal of Pediatrics, 92*, 624–626.

Scafidi, F. A., Field, T. M., Schanberg, S. M., Bauer, C. R., Tucci, K., Roberts, J., Morrow, C., & Kuhn, C. M. (1990). Massage stimulates growth in preterm infants: A replication. *Infant Behavior and Development, 13*, 167–188.

Schacter, D. L. (Eds.). (1995). *Memory distortion.* Cambridge, MA: Harvard University Press.

Schacter, D. L., Koutstaal, W., & Norman, K. A. (1996). Can cognitive neuroscience illuminate the nature of traumatic childhood memories? *Current Opinion in Neurobiology, 6*, 207–214.

Schacter, D. L., & Moscovitch, M. (1984). Infants, amnesics, and dissociable memory systems. In M. Moscovitch (Ed.), *Advances in the study of communication and affect: Vol. 9. Infant memory* (pp. 173–216). New York: Plenum.

Schiff, A. R., & Knopf, I. J. (1985). The effect of task demands on attention allocation in children of different ages. *Child Development, 56*, 621–630.

Schmidt, L. A., Fox, N. A., Rubin, K. H., Sternberg, E. M., Gold, P. W., Smith, C. C., & Schulkin, J. (1997). Behavioral and neuroendocrine responses in shy children. *Developmental Psychobiology, 30*, 127–140.

Schneider, M. L. (1992). The effect of mild stress during pregnancy on birthweight and neuromotor maturation in rhesus monkey infants (*Macaca mulatta*). *Infant Behavior and Development, 15*, 389–403.

Schneider, W. (1993). Domain-specific knowledge and memory performance in children. *Educational Psychology Review, 5*, 257–273.

Schneider, W., & Bjorklund, D. F. (1998). Memory. In D. Kuhn & R. S. Siegler (Eds.), *Handbook of child psychology: Vol. 2. Cognition, perception, and language* (5th ed., pp. 467–521). New York: Wiley.

Schneider, W., & Pressley, M. P. (1989). *Memory development between two and twenty* (1st ed.). New York: Springer-Verlag.

Schneider, W., & Pressley, M. P. (1997). *Memory development between two and twenty* (2nd ed.). Mahwah, NJ: Erlbaum.

Schneider-Rosen, K., & Cicchetti, D. (1984). The relationship between affect and cognition in maltreated infants: Quality of attachment and the development of visual self-recognition. *Child Development, 55*, 648–658.

Schneider-Rosen, K., & Cicchetti, D. (1991). Early self-knowledge and emotional development: Visual self-recognition and affective reactions to mirror self-images in maltreated and non-maltreated infants. *Developmental Psychology,* *27,* 471–478.

Schwartz, E. D., & Kowalski, J. M. (1991). Malignant memories: PTSD in children and adults after a school shooting. *Journal of the American Academy of Child and Adolescent Psychiatry, 30,* 936–944.

Schwartz, N., & Sudman, S. (Eds.). (1994). *Autobiographical memory and the validity of retrospective reports.* New York: Springer-Verlag.

Shaw, J. A., Applegate, B., & Schorr, C. (1996). Twenty-one-month follow-up study of school-age children exposed to Hurricane Andrew. *Journal of the American Academy of Child and Adolescent Psychiatry, 35,* 359–364.

Sheffield, E. G., & Hudson, J. A. (1994). Reactivation of toddlers' event memory. *Memory, 2,* 447–465.

Sheingold, K., & Tenney, Y. J. (1982). Memory for a salient childhood event. In U. Neisser (Ed.), *Memory observed: Remembering in natural contexts* (pp. 201–212). New York: Freeman.

Siegel, S. J., Ginsberg, S. D., Hof, P. R., Foote, S. L., Young, W. G., Kraemer, G. W., McKinney, W. T., & Morrison, J. H. (1993). Effects of social deprivation in prepubescent rhesus monkeys: Immunohistochemical analysis of the neurofilament protein triplet in the hippocampal formation. *Brain Research, 619,* 299–305.

Slobin, D. I. (1985). Crosslinguistic evidence for the language-making capacity. In D. I. Slobin (Ed.), *The cross-linguistic study of language acquisition* (Vol. 2, pp. 1157–1256). Hillsdale, NJ: Erlbaum.

Smith, P. H., Arehart, D. M., Haaf, R. A., & deSaintVictor, C. M. (1989). Expectancies and memory for spatiotemporal events in 5-month-old infants. *Journal of Experimental Child Psychology, 47,* 210–235.

Solheim, G. S., Hensler, J. G., & Spear, N. E. (1980). Age-dependent contextual effects on short-term active avoidance retention in rats. *Behavioral and Neural Biology, 30,* 250–259.

Spanos, N. P. (1996). *Multiple identities and false memories: A sociocognitive perspective.* Washington, DC: American Psychological Association.

Spence, D. P. (1982). *Narrative truth and historical truth.* New York: Norton.

Spence, M. J. (1996). Young infants' long-term auditory memory: Evidence for changes in preference as a function of delay. *Developmental Psychobiology, 29,* 685–695.

Spence, M. J., & Freeman, M. S. (1996). Newborn infants prefer the maternal low-pass filtered voice, but not the maternal whispered voice. *Infant Behavior and Development, 19,* 199–212.

Spiker, D., & Ricks, M. (1984). Visual self-recognition in autistic children: Developmental relationships. *Child Development, 55,* 214–225.

Squire, L. R. (1986). Mechanisms of memory. *Science, 232,* 1612–1619.

Squire, L. R. (1987). *Memory and brain.* New York: Oxford University Press.

Squire, L. R., & Cohen, N. J. (1984). Human memory and amnesia. In G. Lynch,

J. McGaugh, & N. Weinberger (Eds.), *Neurobiology of learning and memory* (pp. 3–64). New York: Guilford Press.

Squire, L. R., Cohen, N. J., & Nadel, L. (1984). The medial temporal region and memory consolidation: A new hypothesis. In H. Weingartner & E. Parker (Eds.), *Memory consolidation* (pp. 185–210). Hillsdale, NJ: Erlbaum.

Squire, L. R., & Frambach, M. (1990). Cognitive skill learning in amnesia. *Psychobiology, 18,* 109–117.

Squire, L. R., & Shimamura, A. P. (1986). Characterizing amnesic patients for neurobehavioral study. *Behavioral Neuroscience, 100,* 866–877.

Squire, L. R., & Zola-Morgan, S. (1983). The neurology of memory: The case for correspondence between the findings for human and nonhuman primates. In J. A. Deutsch (Ed.), *The physiological basis of memory* (pp. 199–268). San Diego, CA: Academic Press.

Squire, L. R., & Zola-Morgan, S. (1988). Memory: Brain systems and behavior. *Trends in Neuroscience, 11,* 170–175.

Sroufe, L. A. (1983). Infant-caregiver attachment and patterns of adaptation in preschool: The roots of maladaptation. In M. Perlmutter (Ed.), *Minnesota Symposium on Child Psychology* (Vol. 16, pp. 41–83). Hillsdale, NJ: Erlbaum.

Starkman, M. N., Gebarski, S., Berent, S., & Schteingart, D. (1992). Hippocampal formation volume, memory dysfunction, and cortisol levels in patients with Cushing's syndrome. *Biological Psychiatry, 32,* 756–765.

Starkman, M. N., & Schteingart, D. E. (1981). Neuropsychiatric manifestations of patients with Cushing's syndrome. *Archives of Internal Medicine, 141,* 215–219.

Stein, N. (1996). Children's memory for emotional events: Implications for testimony. In K. Pezdek & W. P. Banks (Eds.), *The recovered memory/false memory debate* (pp. 169–194). San Diego, CA: Academic Press.

Stein, N., & Boyce, W. T. (1997, March). *The role of individual differences in reactivity and attention in accounting for on line and retrospective memory.* Paper presented at the biennial meeting of the Society for Research in Child Development, Washington, DC.

Stein, N. L., & Levine, L. J. (in press). The early emergence of emotional understanding and appraisal: Implications for theories of development. In T. Dalgleish & M. Power (Eds.), *The handbook of cognition and emotion.* New York: Wiley.

Stein, N. L., & Liwag, M. D. (1997). Children's understanding, evaluation, and memory for emotional events. In P. van den Broek, P. Bauer, & T. Bourg (Eds.), *Developmental spans in event comprehension and representation: Bridging fictional and actual events* (pp. 199–235). Mahwah, NJ: Erlbaum.

Steward, M. S., Steward, D. S., Farquhar, L., Myers, L., Reinhart, M., Welker, J., Joye, N., Driskill, J., & Morgan, J. (1996). Interviewing young children about body touch and handling. *Monographs of the Society for Research in Child Development, 61*(Serial No. 248).

Strack, F., & Forster, J. (1995). Reporting recollective experiences: Direct access to memory systems? *Psychological Science, 6,* 343–351.

Stuber, M. L., Nader, K., Yasuda, P., Pynoos, R. S., & Cohen, S. (1991). Stress responses after pediatric bone marrow transplantation: Preliminary results of a prospective longitudinal study. *Journal of the American Academy of Child Psychiatry, 30,* 952–957.

Suchecki, D., Mozaffarian, D., Gross, G., Rosenfeld, P., & Levine, S. (1993). Effects of maternal deprivation on the ACTH stress response in the infant rat. *Neuroendocrinology, 57,* 204–212.

Sullivan, M. W., Rovee-Collier, C., & Tynes, D. N. (1979). A conditioning analysis of infant long-term memory. *Child Development, 50,* 152–162.

Suomi, S. J., & Harlow, H. F. (1972). Social rehabilitation of isolate-reared monkeys. *Developmental Psychology, 6,* 487–496.

Swain, I. U., Zelazo, P. R., & Clifton, R. K. (1993). Newborn infants' memory for speech sounds retained over 24 hours. *Developmental Psychology, 29,* 312–323.

Swain, R. A., Armstrong, K. E., Comery, T. A., Humphreys, A. G., Jones, T. A., Kleim, J. A., & Greenough, W. T. (1995). Speculations on the fidelity of memories stored in synaptic connections. In D. L. Schacter, J. T. Coyle, G. D. Fischbach, M. M. Mesulam, & L. E. Sullivan (Eds.), *Memory distortion* (pp. 274–297). Cambridge, MA: Harvard University Press.

Symons, C. S., & Johnson, B. T. (1997). The self-reference effect in memory: A meta-analysis. *Psychological Bulletin, 121,* 371–394.

Terr, L. (1988). What happens to early memories of trauma? A study of twenty children under age five at the time of documented events. *Journal of the American Academy of Child and Adolescent Psychiatry, 27,* 96–104.

Terr, L. (1991). Childhood traumas: An outline and overview. *American Journal of Psychiatry, 148,* 10–20.

Terr, L. (1994). *Unchained memories: True stories of traumatic memories, lost and found.* New York: Basic Books.

Thelen, E., Corbetta, D., Kamm, K., Spencer, J. P., Schneider, K., & Zernicke, R. F. (1993). The transition to reaching: Mapping intention and intrinsic dynamics. *Child Development, 64,* 1058–1098.

Thelen, E., & Ulrich, B. D. (1991). Hidden skills: A dynamic systems analysis of treadmill stepping during the first year. *Monographs of the Society for Research in Child Development, 56*(1, Serial No. 223).

Thompson, C. P., Skowronski, J. J., Larsen, S. F., & Betz, A. L. (1996). *Autobiographical memory: Remembering what and remembering when.* Mahwah, NJ: Erlbaum.

Thorndike, E. L. (1905). *The elements of psychology.* New York: Seiler.

Timmons, C. R. (1994). Associative links between discrete memories in early infancy. *Infant Behavior and Development, 17,* 431–445.

Todd, C. M., & Perlmutter, M. (1980). Reality recalled by preschool children. In M. Perlmutter (Ed.), *Children's memory: New directions for child development* (pp. 69–85). San Francisco, CA: Jossey-Bass.

Tomasello, M., & Mervis, C. B. (1994). The measurement is great, but measuring comprehension is still a problem. *Monographs of the Society for Research in Child Development, 59*(5, Serial No. 242).

Trehub, S. E., & Schneider, B. A. (1983). Recent advances in the behavioral study of infant audition. In S. E. Gelber & G. T. Mencher (Eds.), *Development of auditory behavior* (pp. 167–185). New York: Grune & Stratton.

Tulving, E. (1984). Precis of *elements of episodic memory*. *Behavioral and Brain Sciences, 7*, 223–238.

Tulving, E. (1985). Memory and consciousness. *Canadian Psychologist, 26*, 1–12.

Tulving, E., Kapur, S., Markowitsch, H. J., Craik, F. I. M., Habib, R., & Houle, S. (1994). Neuroanatomical correlates of retrieval in episodic memory: Auditory sentence recognition. *Proceedings of the National Academy of Sciences USA, 91*, 2012–2015.

Tyano, S., Iancu, I., Solomon, Z., Sever, J., Goldstein, I., Touveiana, Y., & Bleich, A. (1996). Seven-year follow-up of child survivors of a bus-train collision. *Journal of the American Academy of Child and Adolescent Psychiatry, 35*, 365–373.

Underwood, B. J. (1954). Speed of learning and amount retained: A consideration of methodology. *Psychological Bulletin, 51*, 276–282.

Underwood, B. J. (1964). Degree of learning and the measurement of forgetting. *Journal of Verbal Learning and Verbal Behavior, 3*, 112–129.

Uno, H., Ross, T., Else, J., Suleman, M., & Sapolsky, R. (1989). Hippocampal damage associated with prolonged and fatal stress in primates. *Journal of Neuroscience, 9*, 1705–1711.

Usher, J. A., & Neisser, U. (1993). Childhood amnesia and the beginnings of memory for four early life events. *Journal of Experimental Psychology: General, 122*, 155–165.

Vander Linde, E., Morrongiello, B. A., & Rovee-Collier, C. (1985). Determinants of retention in 8-week-old infants. *Developmental Psychology, 21*, 601–613.

Van Giffen, K., & Haith, M. M. (1984). Infant visual response to Gestalt geometric forms. *Infant Behavior and Development, 7*, 335–346.

Varney, N., Alexander, B., & Macindoe, J. (1984). Reversible steroid dementia in patients without steroid psychosis. *American Journal of Psychiatry, 141*, 369–372.

Wagenaar, W. A. (1988). Calibration and the effects of knowledge and reconstruction in retrieval from memory. *Cognition, 28*, 277–296.

Wagenaar, W. A. (1990). My memory: A study of autobiographical memory over six years. *Cognitive Psychology, 18*, 225–252.

Wagenaar, W. A., & Groeneweg, J. (1990). The memory of concentration camp survivors. *Applied Cognitive Psychology, 4*, 77–87.

Walden, T. A., & Ogan, T. A. (1988). The development of social referencing. *Child Development, 59*, 1230–1240.

Waldvogel, S. (1948). The frequency and affective character of early childhood memories. *Psychological Monographs, 62*(4, Whole No. 291).

Watanabe, Y., Gould, E., & McEwen, B. S. (1992). Stress induces atrophy of apical dendrites of hippocampus CA3 pyramidal neurons. *Brain Research, 588,* 341–344.

Werner, E. E., & Smith, R. L. (1982). *Vulnerable but invincible.* New York: McGraw-Hill.

Werner, H., & Kaplan, B. (1963). *Symbol formation.* New York: Wiley.

Werker, J. S., & Tees, R. C. (1984). Cross-language speech perception: Evidence for perceptual reorganization during the first year of life. *Infant Behavior and Development, 7,* 49–63.

Wertheimer, H. (1961). Psychomotor coordination of auditory and visual space at birth. *Science, 134,* 1692.

West, T. A. (1998). *Infantile amnesia and memory development in deaf individuals: A role for language?* Unpublished doctoral dissertation, University of Minnesota, Minneapolis, MN.

West, T. A., & Bauer, P. J. (1999). Assumptions of infantile amnesia: Are there differences between early and later memories? *Memory, 7,* 257–278.

Wetzler, S. E., & Sweeney, J. A. (1986). Childhood amnesia: An empirical demonstration. In D. C. Rubin (Ed.), *Autobiographical memory* (pp. 191–201). New York: Cambridge University Press.

Wheeler, M. A., Stuss, D. T., & Tulving, E. (1997). Toward a theory of episodic memory: The frontal lobes and autonoetic consciousness. *Psychological Bulletin, 121,* 331–354.

White, H. (1992). *Artificial neural networks: Approximation and learning theory.* Cambridge, MA: Blackwell.

Willatts, P. (1990). Development of problem-solving strategies in infancy. In D. F. Bjorklund (Ed.), *Children's strategies: Contemporary views of cognitive development* (pp. 23–66). Hillsdale, NJ: Erlbaum.

Williams, L. M. (1994). Recall of childhood trauma: A prospective study of women's memories of child sexual abuse. *Journal of Consulting and Clinical Psychology, 62,* 1167–1176.

Windle, W. F. (1971). *Physiology of the fetus.* Springfield, IL: Charles C Thomas.

Windom, C. S., & Morris, S. (1997). Accuracy of adult recollections of childhood victimization: 2. Childhood sexual abuse. *Psychological Assessment, 9,* 34–46.

Windom, C. S., & Shepard, R. L. (1996). Accuracy of adult recollections of childhood victimization: 1. Childhood physical abuse. *Psychological Assessment, 8,* 412–421.

Winick, M., Meyer, K. K., & Harris, R. C. (1975). Malnutrition and environmental enrichment by early adoption. *Science, 190,* 1173–1175.

Wolkowitz, O. M., Reus, V. I., Weingartner, H., Thompson, K., Breier, A., Doran, A., Rubinow, D., & Pickar, D. (1990). Cognitive effects of corticosteroids. *American Journal of Psychiatry, 147,* 1297–1303.

Woodward, A. L., Markman, E. M., & Fitzsimmons, C. M. (1994). Rapid word learning in 13- and 18-month-olds. *Developmental Psychology, 30,* 553–566.

Wooley, C. S., Gould, E., & McEwen, B. S. (1990). Exposure to excess glucocorticoids alters dendritic morphology of adult hippocampal pyramidal neurons. *Brain Research, 531,* 225–231.

Yapko, M. (1994). *Suggestions of abuse: Real and imagined memories.* New York: Simon & Schuster.

Yehuda, R., Fairman, K. R., & Meyer, J. S. (1989). Enhanced brain cell proliferation following andrenalectomy in rats. *Journal of Neurochemistry, 53,* 241–248.

Zola-Morgan, S., & Squire, L. R. (1985). Medial-temporal lesions in monkeys impair memory on a variety of tasks sensitive to human amnesia. *Behavioral Neuroscience, 99,* 22–34.

Zola-Morgan, S., Squire, L. R., & Mishkin, M. (1982). The neuroanatomy of amnesia: Amygdala-hippocampus versus temporal stem. *Science, 218,* 1337–1339.

AUTHOR INDEX

deSaint Victor, C. M., 12
DeVirgilio, L., 106
Diamond, A., 39, 68
Diamond, D. M., 38
DiBase, R., 101
DiTomasso, M. J., 62
Dodd, D. H., 37
Doignon, J. P., 50
Dosher, B. A., 115
Dow, G. A., 27, 50, 123
Dowden, A., 24
Dowden, P. J., 26
Dropik, P., 28, 148
Dudycha, C. J., 82
Dudycha, M. M., 82
Dulit, R., 63

Eacott, M. J., 82, 97, 100
Earls, F., 71
Early, L. A., 22
Ehrensbeck, K., 128
Eimas, P. D., 5
Elbaz, V., 41
Elliot, C. H., 71
Elman, J. L., 9, 13, 14, 15
Else, J., 70
Emde, R. N., 90, 92, 106
Enright, M. K., 22
Erdelyi, M. H., 61
Erickson, M. F., 73
Estes, W. K., 16, 99, 126
Eth, S., 62

Fabre-Grenet, M., 123
Fadil, L., 90
Fagen, J.W., 22
Fairman, K. R., 68
Falmange, J,, 50
Fangan, J., 22
Farinacci, S., 108
Farrar, M. J., 54, 55, 56
Farrar, M. L., 28, 78
Farvolden, P., 60
Femina, D. D., 62
Fenson, L., 92, 95, 96
Fernald, A., 5
Fifer, W. P., 5
Filion, D. L., 39

Finlay, D., 7
Fischer, K., 90, 92, 100
Fischer, K. W., 9
Fitzsimmons, C. M., 96
Fivush, R., 48, 50, 51, 54, 56, 63, 78, 85, 87, 88, 93, 94, 122, 123
Flavell, J. H., 142
Fleck, K., 77
Fleshner, M., 68
Flexser, A. J., 88, 99
Fodor, J. A., 88
Follmer, A., 76
Forster, J., 114
Fox, N., 112
Frambach, M., 9
Franklin, K., 41
Freeman, M. S., 20
Freud, S., 84, 108, 110
Friedman, D. P., 13
Fromhoff, F. A., 93
Fulilove, M. T., 61
Fuster, J. M., 39

Garmezy, N., 106
Garry, M., 60
Gathercole, S. E., 60, 83
Gaultney, J. F., 49
Gebarski, S., 70
Gelman, R., 95
Gelman, S. A., 51
Genter, D., 53
Ghatala, E. S., 48
Gibbons, J., 74
Gibertoni, M., 112
Gillette, A. L., 122
Ginsberg, A. P., 7
Ginsberg, S. D., 71
Goenjian, A. K., 64
Gold, P. E., 67
Goldfield, B. A., 96
Golding, J. M., 41
Goldin-Meadow, S., 95, 96
Goldstone, R. L., 53
Goleman, D., 62
Goodman, G. S., 8, 54, 55, 56, 64, 66, 71, 74, 75, 76, 88
Goodwyn, S., 96
Gotlib, I. H., 67
Gottfried, A. W., 11

Vankov, A., 69
Varney, N., 70
Vigorito, J, 5
Volk-Hudson, S., 37
Volterra, V., 95
von Restorff, R. R., 53

Wadwahan, S., 43
Wagenaar, W. A., 60, 64, 88, 130, 138
Walden, T. A., 8
Waldfogel, S., 106
Waldvogel, S., 82
Wallace, C. S., 14
Watanabe, Y., 69
Water, E., 106
Weber, M., 69
Weiss, M., 101
Weldon, M. S., 110
Werker, J., 5
Werner, E. E., 106
Werner, H., 96
West, T. A., 32, 94
Wetherheimer,, 5
Wetzler, S. E., 82, 100
Wewerka, S., 28, 123, 148
Wewerka, S. S., 27

Wheeler, M. A., 14, 15, 40, 85
White, H., 88
White, S. H., 85, 86, 87, 94
Willatts, P., 37
Williams, L. M., 62, 129
Wilson, J. A., 41
Windle, W. F., 6
Windom, C. S., 129
Wingert, F., 13
Winick, M., 106
Wolkowitz, O. M., 68, 70
Woodson, M. E., 41
Woodward, A. L., 96
Woody, P., 71
Wooley, C. S., 69
Wright, R., 114, 115

Yapko, M., 62
Yasuda, P., 64
Yeager, C. A., 62
Yehuda, R., 68

Zacks, R. T., 38, 39
Zelazo, P. R., 5
Zeltzer, L. K., 74
Zola-Morgan, S., 9, 10, 11, 13

SUBJECT INDEX

False memory (*continued*)
 gist-verbatim memory confusion in,
  46–47
 intrusion in, 46
 in preschool children, 45–46
 retroactive inference in, 46
 suggestion in, 45
Familiarity preference, 30–31
Fetus, response to auditory stimulus, 4
Filtering, of memory trace, 136
Forgetting. *See also* Directed (intentional)
  forgetting
 age differences in, 123–124
  relationship to overlearning measures, 125
 learning rate and opportunity in, 124
 retroactive interference in, 42–43
 storage-based, 154
 of traumatic experiences, 59
Forgetting rate, learning rate independence of, 124–125
Freud, S., 105–106, 108–109
Functional magnetic resonance scanning,
  in identification of neurobiological mechanisms, 14
Fuzzy-trace theory
 of autobiographical memory onset, 87
 false memory and, 44–47

Generalization, in preschool children, 50
Generic representations
 in acquisition and retention, 57, 135
 balance with individualized representation, 140
 discrepant information and, 55
 with distinctive features, 54–55
 gist extraction for, 139–140
 in preschool children, 52
 recall of, 141–142
 vs. individual recall, 65, 66
 in younger *vs.* older children, 54–55
Gestures, in self-representation and communication, 95–96
Gist extraction, for generic representation, 139–140
Gist memory
 developmental course of, 86
 of traumatic events, 66
Gist representations, verbatim representations *vs.*, 44

Glucocorticoids
 response to stress, 68–69, 72
 stress-induced effects of, 68
 structural and functional effects of,
  69–70
Groeneweg, J. A., 60

Habituation-dishabituation. *See also*
  Paired-comparisons
 criticisms of, 30
Harnishfeger, K. K., 39
Hearing
 early development of, 4–5
 fetal, 4
 neonatal, 4–5
Hesketh, B., 116
Hippocampal complex
 glucocorticoid effects on, 68, 70
 in memory, 9–10, 13
Howe, M. L., 89

Illusory truth effect, 108
Imagery organization, impact on recall,
  127
Imitation
 deferred, 25–26
 in early memory, 25–29
 elicited, 26–29
Implicit memory, as aspect of unitary
  memory system, 115–116
Individual differences
 in learning and retention, 122
 in memory development and retention,
  139
 in stress reactivity, 73–74
Infant, age-retention correlation in, 22
Infantile amnesia, 9–10, 82
 historical perspective of, 84–85
 and onset of autobiographical memory,
  87
  language and, 88–89
 shift to autobiographical memory, 85–
  86
Information
 status of at acquisition and retention,
  120–121, 131
 updating of
  past and present in, 136

Inhibition. *See* Behavioral inhibition;
    Cognitive inhibition
  in free- and cued recall settings, 40
  of retrieval, 41
Intentional forgetting. *See* Directed (intentional) forgetting
Interference, in memory updating, 23
Interpretation, in autobiographical memory, 130
Intrusion
  in false memory, 46
  in target event memory, 65
Intrusive memories, of childhood trauma, 62

Knowledge
  accuracy and, 131
  acquisition and retention performance
    in preschool children, 50
  effect on memory, 76
  emotion and, 75–76
  and long-term memory
    in preschool children, 50–52
    in school-age children, 47–50
  memory of, 49–50
  in memory trace construction and reconstruction, 137
  organization and memory of, 49–50
  organization of, 51–52
  retrieval and, 48–49
  storage maintenance and, 49, 57
  stress-reactivity and, 75–76
  trace memory durability and, 49
  updating of past with present, 136

Language
  autobiographical memory and, 86, 87–88
  in autobiographical memory onset, 88–89
  conceptual basis for, 92
  development of
    in utero and in infancy, 95–96
    in infantile amnesia onset, 88–89
    memory and, 89
    role in memory, 88–89
    self-recognition and, 92
Language gestures and, 95–96

Learning rate, independent of forgetting
    rate, 124–125
Learning-retention confounds, 123
Lindhauer, B. K., 85
Localization, of sound, 5
Location, preschooler development of, 37
Long-term memory
  in preschool children, 50–52
  in school-age children, 47–50

Maturation-experience interrelationship,
    neuroimaging of, 14
Meaningfulness
  recall and, 27–28
  and reorganization in storage, 85
  and retention, 138, 147
Meaning of experience, memory as record
    of, 139
Medical treatments
  behavioral measure of stress in, 71–72
  long-term retention of, 64–66
Memorability
  distinctiveness in, 76–79
  salience in, 66–67
Memory
  birth to 2 years of age, 82
  in infants
    behavioral measures of, 119–120
    interpretation, revision, recoding, reconstruction of, 135–136
    opposing tendencies in, 145
    as unitary system, 118–119
Memory constraints
  attentional changes and, 7–9
  motor changes and, 7–9
Memory (declarative) processes, 9–12
Memory development, learning-retention
    confound in, 122–123
Memory systems
  dual, 86–87
  multiple, 87
Memory tasks, implicit *vs.* explicit, 115–116, 118
Memory traces
  cohesive and self-organizing, 144–145
  consciousness accessibility of, 111
  transformation and reconstruction of,
    136
Metamemory, mnemonic strategies in, 48

knowledge acquisition and retention
in, 50–51
knowledge and long-term memory in,
47–52
recall of personal experience by, 93–94
Preschool development
in autobiographical organization, 37
cognitive inhibition in, 38–40
contemporary models and research in,
38–47
in cue use, 37–38
for detail recall, 37
directed (intentional) forgetting in,
40–44
distinctiveness in, 52–56
false memory in, 45–46
fuzzy-trace theory and false memories,
44–47
general trends in, 37–38
knowledge and long-term memory, 47–
52
for location, 37
variables in, 38
Preverbal memory, verbal recall of, 28,
148
Procedural (habit) memory
in conjugate memory reinforcement,
24
early development of, 9–11
PTST. *See* Posttraumatic stress disorder
(PTST)

Reactivation
in conjugate reinforcement, 22–23
in extension of retention, 28–29
retention extension and, 28–29
Recall
accuracy of in preschool and school-
aged children, 94
causal *vs.* arbitrary organization and,
27–28
declarative (explicit) memory in, 24
of distinctive experiences *vs.* familiar,
54
distinctiveness in prediction of, 100
distinctiveness *vs.* emotionality in, 77–
78
of early experience, 82–83
reconstruction in, 82–83

infant
behavioral measure of, 24
interference and, 42–43
intrusion of recent experience in, 46
meaningfulness and, 27–28
meaning of, 25
recognition shift to, 12–13
Recognition. *See also* Self-recognition
early memory and, 20
habituation-dishabituation in, 29
paired-comparisons in, 29–30
shift to recall, 12–13
Recognition memory paradigm, unconscious and conscious memory
processes in, 114–115
Recognition test, of conscious memory,
112–113
Reconstruction
of memory trace, 136
in recall of early experience, 82–83
Reenactment
retention and, 28–29
and storage, 28–29
Reminiscence
at storage and retrieval levels, 151–152
storage-based, 155
Reorganization, of meaningful material,
stored, 85
Reporting failures, reasons for, 129
Resiliency, after infantile deprivation or
trauma, 106–107
Retention
acquisition status of information and,
120–121, 131
contribution of storage and retrieval to
scale sensitivity in measurement
of, 128
correlation with age, 22–23
developmental trends in, 147
and deviation from expected, 55
and individual differences in learning
and forgetting, 122
infants' long-term, 122
information status and, 120–121, 131
long-term
need for models of, 146–147
measurement independent of acquisition, 121–125
novelty preference in, 30–31
reactivation and, 28–29

Retention (*continued*)
  reenactment and, 28–29
  stages-of-learning confounds and, 56
  of stressful event, 71–72
  variables affecting, 22–23
Retention process, storage and retrieval
    in, 126–127
Retrieval
  and autobiographical memories
      early childhood, 84
  in directed forgetting, 42–43
  failure of in trace-integrity model,
      153–154
  inference of, 126–127
  inhibition of in children, 41–42
  knowledge and, 48–49
  modification of, 127
  of trace memory, 98, 151
Retroactive inference, in false memory,
    46
Retroactive interference, forgetting and,
    42–43
Ruffman, T., 94

Salience
  durability of memory and, 130
  and long-term memory, 66–67
Scaling sensitivity
  in measurement of storage and re-
      trieval, 128
Schacter, D., 87
Schemas, learned and stored, 52
Scripts, learned and stored, 52
Selective attention, crawling and, 8
Self-awareness, 18 to 24 months of age,
    92–93
Self-cognition
  and autobiographical memory, 90–92,
      94
  development of
    individual differences in, 100–101
  personalized memory and, 102–103
  self-pointing in, 95–96
  self-referent pronouns in, 96–97
  as subject (I) and me (object), 90, 91
  visual, 95
Self-features, encoding in memory trace,
    99–100
Self-recognition. *See also* Recognition
  of mirror image, 90, 95

Self-reference
  as I and me, 90, 91
  role in memory, 97–98
Semantic organization, impact on recall,
    127
Sensory-perceptual development
  auditory, 4–5
  chemical, 5
  olfactory, 6
  tactile, 6
  visual, 607
Sexual abuse, long-term retention of, 61–
    63, 66
Skin conductance test, of unconscious
    memory, 112–113
Sleeper effect, unconscious memory and,
    108
Sociolinguistic theory, of autobiographical
    memory, 87–89, 94
Sound
  discrimination of, 4–5
  fetal response to, 4
  localization of, 5
Speech discrimination
  infancy, 5, 95
  infant, 5
Storage
  and autobiographical memories
      early childhood, 84
  consolidation for, 68–69
  content of
    modification of, 127, 135
    need for longitudinal assessment of
        changes in, 145–146
  in directed (intentional) forgetting,
      42–43
  of experience as distinctive, 138
  inference of, 126–127
  lack of and failure to report, 129
  modification of information in, 127
  neurobiological development of, 99–
      100
  neuroendocrine effect on, 68–69
  novelty preference in, 29–31
  reenactment and, 28–29
  reorganization in, dynamic, 84–85
  separation from retrieval, 161
  of trace memory, 98, 151
Storage failure, in trace-integrity model,
    154

ABOUT THE AUTHOR

Mark L. Howe, PhD, is Professor of Psychology and Dean of Graduate Studies and Research at Lakehead University, in Thunder Bay, Ontario, Canada. He received his PhD in experimental/cognitive psychology from the University of Western Ontario in 1982, and subsequently has held faculty appointments at the University of Victoria in British Columbia and at Memorial University in Newfoundland. In 1992, he was awarded Memorial University's President's Award for Outstanding Research and elected a Fellow of the American Psychological Society in 1998.

Dr. Howe has established a distinguished research program in the field of cognitive development, the results of which have been widely published in more than 150 journal articles, edited books, book chapters, and conference proceedings. His work spans the development of reasoning, remembering, and forgetting in both typical and atypical populations across infancy, childhood, and adulthood. He has served as a consultant to child protection, law enforcement agencies, and members of the judiciary, and has provided expert testimony concerning human memory in courts of law.